Talk Yuh Talk

Talk Yuh Talk

INTERVIEWS WITH ANGLOPHONE CARIBBEAN POETS

Edited by

Kwame Dawes

University Press of Virginia
Charlottesville & London

THE UNIVERSITY PRESS OF VIRGINIA
© 2001 by the Rector and Visitors of the University of Virginia
All rights reserved
Printed in the United States of America
First published 2001

⊛ The paper used in this publication meets the minimum requirements of the American National Standard for Information Sciences—Permanence of Paper for Printed Library Materials, ANSI Z39.48-1984.

Library of Congress Cataloging-in-Publication Data

Talk yuh talk : interviews with Anglophone Caribbean poets / edited by Kwame Dawes.
    p. cm.
    Includes index.
    ISBN 0-8139-1945-2 (cloth : alk. paper) — ISBN 0-8139-1946-0 (pbk. : alk. paper)
    1. Caribbean poetry (English) — History and criticism — Theory, etc. 2. Poets, English — Caribbean Area — Interviews. 3. Authors, Caribbean — Interviews. 4. Caribbean Area — In literature. 5. Poetry — Authorship. I. Title: Talk yuh talk. II. Dawes, Kwame Senu Neville, 1962–

PR9205.2 .T35 2000
811'.509 — dc21   00-034958

For Lorna, Sena, Kekeli and Akua

Mama The Great and the "Tribe"

Remembering Neville

Contents

Preface ix

Acknowledgments xix

1 James Berry (b. 1924) 1
2 Martin Carter (1927–1998) 11
3 Kamau Brathwaite (b. 1930) 22
4 Edward Baugh (b. 1936) 38
5 Mervyn Morris (b. 1937) 47
6 Claire Harris (b. 1937) 61
7 Olive Senior (b. 1941) 73
8 Cyril Dabydeen (b. 1945) 86
9 Lorna Goodison (b. 1947) 99
10 Ramabai Espinet (b. 1948) 108
11 John Robert Lee (b. 1948) 124
12 Grace Nichols (b. 1950) 135
13 Lillian Allen (b. 1951) 148
14 Kendel Hippolyte (b. 1952) 161
15 Jane King (b. 1952) 173

16 Opal Palmer Adisa (b. 1954) 183

17 David Dabydeen (b. 1955) 196

18 Afua Cooper (b. 1957) 215

19 Fred D'Aguiar (b. 1960) 226

Index 237

Preface

IT HAS BECOME increasingly possible to talk seriously about a tradition of Caribbean writing. This is especially true when we speak of the fiction that has been written by Caribbean authors over the past hundred years or so, but it is more and more apparent that Caribbean poetry has established for itself a tradition that is ample fodder for literary analysis and examination. My desire to compile a book of interviews like this was driven by my recognition of this. I began this project with the basic thesis that most Caribbean authors writing in English today have been influenced by other Caribbean writers to the same extent they have been influenced by the work of the colonizing powers. This thesis challenges the fundamental practices of postcolonial analysis that is often founded on the notion that writing from countries formerly colonized by the British, the French, or the Spanish constitutes literature that can only be defined rather innocuously as "the literature of the clash of cultures."

Wole Soyinka, in the prefatory notes to his play *Death and the King's Horseman,* argues against such approaches to readings and stagings of his play. His protest is convincing enough because he is positing that there exists a readily accessible culture in Nigeria that predates the relatively brief colonial era. This culture, he claims, has a comprehensive series of icons and mythologies that can shape a whole modern literature. While some would object that Soyinka begs the question of the colonial dynamic in the very play that he seeks to protect from misreadings by thoughtless directors of a western European inclination, his fundamental argument is hard to refute: Yoruba mythic structures have existed for centuries and the Yoruba language has a complexity that allows artists to shape a textured and nuanced literature that is quite clearly Yoruba based and realized. Tellingly, this effort at a kind of essentialist rendering of literature and culture cannot be as easily realized in a Caribbean context.

The obstacles involve the history of oppression and cultural coercion that has characterized the relationship between the colonizer and the colonized in the Caribbean. But the relationship has not always been one of contention, anxiety, and resistance, as Derek Walcott reminds us. The Caribbean's cultural makeup is a hybrid one. Arguing otherwise is futile. The question is, what happens to issues of identity and nationality when the process of hybridization remains fresh in the memory? Whereas in Nigeria the indigenous security of a coherent culture and language has made it possible for Soyinka to found his work on paradigms other than those of the colonizer, this has not been entirely possible in the Caribbean because of the absence of that "essential self," that world of beginnings whence a new culture can emerge—a world distant from the colonizer's influence.

Many Caribbean artists and historians have sought to defy the colonial influence and to forge a sensibility based on a kind of essentialist doctrine. This is usually manifest in attempts to locate tradition in Europe, Africa, India, or any place of "origin" for the inhabitants of these islands. Some have made an attempt to hark back to aboriginal sensibilities, and in some islands and regions this is feasible. Guyana's Wilson Harris, for instance, has created a literary tradition that is rooted convincingly in Amerindian culture (even as it draws upon African, European, and Indian traditions), but he remains a unique figure, one that cannot be copied as easily by writers from places like Jamaica where the native Arawak population was effectively wiped out before the beginning of the 1600s. Granted, novelist Erna Brodber and poets Olive Senior and Afua Cooper speak about their interest in retrieving this "Native" past through a spiritual paradigm which effectively recognizes that the earth, the soil, the very landscape of Jamaica contains the spirituality and cosmology of the Taino people. They have found in this project a series of mythic constructs that allow them to appropriate a cultural and spiritual past through artifacts and archeological exploration. But for the most part, efforts by early Anglophone Caribbean writers led to a privileging of European culture (at least in terms of form and prosody) and a somewhat self-deprecating effort to become grafted onto the European tree—specifically, the British tree. Culture was steeped in European values and all efforts at cultural expression took cues from Western models.

The latter part of the twentieth century saw a movement away from slavish, exclusive adherence to the European heritage. Writers like Kamau Brathwaite, Erna Brodber, and George Lamming have tried to offer other models, located mainly in the African part of the Caribbean heritage. This process entailed replacing the privileging of European values with the privileging of the African heritage. But the strength of their works lies in the willingness of the writers to problematize the relationship between the African past and the Caribbean present, for it is in fact a problematic relationship that, in the long run, defies essentializing.

If these interviews had been done with Caribbean writers in the 1950s or the 1940s, the question "who were your influences" would have elicited largely European and American names, and occasionally modern African ones (but only rarely, since accessible literature from that continent was then in its infancy, as well). The effort, then, to forge a new voice effected something that was both positive and negative. On the one hand, the literature that emerged sought to establish new directions, to react to the colonial definition and to resist it, and to create a new and distinctive voice—what Brathwaite calls "something torn / and new." On the negative end, much of the literature that emerged may have appeared far too devoted to that task, so founded on the politics of shaping an anticolonialist sensibility that often the problems and dynamics of craft may have suffered in the process. Because much of this writing was of necessity pioneering, some of it was very successful, and much of it was deeply flawed.

I felt a strong need to talk to writers who are working today to see if, in fact, something has changed since that period. These interviews are very much about craft and about the evolution of a tradition that shapes craft. They are also about some of the intriguing problems that surround the new Caribbean or West Indian literature, not the least of which is the problem of geographical and cultural definition. The fact is that many Caribbean writers working in English today do not live in the Caribbean. This is not new; the same would have been said about the first major wave of Caribbean writers of the

1940s and '50s. V. S. Naipaul, Jan Carew, Kamau Brathwaite, George Lamming, Samuel Selvon, Neville Dawes, Orlando Patterson, and John Hearne all lived outside of the Caribbean; it would have been difficult to live in the Caribbean and try to make a living from writing. They lived in "exile." But they remained quite decidedly Caribbean writers because of the nature of immigrant existence in Britain at the time. A Caribbean-born writer living in England remained Caribbean and was not at all deemed British. The natural course of extended migration and the fact that many families of Caribbean heritage have become rooted in British society has made the concept of a British-born West Indian a reality. Today, large numbers of Caribbean writers living in Canada, Britain and the United States are quite as comfortable about being called British, American, or Canadian as they are being called Caribbean or West Indian.

This collection of interviews reflects the implications of that development. The future of Caribbean writing and critical discourse is going to be devoted to the task of defining what that discourse is. In the 1950s, '60s, and '70s, writers were preoccupied with finding a historical and mythological grounding for their literature—a quest that ultimately led some to speak of the "peasant" ethos (Lamming, Selvon, Salkey), and others to speak of the African (Brathwaite, Reid), Afro-European (Walcott, Baugh), or Afro-Saxon constructs. The new challenge is to make sense of the heritages that are shaping the work of writers who now live outside of the Caribbean and who are opening themselves to a range of ideologies, influences, and constructions of identity that are far more expansive and, some would argue, internationalist. These interviews introduce the problem and suggest ways in which we must begin to reassess the work of Caribbean writers using newer and more comprehensive paradigms.

By asking questions about influences and trying to determine how these writers respond to the question of audience, I suspect that I have begun to tackle the difficult questions around the issues of aesthetic paradigms with which future generations of Caribbean writers will have to grapple. In many instances, the writers have come to a place of reconciliation—one in which they are no longer willing to speak of audience as a finite pocket of individuals who live in the Caribbean. Indeed, many writers speak of audience as a complex mass of individuals activated according to the specific circumstances of writing, publishing, and/or performance. Increasingly, those writers in the Caribbean who understand the meaning of isolation have resorted to another more Westernized and modernist conception of audience—the writer who writes for other writers. This is true of the three St. Lucia-based writers who are included in this anthology. Kendel Hippolyte, Jane King, and Robert Lee are all close friends who have for the past decade been writing consistently and dialoguing about each other's works. Apart from a collection by Hippolyte published in 1997 by Peepal Tree Press, and a collection by King published by Sandberry Press, these writers have not had exposure to an outside market because they have had to sustain their writing through self-publication. There is little doubt about the strength of their writing, but they have been forced to depend on each other as the ideal audience, the critical eye that has helped them to maintain the discipline of strong writing and serious pursuit of literary excellence.

One of the more intriguing discussions that takes place in this volume involves the difficulties of Caribbean poets who live in the Caribbean and struggle to be published. These writers are aware that in order to be "legitimately" published, they must, because of the limited number of local presses and the apparent prestige of international publication, have their works published by presses outside of the Caribbean. But the frustration that comes from not having access to these presses is part of the larger frustration over isolationism that haunts many of these writers and that has had an interesting impact on their work. It has led many poets toward a certain kind of introspection characterized by a focus on formal patterns that are more readily appropriated from Western sources than they would have been in the 1970s, for instance. Thus Kendel Hippolyte can declare that for him "form is everything" when talking about the evolution of his writing.

These revelations are critical to our understanding of what is happening to the Caribbean writer today. But this shift toward a willingness to exploit various forms is paralleled by a less examined area of larger aesthetics that is clearly shaping the direction of the poetry emerging from the region. Most of the writers interviewed in this volume experienced the 1970s in a manner that is worth noting here. Indeed, I made every effort to question the writers about their own understanding of the '70s in Caribbean culture and how that period helped to shape their work. I have isolated the '70s because I regard that decade as a watershed period in Caribbean culture and aesthetics. For much of the Caribbean, it represented a time of political maturation, a period in which the tyranny of ideologies took hold and the Cold War praxis was being played out in full force. The notion of nonalignment took root—a theory founded on the inclination of smaller nation-states to assert autonomy from the dominant imperializing and colonizing powers. It was during the 1970s that the voices of smaller nations began to be heard in the United Nations and that experimental manifestations of Marxist ideologies appeared in several countries. A socialist government, for instance, ruled Jamaica for the entire decade. Political debates were lively discussions about the fundamental issues of political thought and ideologies.

Political rhetoric grew in apparent sophistication even as society plunged into a far less sophisticated quagmire of violence, tribalism, and sheer political intrigue. Political awakening was coupled with a strong cultural awakening. The emergence of the Black Power movement in the Caribbean during the late 1960s led to the growth of African consciousness that was further manifested in the establishment of strong ties between Caribbean and African nation-states. This development was fairly unique in the Caribbean context; previously, the relationship with Africa was cautious and condescending at best and filled with a legacy of shame and mistrust. Caribbean society was embracing an African heritage almost to the exclusion of the European, Indian, and Chinese heritages that permeated many of these nations. In some regions this rise in black consciousness would lead to political violence along ethnic lines (for instance, Indo-black tensions in Guyana and Trinidad during the 1960s and '70s), but this development also led to the emergence of a cultural ferment that generated new and dynamic artistic expressions that drew deeply from an African heritage. It is no accident, then, that the emergence of Rastafarianism and reggae music found greatest expression during the decade of the '70s. Arguably, some of the most trend-setting and innovative literary work done in Jamaica during that period was by the reggae musicians. The industry of reggae spawned an incredible number of new artists who were writing and performing work of some sophistication and with an important element of social relevance and currency. Artists like Bob Marley, Peter Tosh, Lee "Scratch"

Perry, Big Youth, Jimmy Cliff, and Burning Spear were providing the artistic world with a musical form and an aesthetic that was the closest thing to a generic, non-folk-based poetic.

Clearly, this development has had a remarkable impact on the writing of the region. Writers like Lorna Goodison, Fred D'Aguiar, and Afua Cooper, who emerged during this period, have admitted to the powerful impact that reggae music has had on their work. Kamau Brathwaite, although of a different generation, began to see in the music a foundation for a new aesthetic that would eclipse the jazz aesthetic with which he had experimented in the 1960s. Yet these developments represent a larger Pan-Caribbean aesthetic shift that began with the emergence of calypso as a cultural force in the literature produced in the region during the 1930s, '40s, and '50s, long before the emergence of reggae music. The inventive, witty, iconoclastic and radical articulations of calypso would lend a powerful aesthetic foundation to the fiction of V. S. Naipaul and Samuel Selvon and the poetry of Derek Walcott and Kamau Brathwaite, to name just a few. In the present interviews, Jane King, Opal Palmer Adisa, Grace Nichols, and Claire Harris all talk about the importance of calypso in their work. The political upheavals of the 1970s generated a heightened radicalism in calypso that has affected the literature as well. The last twenty years have seen a growing complication and exploration of race dynamics in countries like Trinidad and Guyana, where the tensions that have existed for decades between people of African and Indian heritage have given rise to a fascinating series of musical forms, rooted in both calypso and the varied cultural strains that have come to shape these societies. The poets interviewed in this collection share an awareness of the importance of folk and popular cultural forms in the defining of poetics in the Caribbean.

Anthologies are as much about the writers who are not included as they are about those who are. The rationale for inclusion in this volume was hardly comprehensive or rigid. I was interested in speaking to writers who have established themselves as strong voices in Caribbean writing. But I also found it necessary to interview writers whom I could get to sit with me, or with a tape recorder, for an extended period of time and respond to questions. With the exceptions, perhaps, of Fred D'Aguiar and Afua Cooper, I have not interviewed the new generation of writers emerging all over the world who are writing from a Caribbean perspective. Names like Geoffrey Philps, Marcia Douglas, Shara Macullum, Anthony Kellman, Everton Sylvestor, Rohan Preston, and Claudia Rankine come to mind as representatives of this group.

There are a number of poets whom I would have wanted to include if not prevented by a combination of logistics and the realities of life and death. This list would include Mahadai Das, the startling poet of elegance and power from Trinidad; Marlene Nourbese Philip, the dynamic Trinidad-Canadian poet whose innovations and ideological sinew have offered important models for many young poets working today in the West Indian Diaspora; Merle Collins, who has managed to combine performance and "book" poetry in a manner that is unique and increasingly important; Anthony McNeill, perhaps one of the finest poets to have been produced by Jamaica, who died a few months before I was able to secure a date for an interview; Archie Markham, a British-based stalwart in West Indian writing who has survived in a peculiar marginalized position of Caribbean letters, while still contributing significantly to the shape of criticism and poetic form from the region; Clifton Joseph, a dynamic performance/dub poet based in Canada who brings a stunning intellectual vigor to his poetic acrobatics; John Agard, the remarkable Guyanese-British storyteller, poet, and children's author, who is perhaps the most complexly comedic poet writing in a Caribbean aesthetic; Pamela Mordecai, a poet versed in both dialect and standard English, whose understanding of the publishing world would have lent some useful dimension to the shape of this book; Velma Pollard, the well-published Jamaican poet and fiction writer whose poetry is among the best by emerging women writers from the Caribbean; and Derek Walcott, whose place in this book hardly needs justification.

Ultimately, the traditional caution about writers' judgments of their own work is a good one. I offer that as talisman to the reader of this volume. But I also encourage you to recognize that this warning may very well have been coined by a writer as a red herring that would throw the inquisitive off his or her scent. Thus one must take that, too, with some caution. In the long run, the words of the writers, *talking dem talk,* should speak for themselves.

A final, brief note on methodology. These interviews were conducted in various ways. Most were person-to-person interviews, but several were conducted through letter-writing and via electronic mail. Others were interviews done "solo" by the writers, responding into a tape recorder to questions I sent to them. Each writer was given a chance to review the interviews and make suggestions about changes and additions. The variety has created a lively and interesting range of interview modes.

Acknowledgments

I THANK THE Division of Arts and Letters at the University of South Carolina at Sumter, the University of South Carolina's Research and Productive Scholarship Granting Body, the South Carolina Arts Commission, the Department of English of the University of South Carolina, the Caribbean Writers Workshop at the University of Miami (especially Sandra Paquette for her generosity of spirit), and the following people who assisted greatly in the completion of this project: Fred D'Aguiar, Kendel Hippolyte, Jane King, Robert Lee, Edward Chamberlain, Stewart Brown, Gary Leising, Angella Davis, Phillip Bramblett, Regenia Gatewood, Ellen Arl, Carol Reynolds, Michelle Krivejko, Colin Channer, Rohan Preston, Cathie Brettschneider, Bernardine Evaristo and Spread the Word, and all of the writers included in this book who gave generously of their time. I thank friends James Berry, Ramabai Espinet, Grace Nichols, and John Agard. Jeremy Poynting, Hannah Bannister, David Dabydeen, and Cyril Dabydeen offered hospitality in the United Kingdom, Canada, and Florida during my trips to conduct these interviews. Thanks also to the Poetry Library at the South Bank Centre in London for the wonderful collections that were invaluable during the research stages of this project. I especially want to thank Jean "Binta" Breeze and Linton Kwesi Johnson, who gave support and sacrificed time to conduct interviews with me that were wrecked by technical hitches with my equipment. I promise that I will repay. I will. I would like to thank anyone else who helped in some way to make this book possible. Finally I must thank my family: Lorna, my wife, and my children Sena, Kekeli, and Akua for their support in this project and for the time they allowed for me to indulge myself.

Two interviews in this book have been published previously. Lillian Allen's interview appeared as "360° Black: A Conversation with Lillian Allen" in *West Coast Line* 22 (31/1), Spring/Summer 1997, pp. 78-91. David Dabydeen's was printed in *The Art of David Dabydeen*, ed. Kevin Grant (Leeds: Peepal Tree, 1997), pp. 199-221. I am grateful to both publishers for permission to reprint.

James Berry

BORN 1924

JAMES BERRY WAS born in rural Jamaica in 1924. The fourth of six children, Berry left Jamaica at the age of eighteen for the United States as part of a wartime contract labor scheme. After a four-year stay in the United States, he returned to Jamaica deeply bothered by the treatment of blacks in America. He continued to live in his coastal village until 1948. Tired of the limited possibilities in the island, he traveled to Britain. In London, Berry worked during the day and studied at night to gain a marketable skill. He trained to be a telegraphist and worked as one for twenty-six years. Since beginning to write seriously in the 1960s, Berry has devoted his life to writing.

His writing has earned him a great deal of attention in Britain and the United States; his numerous awards include the Greater London Arts Association Fellowship in 1977, the National Poetry Competition Award in 1981 for his poem "Fantasy of an African Boy," the Grand Prix Smarties Prize for his book *A Thief in the Village* in 1987, the Signal Poetry Award for his collection of young people's poetry *When I Dance,* the Order of the British Empire for service to poetry in 1990, and a Society of Authors Cholmondeley Award for Poetry in 1991.

Berry edited two important anthologies of Caribbean and black British poetry, *Bluefoot Traveller* (Limestone, 1976) and *News for Babylon* (Chatto & Windus, 1989). He has also edited several anthologies for children, including *Classic Poems to Read Aloud* (Kingfisher, 1997), and has published several books of fiction and poetry for children and young adults, both in the United States and in the United Kingdom. His poetry collections include *Fractured Circles* (New Beacon,

1979), *Chain of Days* (Oxford University Press, 1985), *Lucy's Letters and Loving* (New Beacon, 1982) and *Hot Earth Cold Earth* (Bloodaxe, 1995).

Berry lives in England.

KWAME DAWES: What is the fundamental rationale for your impulse to write poetry? You write fiction and you have done some drama. But why poetry? What is it about the poem that compels you to create in that form?

JAMES BERRY: I think, first of all, in my case there was a very early impulse to express myself on that kind of heightened level. I think it is something you feel in your guts. Because from quite early, maybe ten years old, I tried to write poems. We weren't taught poetry at school. We were taught to recite one or two British background poems that didn't have anything to do with our own surroundings. The particular one I remember is the moral, character-building poem about Bruce of Scotland by Eliza Cook. It was the Bible, the Psalms, that moved me deeply. There was something alien, I felt, about my life—its poverty—and what was available to me. And, pretty early, I suspected that there was some sort of stigma, some sort of something unfavorable about my parents, myself and my people, in regard to the way we were regarded by the world and by those in authority. Nothing praiseworthy about black people appeared in my school books. Of course slavery was hardly ever talked about. It was treated like a shame to be concealed. It was like that both at home and with authority generally. So you didn't understand. And, remember, my house was practically on the site of the old slave mill. So we used to play on the ruins of it. The children of the one white family in the village—like their parents—had an attitude of disrespect towards my father. He used to help the white woman with her horses, and did other unpaid jobs, and the children disrespected him, and this affected me. So there were all these things. And all these things put me out of place, you know? I saw it from quite early. And when you tried to talk about these things, there was no response.

We had Anancy stories from Africa. We had the proverbs. But that reality of day-to-day slave life—the stories, the agonies and disgrace that came from plantation life—all were suppressed in the memory. People just would not inform on that hell. And so how it all happened was not passed on. Yet I have just written a very long poem about it, and it will be in my next book, *Hot Earth, Cold Earth*. I call the poem "Letter to Mother Africa." It's complaining about Africa's part in slavery and about the absence of Africa in our lives and why Africa did nothing about it. I feel I cannot make excuses for Africa, but must deal with the reality.

So, you see, I grew up with a kind of heavy loneliness in me. And yet I have four brothers. And I enjoyed them and enjoyed boyish things. I enjoyed my brothers tremendously. We had our piece of land. We had our animals. We grew our food.

The children in my time had to help, had to work, even made our own toys. I was a thoughtful child. I grew up with my home people calling me the "brainy" one. But I never saw myself as "brainy" at all. I was just thoughtful and asked questions. It was also true that I got on well at school. And I yearned for higher education. But I was never going to get it. We had no tradition of advanced education in my family. My father was too much identified with his plantation personality. And, you know, from that sort of culture, you don't think about education. You don't think about earning money. You don't think about your place in society and what that absence of education was going to do to you. So we grew up disliking my father gradually. These kinds of pressures pushed and shaped my instinct to write. As I got older, I began to examine these feelings.

I went to live in America to work as a seasonal farm worker in 1943; the condition of black people absolutely appalled me. I was not really aware of it. I was not taught these things. I was only eighteen years old and was shocked and distracted by the way black people were treated. I could not believe it. When I went back to Jamaica, I knew that I had to dig deeper into our own British history and that background. I began to research it and look things up for myself. Not long after my return home, I came to England.

Of course, this was when I had libraries at my disposal for the first time. I was able to see what I felt in my guts, and I didn't at all understand: our history and our position in the world! I saw how everything went against me. All my reading now reinforced my feelings: we were different, but never inferior! And that falsehood was never to be accepted. Never! Yet, you were never going to change anything by just shouting about it. You had to contribute working ideas within the society; you had to create new institutions yourself. You had to change traditional, cultural, institutional patterns of thinking. You had to help society become something more positive and creative. You had to help humanity as a whole to be lifted from basic instincts. So, that was how I started.

I wanted to tell stories. I wanted to turn my feelings into poems. I wanted to realize that heightened voice of poetry that was suited to the kind of emotion and energy I felt within myself.

KD: In one of the notes on your work, there are some poems which are described as the "fifties" poems, poems that you wrote in the '50s. Is that when the active writing began?

JB: Midway '50s. Coming on to the '60s, *Lucy's Letters* and *Fractured Circles* arrived. They all were written during that time and into the early '70s. I really became very interested in short stories and I thought I was only going to write prose. I went to a lot of workshops and did lots of explorations on the short story. I started writing short stories and had some success. Radio took my stories and one or two magazines. This was way back in the '60s and '70s. I broadcast short stories on radio and had a few published as well. People offered me courses to write for television and to write plays, but mainly it was the short story form that took my attention. Then I went to a workshop with a woman friend.

I really went to that workshop because it was my first date with her. She was mad on poetry. Her group was studying T. S. Eliot. Now, I had never heard the name because, as I said, my focus was settled on story writing. I had never heard the name. And the people in the writers' group were all highly intelligent people. All great readers. And they were reading and talking about T. S. Eliot. I was never more moved. It compared only with reading the Psalms. Later I realized it was not so much the meaning in the work, it was the quality of sound and quality of music that affected me so. A week and a half later, I was vacuum-cleaning my sitting room, and suddenly, I felt this poem come on. I got a piece of paper and wrote it down. It came in dialect. I don't think I ever tried to publish it, and I don't remember it by heart. But it was a poem about looking at myself. That was how it started. From then, I had this tremendous desire to write poems.

KD: What you said about the first poem that came out in dialect is interesting. I know the dialect form plays a critical part in your work, and it has been there in your poetry from the beginning. In your prefaces, you often talk about the treatment and attitudes to patois, dialect, Nation Language, and so on, both in Jamaica and among Caribbean people living in this part of the world [the U.K.]; how do you react to the negative response that many people have? How do you respond to the elitist attitudes that denigrate the dialect even among Caribbean people?

JB: It's who and what we are. Just as we have had to teach Europeans to recognize that black skin is as natural as white skin, that it's God-given, nature-given, culture and race given, we have to keep on valuing who and what we are. It is important. You don't develop value for yourself, and also help others to value you, by rejecting intrinsic parts of yourself. That first sound a baby hears must be important. Yet I don't want to separate my African-Caribbean self and that self of mine that obviously shares a Western (and particularly British) culture.

We have to keep on claiming and reclaiming our voice and language. We need to use them to make our distinctive contribution to life. It is for this reason that I authenticate my characters with their own voices. I keep on introducing and reusing African and Caribbean proverbs in my books. Our voices with their own wisdom have their own place. It is our duty to bring the vibrancy, wisdom and pleasure of our own culture sounds into the mainstream. Yet I don't think if I go about saying, "My Nation Language gooder than everybody else language!" it is going to make any desirable impression or difference in the world. You have to creatively present it. You have to use it creatively. Yet we Caribbean-British people do have two languages, as far as I am concerned—standard English and our own Nation Language. For me it is vitally important that I represent these two distinct voices and give credit to both to the best of my ability.

KD: You write with a clear passion for exploring the dynamics of living as a black person in this world. The English world is your most immediate backdrop, even though there are a lot of poems that are "returns" to the Caribbean and to Jamaica, etc. And yet, inherent in some of your most popular poems, like the "Lucy" poems, is a sense of dichotomy—a bifocal view of landscape: rural Jamaica and urban London. How do you work through that dichotomy?

JB: While I feel a belonging to the whole world, I do feel a strong rootedness in Jamaica, and in part, it is because of the history—that so little has been done. I feel that there's much to be said, which is good for the upcoming generation and good for Europe to know and understand. That we express history through our written experience is very important. And so, the landscape, the Caribbean landscape, holds me. But, at the same time, I realize that I've been very much enmeshed with England. The experiences of these two landscapes hold me to their histories, both with agonies and a love I must not allow to get swamped by pain. I feel I must somehow try and link these two places together, as my home on earth. I must then use both my standard English and my Caribbean Nation Language in my writing. I am working on a novel, and in it, both will be represented.

When I look over what I have done, what I have written, and what I really want to write, I feel a little disappointed that I have not written more prose. I started writing late, but I also spent a lot of time developing short story skills. There is really much to be told about black people in Britain, in prose. And since I have been here from more or less the beginning, in the late '40s, I feel disappointed that I have not done more in the way of stories. But when you take up writing poetry, you realize poetry takes a long time to write to your inner satisfaction. And, also, I very much enjoy writing for children. And probably will keep on doing so. So I am hoping to do more prose, exploring two levels of landscapes, two aspects of the world. We have to create European characters in situations that will stretch them beyond their automatic love and advertising of themselves. Black people have the hardest job in the world to extend their human spirit and get others to extend theirs to include them. We need more and more to create fictional situations that may help us all to extend our human spirit beyond automatic look-alike group love. There is an inclusive world of global development and abundance to be tackled. And all this is why people who are merely politically correct think that there's much about my thinking which is "white-minded." Foolishness, dat! Absolute foolishness. Rubbish! Nobody is either black- or white-minded. A person is simply biased and stuck tribally, culturally, or both, with certain similar basic and flock instincts, like any flock of birds or pack of wild dogs: that's how I see racism.

KD: I think part of the reason that you do get flack from that quarter is a failure by many to recognize the use of irony in your work. In a poem like "I Am Racism," one would expect a "rant." If you don't get the "rant," one begins to question the mettle of the poem. And yet, there is a sense in which the poem is a "rant." But it's controlled and subtle.

JB: I try to engage the mind. The poem "White Child," for instance, you would be amazed the impact it has had on white people, because I set up a mirror and let people see themselves. I avoid attacks and confrontations. I try to put something into heads that I believe will reappear again and again for reasoned examination, or I try to present something quietly beautiful where it is unexpected. Remember the Bible passage—"the darkness and the light are both alike to thee."

KD: You have been an avid and indefatigable anthologist of Caribbean and black British writing. What are you looking for in your anthologies?

JB: I have just done a new anthology for Kingfisher Books which is called *Classic Poems to Read Aloud*. It is for the general and educational market. They asked me to do it because we have come to this time when black people need to be represented within classical literature. And I was able to find Caribbean poems, African poems, Asian poems and so on and use them in this anthology. It is published both here and in the States. It is important because of how it shows and represents change. It shows how battles won can be reflected in political, social, cultural, educational, institutional change. Placing poems like Blake's "Tyger" next to an African Dinka piece, two animals doing different things, has been interesting. I am on the verge of putting together a new black British anthology because *News for Babylon* has been remaindered. I have just talked to Bloodaxe publishers. Myself and an Asian guy, Mahmoud Jamal, are going to do a new version of *News for Babylon*, in which British-Asian poets will also be represented.

I am looking forward to that. Now, what will I be looking for? Archie Markham, in his *Hinterland*, said that when James Berry did *News from Babylon*, he put in everything that was out there. It was not really like that. First of all, an anthologist brings many poets' work together in one book to provide both artistic exposure and a marketplace for important, active and particular new poets. With the new anthology planned, my position is different only in the way that my poets will again represent new cultural groups in the U.K.

What am I looking for? In my last big Caribbean-British anthology I wanted to represent the voices I'd heard and knew about. I had known all the poets' work. Most of them I had read with, or I had heard them read at other readings. Some were more developed than others. A few were going to become established quickly, like Grace Nichols, John Agard, David Dabydeen, and Fred D'Aguiar. But, mainly, it was the desire to participate and express our Caribbean experience to the British public generally, and our new community. And I wanted to give as wide a range of these new voices as possible. I looked for the best pieces that, from my point of view, these poets had. Most were very angry indeed. Some only had two or three pieces and I looked for the best one. I even couldn't help representing one or two school-age contributors: one, particularly—Vivian Usherwood—was a very gifted young writer. In fact when we do this new anthology, I want to include some of his work again. He died at the age of nineteen. He wrote these poems when he was fourteen to fifteen years old. Most poignant, most sensitive! One of his poems is titled "My Name Is I Don't Know." A contributor such as Ben Zephaniah was still on the edge of things. Great to see how his work has come on in leaps and bounds. At the time of putting *News for Babylon* together, it was difficult to find any of Ben's work that really did him service on the page. But I didn't at all want to leave him out. Even years later, E. A. Markham didn't include Zephaniah at all in *Hinterland*. I felt I had to use a new sense of evaluation to highlight important and relevant qualities in our new Caribbean voices. I felt I had to look and see what aspect of our Caribbean experience the poet's mind has locked into and the place for the voice. It was not only the literary that I looked for. I also looked for the individual relevance of that voice in the scheme of things. And I wanted everybody to be there. This time, we are likely to drop out a number of those poets who were in *Babylon,* and no longer write poems. This time I may reduce, I think, some of the pieces from the previous contributors and bring in some new work from them. Of course, essentially new writers have come on the scene, and there will also be Asian-British contributors.

KD: Are there any developments that you are seeing in black British writing today?

JB: Some significant new women have come in the writing—Grace Nichols and Jackie Kay, for instance. John Agard's work continues to develop. Fred D'Aguiar and Caryl Phillips have arrived. Our situation in the U.K. calls for a new focus to develop relevant literary skills to meet new challenges in a strong literary culture. We are challenged to find new ways to help stimulate a widening of a new human consciousness. We are challenged to belong to the world fully. David Dabydeen is an academic, an intellectual and a talented poet and educationalist. Grace Nichols' talent promises much. The moment she showed me the manuscript of *I Is a Long Memoried Woman,* I said, "You've got a classic here. This is gonna be a classic the moment it's published." People say since she's done that she has done nothing interesting, but I don't think that's true. I think that her *Fat Black Woman* is creative and rebelliously interesting. I expect her next big book to be equal to *I Is a Long Memoried Woman,* because she is a great thinker. We do explore things together. She amazes me once she switches on with her kind of mind. And I like it too that she has broken through just the "black only" bandwagon. That makes her far more interesting. And people listen to her.

KD: Your poetry is constructed around a series of lines that are often self-contained expressions. You build on each line, layering upon layer. What is the process? Is the process, for you, one of pouring out words and then trimming to find the poem, or do you work slowly, waiting for the poem to emerge?

JB: First of all, ideas come and I make notes. There are those pressures of hot feelings, ideas that want words. Ideas come in many ways. And, of course, you are a source of certain contentions within yourself, and they grow, develop, and add other dimensions. There are threats and conflicts embedded in society that I may feel impelled to address in a poem. More important are the created wonders and joys of life that swell up a desire to enter and somehow rediscover. Also there is that desire to discover for oneself. Then too there is that desire to record personal experiences. Once I decide a subject is mine for a poem, I make notes. Whether I'm writing it down immediately or not, to develop an idea, I give all my mind to it, making notes till I think I have all the material. I then sit down and put the poem together. Its music may well have come with its inception. So I make notes before I really begin to write. Let's say I am writing about a bird. I like to get in my poem the spirit of the bird expressed in its physicality. I want the poem to suggest the sleekness of the body of the bird, the way nature designed it to fly through the air. But, as I say, I have to first know what my subject is. Of course, there are sometimes when I don't know what it is about until I have written it.

Sometimes I am working on something else and an unconnected image may come to me, like, "a saint in bliss, curled in a face of fire." And I am fascinated by it. So I type it down. Then the full poem emerges later. But normally, I have to first understand my subject. I think about it a lot, I walk about, thinking about it. And I make notes. I like my poem to be as clear as Blake's verse. And if it's going to be subtle, it must be as subtle as "The Sick Rose." Because "The Sick Rose," I think, is one of the world's greatest poems. But also, as I said, I like the music of my poem to be well integrated with it. Its rhythm is most important. I like it to have its own kind of swing. Once these things are in place, I begin to write. I begin to put it all together. And may well revise a lot. Yet, I might write it all in one session. But I never send my poems out immediately. I have to keep them and look at them. When my poem looks to me as if I had not written it and I can think, "That's not bad. I think I like that," then I think I can let it leave my hands.

Martin Carter

1927–1998

MARTIN CARTER WAS born and educated in Guyana, where he was highly regarded as one of the most significant and influential voices in literature. His example was a distinctive one in Caribbean letters as he represented one of the most effective writers of engaged art working in this region. His work landed him in a great many political problems in Guyana, and his poems have become, for many Caribbean social movements, anthems for change and political reformation. In this sense, Carter must be read along with such poets of this hemisphere as Pablo Neruda and Nicolás Guillén—all committed poets as devoted to the power of the craft as they are to the cause that drives the craft.

In 1954, his seminal and best-known collection, *Poems of Resistance from British Guiana,* was published. This slim volume of decidedly political poems has become a veritable classic in Caribbean writing. The poems in the volume reveal some of the trademark qualities of Carter's writing—a fascination with form, a terseness of language, and a distinct sense that the poem represents a finished artifact—a moment of epiphany that enlightens, but a moment that is contained and marked by the ordering of form.

His later poetry continued to explore similar themes even as Carter developed his interest in form, and, to some extent, myth. His volume of *Selected Poems* published in 1997 (Red Thread Women's Press) received positive critical attention. While he is recognized by a number of critics as an important Caribbean voice, his nearly constant residency in Guyana may have reduced the level of attention that he has received internationally.

Carter died in Guyana in 1998.

His other poetry collections include *The Hill of Fire Glows Red* (Miniature Poets Series, 1951), *The Kind Eagle: (Poems of Prison)* (1952), *The Hidden Man: (Other Poems of Prison)* (1952), *Jail Me Quickly: Five Poems* (1966), *Poems of Succession* (New Beacon, 1977), and *Poems of Affinity: 1978–1980* (Release, 1980).

This interview was conducted by Fred D'Aguiar.

FRED D'AGUIAR: Martin, if I can begin by asking you something about craft. What struck me over the last few days, hearing you read different poems from your *Selected Poems*, is how carefully put together your poems are. Now that's a general statement; poetry ought to be put together. But there also appears to be a design which I think relates to the notion of a craft, where the poet is facing his or her maker, and the maker is an obligation to the craft, something you inherit, which you pay attention to, and which you obey. Could you say a little bit about craft?

MARTIN CARTER: First of all I would describe it in a term, or a conjunction of terms, what I call "prosodic craft," as against any other kind of craft. In other words, I'm specifying a type of craft I call "prosodic craft." And the elements in prosodic craft as I understand it, and as I try to embody it, is unity in a way, of what I will call verse meter and prose rhythm. Now, obviously, if I'm speaking of verse meter and prose rhythm, I'm speaking of two things that can be separated. And therefore what we have to look for is a third term. And the third term I'll use is harmony. So that my conception is craft, to use a word, which I said was prosodic craft, ends up as harmony. Now, this harmony is not harmony in a sense of music. It is a mathematical sense of coordination, where things are coordinated rather than combined. So that, to refer back, you get the coordination of verse meter and prose rhythm. In the history of prosody, there has been something called logaoedic, from the Greek *logos* meaning prose and *oide* meaning song. In other words, you get the thing called prose song. But that is strictly meter where you get a combination of trochees and spondees and so on in the same poem. I'm speaking of something else where we get what I call harmony, which is a coordination of verse meter and prose rhythm. The best examples, I think, of harmony—or readily available one I can mention—is Shelly's "Ode to the West Wind," which has so much in common with another one, a paradigm of it, Milton's "Lycidas." So that is what

I mean by prosodic craft. To which there is no rule. There's no rule in which you say, "Use verse meter in this sense or prose rhythm in this sense." It is the coordination that is important. The coordination of verse meter and prose rhythm.

FD: I'm glad you mentioned "West Wind," because that ode is in terza rima and iambic pentameters. Now in that formula, the idea is that the poem clearly demonstrates that the form liberates meaning and that the poet as a writer isn't strapped to that form at all, but it works for him in its ways. How does that compare adversely, or how do we get out of form and still retain meaning?

MC: We have to distinguish between what is known as *vers libre* and free verse. *Vers libre* was the name given to a movement in the late nineteenth century in France. Free verse must be distinguished from blank verse. And free verse, its meaning depends so much on who is using it, at what period, and what conviction. So that I prefer not to use either term, *vers libre* or free verse, which I think are specific appellations given to a certain type of writing. I can give no name to it other than to say that what you get when you come in contact with what I call prosodic craft is harmony. And I would not want to say harmonious verse, because by definition, verse should be harmonious. So I don't want to make a tautology. And I said an example is Shelley and also Milton. What it does really is make it free, free for variations. In other words, you can have a line with nine syllables, and at the end of that line, the syllable can be taken up by the first syllable of the following line without a break. And yet, at the same time, in that following line, you'll have an end stop. And now the next two lines will be possibly a reverse of that. But together, they make a harmony, because they harmonize. And you get, in other words, a structure within a structure. So that in total the poem may appear to be free, but internally, it is very closely organized and closely knit. And one of the effects that you get is (and this refers to a thing that I think we'll come to in due course), what happens here is that you get a lot of assonance and internal rhyming, which is not stressed in the reading of a poem, but which occurs. As a consequence, the reader is reminded almost of his own speech. Only that this speech is coming in a different way to him. But when you get, for instance, a rhyme occurring in the second word of a given line and in the eighth word of the following line, the spatial dislocation, if you like, is now reconciled of the lines. So that not until you reach the second line right down to the eighth word, let us say, that you pick up again from the line that followed it, that preceded it. And that unifies the two lines in a way that you cannot do any other way. Now that depends a great deal on what I call verse sense, which is something that can't be taught. I mean you can't teach anybody verse sense.

FD: The poem communicates before it's understood — is that part of this?

MC: That's part of it, yes.

FD: As a poet, you're seen as a national poet in the sense that, in Guyana, when people think of poetry, your name comes up immediately as the poet who appears to have captured in this half of the century what it is that Guyana had been through, is going through, psychically and metaphysically and everything, which is okay. But it suggests also that a community, or whoever is assessing your work, or to whomever your work is communicating, there appears to be a covenant of some kind or something that is an unwritten contract or agreement between you and the community. This could be a trap, obligation, it could also be something that may follow you and they see the poem and there's nothing there written, and there's no trap really. But how much of a sense do you have of that, especially given the Guyanese context and so on?

MC: First of all, I think the word national is a misnomer. It is totally irrelevant to what you're doing. And if any adjective be put to it, Guyanese would be the only adjective that is permissible. But to say that a man's a national poet is making a conjunction of incompatible things. So I would not acknowledge that term national in the first place. The second point that you are making — that people may repeat, and then may write or say that something that has been written represents something else — comes back to craft, really, to a great extent. As I said, earlier, just now, you get a sound occurring, let us say, very early in a given line, and another sound occurring way down in a following line. And those two sounds connect the two lines. So one line may seem to be of a different direction than the other line, yet they are connected by an element in both lines. It could be summed in one case and it could be anything else and one doesn't know. What I think they mean when they say it stands for this and it stands for that is that it somehow reminds them of their own speech. Not their, not all of their speech. It reminds them of tones, tones that they themselves have not been able to describe or express. But somehow you get, what is the best word for it, reverberations, I think that is the best word for what I think they call different things. And they use other names because those names are available, easily available. People may understand what they say, but they don't mean that really. As I said in the first case, applying words like nationalism and so on doesn't really help anyone to understand.

FD: So you don't think you can have a poet who might coincide in his writing with a movement that would cover a fixed geographical space? For example, the evolution of Guyanese thinking as a geographical reality as distinct from British Guyana. Now a poet coming out of that might be seen to spearhead the articulation of those sentiments where in the populace they can't quite put the words in it, but they recognize the sentiment when they see a combination of words in a particular order called a poem written by you. And they take this poem and say, "This is what we mean by us as distinct from you." When that happens, the poem has taken on a communal kind of life, which means that you become, as a single person writing this poem about language as a medium, it appears that you've tapped into something much bigger than anything you could have been thinking about consciously as you put the poem together. How much do you subscribe to that notion of the poet as a kind of medium or whatever it is that's going on there?

MC: In a poem I wrote, which puts it as I would like to put it, there are lines, and then these lines occur: "If these are riddles, then riddles bite themselves." By that I would want to mean, in the terms that you read out, that there is a stage in the production of a poem where you don't know what you have written, and it's not until you are finished that to some extent, you realize what you have done. Now even that is limited, because there have been many cases in which, by accident, or by someone calling my attention to it, that I've gone back and looked at a poem or poems, and I have discovered things which I am quite sure I did not have in my mind at that time. So what you are saying is correct in that it is possible to pick up and to say things which are present to you without you yourself being deliberately aware of them. Or if you want to use the word, consciously aware of them. Now I think that happens with the readers, too. For instance, I'll give you an example, a very simple example, but it makes the point. There's a poem in which I had a line ending in "want." Something-something "where it wants." "Where it wants." Now read at a certain level, "it wants" would leave the word *to* understood. But someone could come to you and say "where it wants" meaning "where it needs," instead of "where it wants to," which is an intention. So we have a need substituted for an intention. Well, and yet when that comes to you years after the poem has been written, you go back and read it and you are corrected by that response from someone who is not in the slightest bit interested in that level of the poem. So that an unlearned person, a person without experience in these things, can come up with something which is very enlightening. I am reminded here of a quotation which I'm very fond of from Paul Lenin. I'll try to remember it as close as I can. "Never gladly the poet keeps his lure on the shield, but likes to join with others who help him understand it." I think it applies, it is a very beautiful statement, makes a lot of sense too, in the light of what I've been saying.

FD: I know language is there, and you use the language that you breathe and live. But over there in Britain there's certainly been a distinction between something known as English, which is something the Queen might be speaking about . . .

MC: British English.

FD: British English, all right, and this happens in the Caribbean and overseas, there's obviously differences there. Now when people talk about poetry coming from the Caribbean, language is one of the early indicators of the poems, where the poem's born and how the poem travels as well, in terms of its meaning. What's your view of standard English?

MC: I would make a distinction here quickly between language and poetry. And would suggest that we deal with the problem we've raised in terms of linguistics rather than poetics, about which I make a serious distinction. If this is permissible, then it is not difficult to understand the nature of the problem. And the nature of the problem is what is known in linguistics as dialect. And the sense of a geographical dialect. There's a dialect here in Plymouth different from the dialect in northern England. And I use the word "dialect" there in terms of geography and the geographical category. And therefore, as I said earlier, I would deal with this matter of dialect purely at the level of linguistics rather than poetics. When you enter poetics, the concept of a dialect is subsumed in another concept, depending upon what you are talking about. There's no general concept that subsumes dialect. Dialect has a meaning in its right, and it has an analogy in poetics.

FD: Okay, I see what you mean. So there's the language of contemplation of a poet, say, in Guyana like yourself, where "The University of Hunger" begins with a question that's also a statement.

MC: That is very interesting.

FD: There's no question mark after the first line.

MC: It isn't a question.

FD: No, no, it's not a question, it's a statement, but it also has an inquiring feel to it, too.

MC: That's because it starts with "is." All you have to do is put out "it," which is understood in front of "is." It becomes a statement. If you take off the "it," it can become a question. But I have no question mark at the end. Therefore it becomes a statement.

FD: Which is what I like, because you come to the end of it and go back . . .

MC: Then you have to go back and read it again.

FD: Which makes it not just an image, but you are drawn to the sense that this is a moment of contemplation. That you couldn't, for example, it's unparaphraseable. There are other things about it that it tells you. It comes from a language born out of contemplation. It's not a universal language, for example, I wouldn't recognize that dialect here. I would think, "Now, this is not Plymouth speech, it's somewhere else." That tells me that at the moment of creation where this thing happens, it comes out of a language that seems to belong to a region.

MC: But at the same time, there's no one in the region who would speak like that. No one in Guyana would speak like that. The poem as a whole, you can't take out a part of it, you have to speak of the poem as a whole.

FD: What idiom is it? Is idiom . . .

MC: Well, idiom, that's another thing again, because you come back to linguistics, you see.

FD: All right, okay, but say . . .

MC: Then you move into poetics, you're giving it another order. And my contention is that while it may have traces of its origin we are not to allow ourselves to fall into the genetic fallacy of confusing the result with the source. So while the source may be the dialect in linguistics, as a linguistic category, the result is a poem in the poetic category. So they're different categories, all of both are applicable, and one thing could be understood in whatever category you are dealing, you want to understand it in, but I would like to suggest that when we move from linguistics and move into poetics we are dealing with things that I call emergences, which no poet, I think, really sets out to do. But what happens is the poem is a result. Now in linguistics there is the conception of the sentence. The sentence considered as the systematic object of linguistic inquiry. And a happy thought has just occurred to me to repeat something I saw once in which a sentence had been defined, and been defined as follows: "A sentence is the result of a grammatical process which is not available to us before we have begun." In other words, it's only at the end or only in the projection of a poem that you know a poem is produced or has been produced. You can't say in advance, "I am going to produce a poem." In other words, the poet himself discovers that he's written a poem only at the end. And that is why so many poems are thrown away, because we discover that it isn't at the end.

FD: What about the beginning that gets you into that process of discovery? Is it an image or thought or an idea, what is it that gets you there?

MC: It depends. I think that one cannot put one's finger on what it is. It could be anything. It could be anything at all. I cannot accurately say, in any of the cases, what it was that brought this about. It's a kind of realization really, that something that may be of another world, is also of this world. So that what you have here is a constellation occurring, a constellation of words occurring. And a reader of a poem can realize one aspect of that configuration at one point, and at another point, read another aspect of it. I suspect that after the poet has finished the poem, he becomes a reader of it, and he goes through the same thing that any other reader would go through. He's only a privileged reader. That's his only distinction from another; the person who has written the poem. So a poet becomes a privileged reader of his own poems, and I use the word "privileged" in the classical meaning of the word. That he has a right to think that he's reading it properly.

FD: This is good. It suggests an estrangement as well, once it's launched. What is that process of estrangement? Of the poem being strange, of you being strange to it as well? What is that exactly?

MC: Well, I think that happens in the process of being written. You are strange to yourself, you see? And I have a line exactly like that. "Stranger to themselves." It's a line in some poem. And these things occur all the time, see, because how we talk. I remember lines that previous to this talk I would not have associated with the questions you ask. But now that you ask the questions, the lines take on a meaning which, apart from this discussion, they would not have taken on. Now this could happen overtly or silently, and one may be walking down the road and a line flashes in his mind, unwritten. And it may be something that had occurred. Maybe the same time or some time before. And it may even occur in the future, one doesn't know.

FD: The other thing I've noticed in poems like "Bent," which we've already spoken about differently, but the old woman who's at the end of her life, her value is not very much in the society. She appears to have no value, but there's a moment when you describe the curve in her back, and you give her a cosmic and global value by having the curve in the sky, she's matched to that. So she becomes bigger than herself and has a kind of noble and massive relationship to the cosmos, almost. Now that process, in the course of a line, we travel all these light years. It's a lovely curving image and it can only be done in a poem. What is the will that's driving the writer to do that kind of thing, to see the value where there apparently is no value and to make those connections? How do you account for that will and that process? Is there an account?

MC: I'm going to put it badly, because I'm just speaking easily. And possibly I'm putting it badly because I just can't put it better. I suspect it's a question of preservation. That in formulating or expressing or embodying something in that way, one is preserving oneself. And making oneself available not only to oneself, but to other people, too. In doing so, you make other people available to themselves. So it's always this double, double traffic going on, if you like using that word, all the time. And it is dynamic, in other words. That's the best word I can think of for the moment. There's no stasis. It's moving. It's always moving and changing, turning on itself as it were. So in the case of the woman who has now become, I think the line goes, "Her bent back . . ." the sky blue imitates her bent. I mean you reach a stage where there's nothing more to say. It can only be understood, it cannot be explained or paraphrased or anything else. It can only be seen. I am using the word "seen" in a sense of mental sight.

FD: So in fact grasping it, we grasp the whole thing, and it's hard to take it bit by bit.

MC: We can't take it bit by bit.

FD: There's a kind of seminal-like will. To go back to the poem, the image almost draws you back...

MC: Asks you to come back...

FD: ...to the conversation in various ways. The way it's stated is quite haunting, and the sense of it being totally understood but when it comes to be articulated in a linear way, then we get into problems of compartmentalizing it and what have you. Is there a dilemma between this holistic thing, where it's an attempt to get something holy, and it's understood, and the will to explain it? But in the fact that we work in linear sentences, are they working against each other?

MC: Well, both against and for. This is what I meant by coordination. Let me go back now to where we started in the sense of the distinction I made between verse meter and prose rhythm, where what may appear to be rhythmic is translatable into what may appear to be metrical. So at any given point you can't say that this is metrical or rhythmical, and the reason you can't say metrical is mode. And that is why I introduced the word harmony. Using the word harmony in the strict meaning of a joint ordering. That's what it means in Greek, to order jointly. And to order jointly means to coordinate. So that is what I mean. But again, it is not available to us until it is finished. You can't say I am going to write a harmonious verse, or a harmonious poem. It is after the poem is produced that you can say it is harmony, that harmony is invested here.

FD: I understand.

MC: If we reduce poetics, using poetics as a science, using science not in the commonplace, incorrectly used way, because in the nineteenth century science was considered to be physics, but the emergence of subsciences and so on, the idea of the exact science is blown. I mean, there's no such thing as exact sciences. As a matter of fact, in some cases, the vaguer the thing is, the more scientific it is. Because it takes in possibilities that have not been even noticed yet. Unforeseen possibilities are available. And to be scientific is to be aware of those unforeseen possibilities.

FD: Sounds like poetics as well. As you're speaking.

MC: Precisely. Well you see what is going to start happening? You start moving poetics into systematics if you use the word "systematics" to represent science. And I am convinced that they are very close together.

FD: In a sense, they are both about inquiry.

MC: Inquiry, and the way that things happen. The word I will use is cognition, and the question of cognition as a total thing.

Kamau Brathwaite

BORN 1930

KAMAU BRATHWAITE WAS born in Barbados in 1930. He began writing poetry and occasional fiction while a student in England, and appeared regularly on the important BBC *Caribbean Voices* series that launched the careers of many Caribbean writers living in "exile" in Britain. Brathwaite lived for nearly seven years in Ghana in the late 1950s and early '60s, and found himself "de-educating" himself from the European assumptions of his early education into a discovery of self through his experience of Africa, as chronicled in *The Arrivants* and in his recent Rwanda poems and some of the *DreamStories*. When he returned to the Caribbean to teach, first in St. Lucia and then for almost two decades in Jamaica at the University of the West Indies, Mona, Brathwaite was busy both as a historian and as an artist interested in constructing a series of approaches to West Indian literature. His critical work is virtually foundational to an examination of a Caribbean aesthetic; his experimentation with music, popular culture, and various forms of poetic expression has proved influential for a significant number of writers. Brathwaite's work is challenging because its meaning resides as much in the sounds of his words as in their semantic construction.

Recently Brathwaite has stretched the boundaries of poetic convention with his foray into what he calls the Sycorax writing style, in which he explores variation in font and type sizes in constructing what approximates to a kind of "concrete" poetry (he prefers to call this "hieroglyphic" or "mural" writing, as will be seen in the interview).

His poetry collections include *The Arrivants* (Oxford University

Press 1973), *Other Exiles* (Oxford University Press 1975), *Mother Poem* (Oxford University Press 1977), *Sun Poem* (Oxford University Press 1982), *X/Self* (Oxford University Press 1989), *Jah Music* (Savacou 1986), *Black + Blues* (Casa de las Américas 1976; rev. ed., New Directions 1995), *Soweto* (Savacou 1979), and *Middle Passages* (Bloodaxe 1992 and New Directions 1993). More recently Brathwaite has published several works, mostly poems in dread style, about what he calls the Time of the Salt: *The Zea Mexican Diary* (University of Wisconsin Press, 1993), *Shar* (Savacou, 1990), *Trench Town Rock* (Lost Roads, 1994), and *Dream-Stories* (Longman, 1994). His poetry has been translated into Spanish, French, German, and the Sranantongo language of Suriname.

Brathwaite left Jamaica in the early 1990s and now spends his time between Barbados and New York, where he teaches comparative literature at New York University.

NOTE: *The form of the interview published here reflects Brathwaite's strong reservations about the interview genre even when, as here, there is opportunity for editing and revision. He contends that the interview is too often a form of interrogation, in which the interviewee is subjected—unlike in a conversation—to a barrage or series of unforeseen questions to which he or she is expected to respond "intelligently," "knowledgeably," "authoritatively," and "on the hoof," as it were, when in fact most answers to questions involve a lifetime of response, one "answer" being only a layer trail to so much else. In his own words: "The danger that what the interviewee says in the threshing room of the interview will later be misconstrued in its cold or cooler blood, as it were, and each proper name called, except perhaps in immaculate praise, is fraught with the danger of animus and/or interposition or failure.... And most of the absolutes have to be revised, quite rightly, as 'most/many/some/several,' etc. And sometimes the critical 'they' means even more 'we' and even more I and I—'mwe'—one trying to talk about not being able to talk about what one can't really talk about."*

In this interview, therefore, following the now-familiar Brathwaite practice, the original has been considerably refracted: although the spirit and intention and "verbatim" of the original have been preserved (especially the spoken even if "ungrammatical" construction), some of the at-the-time strangulated or not fully or properly expressed threads of thought have been "interfaced" into the text, a process that out of respect for length (the original interaction in New York went on for almost four hours) has been confined here to only three or four of the topics and issues raised.

For Brathwaite the ideal is finally to build up the interview, as if it were the generative humus, into something approaching a book or monograph, with notes and movements through time, bringing aspects of the interview up to date or restoring them to their context in what he hopes will be a "new form of literary testimonio."

He argues that the abiding endeavor is not only to express opinion, which is the usual interview nexus, but to use the flow of opinion as a contribution to the body and spirit of our literature.

KWAME DAWES: I'd like to begin with your perception of where things stand now with Caribbean writing. A broad question: do you see this as a time of significant productivity in creative writing in the Caribbean or are these declining times?

KAMAU BRATHWAITE: What has happened in the Caribbean is that the "great days" were the days that we were published as the exiled writers; therefore, there was a lot of publicity coming out of London. Now this has faded and the impression would be that we are not really producing all that much. But when you go into the Caribbean you come across a lot of youngsters who are actually writing and thinking and carrying on but they are not "going anywhere" because they are not getting published, okay? So I think we've reached a crossroad situation where it is long overdue that we should have had a serious publishing venture inside the Caribbean. [Ian Randle has since the time of this interview published several volumes and at least two collections of plays. —KD] Without the publishing house you can't really have a literature. And with the collapse of the exile writing (some are dead now and some who are still writing are kind of repeating their positions) there will be no dramatic development as far as I can see, after that first generation of writers in London; and there has been no effective influential dramatic development *within* the Caribbean since the brief Cultural Revolution of the '70s. It's not that there is no activity but that there is a shortage of presence.

KD: Of course there is self-publication. Robert Lee and Kendel Hippolyte in St. Lucia, for instance . . .

KB: And they are wonderful examples of it. And before that, up to the mid '70s, there was the remarkable contribution of A. J. Seymour and the Guyana writers in this area. But you see, despite their activity as self-published poets, the general Caribbean does not know what's *happening*—and this applies even more for the more recent St. Lucia effort as it was in Guyana, where at least Seymour's *Kyk* and its link with *Bim* and the BBC kept us in touch with what was happening. Now we hear names but you don't really know what they doing, and I think there is a problem. Unless there can be some organization where the people who are writing can be heard, like *Kyk* and the BBC's *Caribbean Voices* and Frank Collymore's *Bim* used to provide, we're going to, as the Poet says, "blush unseen."

KD: Do you think that the defining place for Caribbean letters is located primarily in how the work is disseminated?

KB: Unless an individual has *access* to what is happening, despite the publication and despite the "dissemination"—i.e., distribution—you are ignorant. You can really only go by what becomes available, and what is becoming available is very limited and is also very selected. For instance in this present phase now, a woman is going to be published over a man. At least it seems so to me. The literature conferences that are being held throughout the Caribbean, and elsewhere, are mainly devoted to women's writing; or if there are "transgender" conferences, they are preponderantly more women only.

That is giving a false impression as to the energy of the Caribbean. This gives the impression that only or mainly women are "saying something," when in fact that's not the case; though since with the Revolution women are at least released into increasing confident experiment and self-expression, a great deal of the creative writing *is* going to be from women. And the three awards from the Central Bank of Barbados, for example, the first monetary awards given by the Bank (March '99) in an effort to encourage creative writing in Barbados, are all won by women—with unquestionably fine records of previous good work in the island.

The other problem we have in making an assessment of our "literature" is to do with our main publishers—the metropolitans. The Metros—who then influence what we in the Caribbean come to define and accept as "literature"—the old colonial situation—have settled on only a few, three or four only, "major" people who they will publish and push. Right now it's Walcott, Naipaul, Kincaid, Caryl Phillips, and perhaps Edwidge Danticat. And this means that the "younger writers"—and people like Roach, Martin Carter, Bongo Jerry, N. D. Williams, and James Carnegie, those fellas who are writing in the middle '70s and who really produced *in the Caribbean* some radical work, have not gone any "further" because I suspect that if they did send anything to London, it would not have been published and if they sent it to New York they wastin time; because is only in the last few years—let's say from the early '90s—that the U.S. has started to look at Caribbean literature, and even now, is highly selected and limited. I mean, even Harris is not published in the U.S.!

KD: No, he's not...

KB: And it shows you the kind of bias there is... an anthology of rejection letters would make very interesting reading...

15 MARCH 1994

Dear Professor Brathwaite:

Herewith your *Barbajan Poems,* which I enjoyed immensely. Yet despite my enthusiasm and appreciation for your work, I must, reluctantly, let you know that it is not right for [our] list. That is to say, some of the more exuberant passages that are specifically "poetry" have their greatest strength and arid weakness in the same brilliant layerings, emphasis on polyglot, orthographic playfulness, portmanteaus and vernacular. The Humor and insights and sheer enjoyment that much of this brings is indisputable, though, at times, I found it distracting and misleading, even opaque. Surely this could be revised and made more narrative, thereby shaping a more coherent story of your life, without losing your great talents for rhythm and mood. I'd hesitate to suggest that the poems be used less prominently, but feel strongly that you flesh out what goes around them.

I'm terribly sorry, and wish you the best of luck in placing this somewhere else. I'm confident you'll find a braver publisher than me. My hunch is that you will do just as well—and will most likely sell just as many copies—with a smaller regional or academic press. That said, I would be eager to read anything you write in the future.

KD: And speaking of anthologies, have many anthologies of Caribbean literature appeared in the United States?

KB: One or two, with some very nice things; but they not available to the generality of Caribbean readers—not even, it would seem to Caribbean—certainly not in the Caribbean—reviewers, critics, booksellers, and librarians. Therefore they don't have the impact that *Breaklight* (ed. Andrew Salkey, 1971) had, for instance, or the Seymour anthologies (A. J. Seymour, ed., *Anthology of Guianese Poetry* 1954; the *Kyk-Over-Al Anthology of West Indian Poetry*, 1952, 1957), *New Writing in the Caribbean* (Carifesta, 1972) or the *CQ*'s (*Caribbean Quarterly*; see especially the 1958 issues edited by Philip Sherlock and Andrew Carr).

KD: You've talked consistently about the communal role of the artist and the artist vis-à-vis the community. In your analysis of *The Hills Were Joyful Together* and *Brother Man* (by Roger Mais) this is the distinctive quality you speak of. To what extent do you regard this as the ideal posture of the poet in societies today?

KB: I would think that that is still there — the communal quality — especially within the dub poets who depend very much on group support in their writing and performance. Most (or is it many?) of the other poets in the Caribbean have never really been people-people. I think they have always been more on the Keatsian thing about the isolated persona, the isolated muse. Some have openly said that they don't rely upon community for their inspiration and their voice. And I think that this is limiting our production of poetry in the Caribbean, because unless you have an "ego," it looks as if you don't get heard.

But I can't see at any level, at any time, not only in the Caribbean, not only at any period, how any artist can really grow and flow unless he/she is in touch with their community, and is writing out of that community's experience and flowing it back into that community's spheres. I think that you can have the individual geniuses who write in an abstraction, but that's going to be very successfully rare. And in the Caribbean where we need to bring the fragments together, it's almost impossible to remain separate from the climate alone, from the heat, from the vibrancy of the colors — they all demand description — and not only from the individual but also from the community point of view and vision.

In any case, these details of our environment really haven't been properly described since early Naipaul and Lamming and even that was only a hint of a beginning (though we've had a culmination now in Walcott's *Omeros*, 1990) — so that one of the first calls of the writer is to simply describe what is going on through the window. And if you not doing that, you might as well be on the djuggs or something else equally "antisocial," though again we must recognize that the new djugg culture and its artistic offshoots and shootings is itself highly community based and supported.

Above all we have to recognize that there has been what is being called now a "paradigm shift" in our expressive culture, so that much of what writers and especially lyrical poets are saying is being said and done far better and far more community-relevantly by reggae, kaiso, an' soca artists and of course has always been potently well done in the folk and *vodoun* tradition from which much of the popular secular music now directly comes. I mean which "literary" writer could do better than Sparrow's *high pothetical* (or high pathetical) *ass*. When one hears that cricket kaiso, "Cricket in the Jungle," where the team is picked according to attributes—the umpire is the parrot up in a tree, the wicket-keeper is a crapaud squatting down, the snake is in the gully, etc. etc. etc. And what better metaphorical telling than Sparrow's "Lion and Donkey." At first "Lion foulin but the Referee inn callin," but as the tables turn—

> Hear de Referee—
> **Dat is foul, Donkey, dat is foul**
> Donkey tell de Referee—
> *Yes uh know*
> **Dat is foul, Donkey, dat is foul**
> *Maybe, but dis is the one foul dat cd crow!*

THE SECOND GENERATIONS OF EXILE(S)

KD: Before that though, I want to take you up on exiles—exiled writers. You have talked about the exiled artists of the '40s, '50s, '60s, but clearly there is another kind of "exiled" artist today, one who is no longer exiled in the same manner. I mean, if you take Claire Harris or Dionne Brand in Canada; Claudia Rankine or Rohan Preston in the United States; or John Agard and Grace Nichols in England, we have to use other terms to define their situation. It is different...

KB: One would have to do a very careful study to answer this question—and as far as I know, no one has so far tackled it—this important consideration of the orientation, the sensibility, and the contribution of the second-generation exiles to the Caribbean. So that again we come to the question of dissemination of information—what are they doing? I mean, we so seldom see this work and hardly ever read about it in the paper and journals that we have access to.

These "second exiles," although many of them are born in the Caribbean and write on Caribbean themes from Caribbean memory and often in Caribbean "language"—riddim, idiom, images, climate, etc.— and of course are fiercely Caribbean, etc. etc. etc.; they nevertheless are faced with/and respond to their new environment—which many increasingly perhaps unconsciously accept as their environment— home—despite the caveats—in a quite different way from say Selvon and Salkey in first-generation London. And this new environment, as it becomes increasingly home, also challenges these new exile Caribbeans, naturally, with themes and forms other than the "olde traditional" Caribbean of Pan, Yard, Church, Migrant, and the would-be nativist revolutionary in a society losing—no *selling*—its "unspoiled soul"—and unable to sell its bananas.

Contrast this with the new urbanate high-tension forms in the poetry of [Marlene] Nourbese Philip and Claire Harris, for example. Nalo Hopkinson's novel, *Brown Girl in the Ring* (Toronto 1998; Nalo is Slade Hopkinson's daughter), although titled with a Caribbean folksong, is really science—what she calls "speculative"—fiction. After Dionne Brand returns from the Grenada Revolution, she becomes involved in areas of writing far removed from Caribbean Yard— even though, thank God, no Canada can tek Yard outa the sista. And all this while the nativist concerns of the CaribbeanCaribbean become increasingly different from that of the second exile generation. We hear in them—despite the "global village"—a different and sometimes—I not happy with this word—alien accent. This, for instance, is from Claudia Rankine's "elsewhere, things ten," from I assume a book published by the University of Illinois Press, which I find on the Internet:

> Think of me somewhere dumb,
> open heart, open
> corridor into—
> whispering, okay. okay.
> And afraid. Alone
> and not. Afraid
> with no more room, falling
> into nowhere else

A CaribbeanCaribbean reader could in many ways "miss" this— which brings me back to the crucial need for information about the different Caribbeans among the different Caribbeans. I mean, I need to know in some detail what Claudia is writing and how/where I can find her work. We need conferences on this; above all we need inter-conversation and a *journal*—and perhaps an Internet link—to bring more news and knowledge of these several Caribbeans urgently about.

In the CaribbeanCaribbean right now, there is desperate need for a Restoration of the Caribbean—its sense of history and its history of voice. And I say "desperately" because every time I go back to the Caribbean (and since this interview, I've taken a two-year "sabbatical" there and intend to stay as soon as I can), I am aware of increasing materialism, of crassness, of a collapse of values—you just have to read what I had to say in *Trench Town Rock*. Having to write like that isn't easy, but it's the truth we must face before there can be any redemption.

I mean there is such a rapid destruction of the environment on which the artist has the whole purpose of his/her life built. But with the increasing superhighway graveyards, hotels squatting on our metaphors, structures obscuring manscape; from chattel house to castle—an architectural fantasy of "bigupsy" . . . So that with this I think that the writer is going, in the Caribbean, to go more and more into an increasing kind of silence. Which is perhaps another way of saying that there's not much "new native Caribbean" to report; while Claire and others you mention, especially I think, those in North America, have increasingly other concerns and don't—can't—contribute to the Restoration of the Caribbean Cosmos—though they are contributing to our Redemption—in the same way as the first generation of exiles did. Selvon and Lamming from London created creative echoes back in the Caribbean. Whatever else is happening, that's not happening—despite independence—via the second generation of exiles today.

KD: Is this not simply the crisis of exile?

KB: Is not simply the crisis, is actually the condition of exile.

THE CARIBBEANCARIBBEAN

KD: Okay then. Would you like to say a little more, expand, on your sense of "CaribbeanCaribbean"—"native Caribbean"—its problems and the responsibility, the relationship of the writer, to these?

KB: For me, you either continue to write what you knew when you were at school, basically, or you go forward and write where you are now. Write about what you have here now. But the larger "Caribbean issue" still remains to be dealt with.

When I talk about Caribbean literature I'm talking about literature which addresses and informs and comes out of what I call Caribbean Cosmology. The nature/natural of the Caribbean. Our sense of our space/time . . . The relationship of landscape to time, the movement of landscape and manscape in time and to time's riddims; our sense of our history out of this and the details of that history, iconographically expressed. The paradoxes, violences, and futures of society; people's relationships, integuments, physical, social and spiritual; the language we speak among each other and how this relates to Nature.

All this is a thousand years of work to be done. And when there are gaps in it (slavery, colonialism, underclass struggles, etc.), it means that generations of us are not going to be described. We haven't even been able to describe that crucial genesis period before Independence—the '30s. Mais and James did a little but they were limited to their sense of Yard. Mais only becomes engaged with Cosmos in his last novel, *Black Lightning*—which in itself is a wonder, even though he kind of deserts the kind of Caribbean social reality I consider our base.

The historians haven't done it yet either. And with their present archivally oriented training, I don't expect we'll cover very much ground in their area either. So that these things (our History) now become rumours and they are distorted by people who don't really like and don' really appreciate even the little that we've accomplished in the postindependence years.

The approach to Cosmos is connected with Shadows (Art), Music and Language. I mean, you wouldn't have to be away from the Caribbean for a year to realize that you've lost pace with how people are speaking and the body-language and the dance music of that speaking—the poetry. It's such a quick growth of thoughts and insights and images that if, as I say, you not *here,* it leaves you behind, you're left behind, like you bline, catching up with yesterday's nostalgia. For I mean that if you don't know/hear the native language/music, you can't write *new.* You can of course continue to write old verse but the real verse, the new verse, goes along with how life grows around your house, and inside you house and down the lane or (perhaps more difficult) terrace of your neighbours. Without this, you not really producing (much) new work and no new radical forms or excavations.

So therefore, coming back to your first question, about how does/can the new exile relate to the Caribbean, let me look, if you don't mind, since you're here—but I not saying this because you here but because I know something of your work—you at least have been making it available! And hence have made conversation about it possible—your *Jacko Jacobus* (1997).

You, I find, have found a way of connecting back to the native Caribbean by using a well-known (biblical) story and relating it probably to your own life-experience. And you are able to write a fantastic account of Caribbean sensibility, both in the Caribbean and in the space of exile beautifully; that reflects a particularly personal and Caribbean theme. But since you had left the Caribbean yourself, you could not write the kind of *yard version* that someone in the Caribbean would have done. *JJ* had to be *pitched*—literally and tonally—outside of its exile. It constantly and consistently tries to return and connect. . . .

But the actual details of the *yard part* of the work are not there, because you are not here, okay? And the people who are here—in your novel—don't seem to be able to create the kind of "yard structure" that in a sense one senses they wish to. But then you transcend this with ritual—secular Caribbean ritual, if I may put it this way, in which the Father tries to return to the Son and the Son to the Father, the One becoming the Other; and through this ritual, you make a Caribbean link with what I call Cosmos; and you have been able to reach this sense of ritual and find the form/language for it, through your sense of reggae as I earlier did in my work with jazz.

And then there's Erna Brodber who is continuing in a new sense, the old nativist Caribbean what she calls *koumbla* tradition.

THE NATIVE EXILE

But most of the writing I've been seeing—mainly unpub work—in the Caribbean—it is very surprising that people are still so very Victorian. It is amazing. But then, despite the ScrewFace and Gorgon, our society remains very Victorian. Or perhaps "Victorian" was more ScrewFace than we think! And by Victorian I mean, in terms of literature, pre-Wilson Harris.

And to make this worse, very little that one does, writes, is not even ever *seen*. So that we're now faced, in the Caribbean, with a generation of *native exiles* . . . One of the great ironies of the postindependence twentieth-century Caribbean.

Hence the new cult(s) of crime, violence, djuggs, freak-out, burn-out, road rage, and the inability, it seems, to play magically anymore in the Caribbean culture sport of the cricket. And I think that when you reach this stage of native exile on the increasing widening scale that's here, the society is in serious problems.

I don't know enough about Cuba, but I suspect that on the verge of their great Revolution, you had this same/similar condition of native exile, resulting in implosion and, in their case, liberating revolution involving violence. It don't follow, even if we too have an implosion, that it will lead to revolution or to liberation. But we might just have more violence and the enjoyment/exploitation of it; the psychosocial justification of it—the violence of like earthquake and volcano—already erupting symbolically along the Caribbean chains—the deformation of the person and the personality—KICK-EM-JENNY!—and our fomentation into magmatic interpersonal cruelty. It's a deformation of grancharge reggae and kaiso—way of mocking other people an' makin yoself gloat greater than you are.

I suffer this when someone—someones!—break into my house in Kingston—three gunmen. And the way they carry on, I could tell that the whole thing was a kind of masturbatory exercise in the threat of torture and violence. These guys were trying to get a high on the situation they were able to create at my expense. They themselves were not creating anything, right? They were *consumers*. They were not interested in criticizing my lifestyle—except insofar that I didn't have no gun, had, they thought, the money they felt they should have, and was at their mercy—which in their eyes made me a *bwoy!* I mean, they had not broken into my house in that thunderstorm because I was Robin Hood or a wrongdoer. Or because they were Shango! They come in there to have a pleasant evening writing physical anti-poetry upon my mind and body . . .

What Caribbean literature and what kind of Caribbean is coming out of this dumb domino?

KD: And you suggest that the literature that comes out of that needs to bring vision to that violence, needs to bring an understanding of that disruption, a conscience?

KB: And it also challenges our criticism to "place" this new art, these new artists . . . and all that this implies.

[The interview went on through dub; Bob Marley and Mikey Smith; Rohlehr as critic of KB's work and Rohlehr's problems of publication; the University of West Indies; the question of KB in both history and literature (KB was a professor of history at UWI and is now a professor of comparative literature at New York University); more on Caribbean cosmology; KB's new African poems and the images of Rwanda; and more on publishers, including the remarkable contribution of Jeremy Poynting's Peepal Tree Press at Leeds, England, since 1994. It ended with a discussion, initiated by Dawes, of KB's material writing.]

THE LONG POEM

KD: I have never read anything where you talk about your writing process. How you construct "the long poem" . . . Is the long poem a series of sounds that become a long poem or is it a projected map that you can follow? How does it relate to the idea of the novel?

KB: You know, I have never been asked that question before . . . so I will have to think it out . . . It begins with a vision of where I thought we were going. Having said that we should be going into whatever horizon that was—which is what we were not! Then the question was, "Where were we coming from and why are we not going where we should!"

Rights of Passage is constructed as a kind of answer to this question. And then there was a kind of response to this in that I wanted to talk more about where we were coming from—so I went back to my experience of Ghana in the poem *Masks*.

And then the third poem of the trilogy, *Islands,* is pitched into where ever we are going or should be going. . . . And not only that, but as soon as I thought of all these ideas of *where/why do we want to get there and therefore how is it that we not,* so many images presenting themselves, that I could see that it would take time to talk it out, write it out. It couldn't be anything "lyrical" in the old traditional sense; nothing "short." There were too many factors involved.

KD: And this would have operated in the second trilogy as well?

KB: Yes. Because there I go to Barbados. This is the first time I was back in Barbados very seriously. I got a sabbatical and I was assigned to be there for a year. I left Barbados in 1950. All that time I might have come into Barbados just a few days, but in 1970 I'm there now for a year. And I got a Guggenheim so I do have time to write. I had just come from CARIFESTA, but the thing that's at the back in my mind is that having written these three things—the first trilogy—there is an absence of my family—my family—in the work. It's amazing. Right away, I say, "Hey." I mean, I owe so much to them that how come the poem doesn't deal with them? And at the same time, since I was back in Barbados, I made the link between Barbados and my mother. I remember on the beach at Bathsheba there facing Africa (because that was part of that too). And I write in the sand: MOTHER POEM.

And I knew that the poem would be that. And it would be exactly what and where I was at that moment—the sun, sand...

KD: Yes.

KB: The sea.

KD: Yes.

KB: The mountains behind me.

KD: Yes.

KB: The islands the coral and the mother... And therefore I sit down and all these things were already living in me, and they begin to work themselves out.

And after that then there was *Sun Poem* which was... my father's ... the male kind of point of view.

X/Self is different again. Frankly, I sometimes feel that it's not a true third part of the second trilogy. It's a big departure into something entirely different. It's as if there are two poems here, *Mother Poem and Sun Poem,* that are satellites of each other, but the third, *X/Self,* goes somewhere else. [For detailed remarks by KB on the disjuncture of *X/S* and its place now in the architecture of his more recent trilogies, see Kamau Brathwaite, *Conversations with Nathaniel Mackey* (We Press, 1999).]

KD: I remember when we talked way back—early in 1983 or so... '84... We talked about jazz. We were talking about *The Arrivants.* I'm almost certain that at some point the question of the appropriateness of jazz became an issue. You already had, at the time, a whole slew of work that could be called a precursor to a lot of dub poetry and reggae riddim poetry. How does reggae begin, from where you sit, to define an aesthetic in the context of the Caribbean, or in the context of Jamaica?

KB: (Had I known at the time that KD's question here is specially formed, since he himself has embarked on the study and practice, I might have cut the cloth of this answer more closely . . . again the need, as we say above, for information, more conversation, among us.)

I started out with jazz, as you say. Don't forget I had been out of the Caribbean for most of my "grown-up" years in England and Ghana. So that the only music that I used to listen to was this jazz (not really true—but jazz is what most influences the poetry, certainly of *The Arrivants*). And therefore, whatever jazz was doing meant poetry for me. But what's interesting is having got that trigger of jazz and being back in the Caribbean where you don't hear jazz, I began to hear this *kaiso*, in St. Lucia *cadence* and *La Rose;* in Jamaica *ska, mento, pukkumina,* and then *reggae,* etc., and they led me now into the folk elements of the culture and therefore into the folk possibilities of the poetry.

When I write (in *Rights of Passage*) the poem "The Cabin"—look at it—I didn't know anything very much about slave cabins in the Caribbean. So I fall back on Harriett Beecher Stowe (*Uncle Tom's Cabin*). But at the same time I was writing (1963-64) the poem, I was hearing the music coming out of the Kingston cabins, and this leads me, in *Islands,* to whole rhythm changes—*developments,* rather—in my work and through these new riddims (poetry as teacher) and the disc of history to a widening knowledge of yards and cabins.

And therefore (to try answer your question), the aesthetic that reggae will present is an aesthetic that allows or encourages or reflects a local statement, a nativism. Jazz represents, in the Caribbean, a plantation and American urban aesthetic—it has that wide spectrum and dynamic. But when you want to come to your yard—your own thing—you have to go back to the music that comes out of your yard. Because, the only way you can describe the woman going to the hospital, in the casualty, with her bleeding child and no doctor not there to even *look* at you in that cold midnight hour—that lonely silence of the waiting room. And you watch this woman, with her helpless dying child beside her bleeding to death . . . and all she can do is hug herself to her stomach, her belly—binding her belly against all these midnights and centuries of neglect and indifference with her frail strong arms folded around herself since this is all she has . . .

For this the only music is *mento*, is Bob Marley's "Woman hold your had an cry." There's no other music—no words—that can say what this mother's gestures mean.

NEW DIRECTIONS: SYCORAX

My big regret is that Caribbean criticism has almost totally disregarded my work since *The Arrivants* as long ago now as 1973, even though they are still trying to absorb its riddims, structures, and *Iwa*. But in the effort to deal with *The Arrivants*, and the stereotyping that their laziness and lack of knowledge has resulted in, it could be as if Brathwaite has written nothing since *The Arrivants*; or that *Ancestors*—the title of the rewritten second trilogy which should have been published by New Directions but it seems they run into problems with my *Sycorax video style*—so it seems we won't even be seeing soon the new second trilogy, not to mention the work that crucially follows from this.

KD: So Sycorax becomes a problem?

KB: As she is for Shakespeare!

KD: Indeed!

KB: I come to Sycorax during my Time of Salt: death of Zea Mexican 1986, loss of Irish Town Library of Alexandria 1988, murder by Kingston gunmen 1990 . . . just look at the dread frequencies of these catastrophes. My writing hand becomes a dumb stump in my head . . . I mean I can't write or utter a sound or metaphor. But Sycorax comes to me in a dream and she dreams me a Macintosh computer with its winking *io* hiding in its margins which, as you know, are not really margins, but electronic accesses to Random Memory and the Cosmos and the *Iwa*.

And she dreams me these stories (see *DreamStories* 1994)—what Rohlehr calls "Night Journeys" or "Night Healings"—and shows me how to find *jo* to write them out on the computer. And the two together introduce me to fonts and the fonts take me across Mexico to Siqueiros and the Aztec murals and all the way back to ancient Nilotic Egypt to hieroglyphics—allowing me to write in light and to make sound visible as if I am in video.

She abolishes, as I say, the traditional margin and the boundaries of books *and publishers don't like that*—just as they don't like Sycorax and her sons Mike Tyson and Caliban.

Edward Baugh

BORN 1936

WHEN EDWARD BAUGH's first and only collection of verse, *A Tale from the Rainforest*, was published by Sandberry Press in 1988, he had long been recognized as one of the more skilled writers of verse in the West Indies. Baugh, born in Jamaica in 1936, somehow focused his time and energy, not on the rather self-absorbed pursuit of getting his poetry published, but on developing a remarkable reputation as a professor of English literature and as a formidable critic of West Indian writing at the University of the West Indies in Mona.

Baugh's poetry reflects a writer with an intensely dogged wit who is constantly aware of the masking and pretense that characterizes the art of making poems. Irony is a dominant feature of his work, but it is largely a bearable irony since the victim of ironic commentary is almost always himself in relation to the reader.

Edward Baugh lives in Jamaica and teaches at the University of the West Indies. He continues to write and publish his poetry in periodicals and journals all over the world.

KWAME DAWES: Why only one volume? Is this a case of the peculiar pressures of being an active academic in the Caribbean, the kind of pressures that make it difficult to pursue the writing and publishing of poetry, or are there other reasons for this seemingly modest publication output?

EDWARD BAUGH: The fact that I have published only one (proverbially slim) volume to date is owing in the first place to my not being a prolific poet. In addition, I am not much good at "pushing" my own stuff. The fact that even that one volume appeared was due almost entirely to the publisher's initiative. For a long time I'd also had a sort of perverse, superstitious policy that I wouldn't attempt to put out a collection unless I also had a lot more poems in reserve, because otherwise I might never write another poem after the collection came out. I think I have enough poems now for a second collection, but I haven't done anything about that yet.

As to the not being prolific, I suspect that's just the way things are with me; I wasn't blessed with a heavy dose of the creative adrenaline. But it's also true that the demands of my work, teaching and administration, and the fact that I am probably too obedient to those demands, have rather limited my "space" for writing poetry. Once or twice in my life I've felt that I was being caught up in a creative surge that could have lasted and gathered momentum, but then routine work would interrupt, rather like Coleridge's "person from Porlock" who knocked at his door and put an end to "Kubla Khan" or whatever.

KD: In your collection *A Tale From The Rainforest*, there are a number of poems that make direct reference to Shakespeare, particularly to *Hamlet*. I know that for a number of years you were a fairly serious actor in Jamaica. Would you regard the qualities of drama—dramatic monologues, character definitions, and the engagement with narrative (stories really)—as important elements in your work and in what interests you about poetry?

EB: Yes, I'm pretty sure that my feeling for theater, for acting, and my little experience at it must have had some influence on my poetry. A poem has to be *heard*, if only in the silence inside one's head. And every "I," even the most seemingly personal and confessional, is a "character" the poet assumes.

KD: How long have you been writing poetry? What prompted you to start writing in this form?

EB: The first poem I can remember writing was a short, Romantic-type lyric about sunset, written when I was in fourth form, i.e. about twelve, for some competition or other. I can't really say what prompted me to start writing poetry. Perhaps, essentially, it was the sound, hearing "the sound of verses," a gut experience.

KD: Do you write on a regular basis or do you turn to poetry as a way of making sense of things? Is the process itself enough, or is there a need to share the product with others?

EB: No. As you will have gathered from something I said earlier, I don't write on a regular basis. Poems come or they don't, in their own time. Sometimes I have an idea, or a line, and I worry away at it for a long time, off and on, but whether it ends up being a poem or not is unpredictable. I don't think that I write to make sense of things as you put it. Whatever sense I make of things is what I would have made even if I didn't write poems. It's just that some experiences, the savoring of them, seem to want to be sharpened, fixed, shared by way of memorable speech. In some cases, too, I come to terms with an experience, I lay the ghost of it by writing it. That is true for instance of the poem "The Carpenter's Complaint." The sharing of the experience, which I mentioned just now, seems to be only too natural a motive. I can never quite understand or believe people who say that they write just for themselves. They may actually believe this, but I think that they're fooling themselves. The very act of writing, the very impulse, is an outgoing from oneself.

KD: You have written about the writing process (at least I think it is writing that you are writing about) as a kind of journey ("Getting There") to find the muse. But it is a treacherous and painful journey with the potential for getting lost in the process. Yet the destination is "Silence," a place of serenity and assurance. Is this the ultimate destination in writing—a quest for resolution and peace? One senses this kind of quest and resolution in "The House of Poems," "A Tale from the Rainforest," and "Warner-Woman," to name a few. I am reminded of Goodison's mythical "Heartease."

EB: The fascination with silence is something I am happy to find in some other poets. It is as if speech/poetry and silence exist in a symbiotic relationship. Or as if, as you suggest, one worries away at words in the vain hope of reaching a state of being in which one does not need them. The obsession with words and with wanting to establish a presence through speaking goes hand in hand with a deep distrust of words. They can seem like the ultimate futility. I suppose language and poetry are functions of, and consolations against, our human imperfection. I can't imagine that there is any need for poets in Heaven. There, I should like to think, being flows into and out of being in pure, wordless music.

KD: The iambic crawls into your poetry a great deal. At times the pattern is very deliberate ("There's a Brown Girl in the Ring"), and sometimes it is more subtle; but most of the work I have seen is committed to the line of ten feet or more. Long free verse lines that rarely, if ever, shift to the staccato of single-word lines and so on. A number of American poets have adopted a pattern of lineation that entails replicating the natural breath where line breaks are defined by the breathing patterns of the poet. Is this something of what your poetry moves towards, a kind of replication of the natural voice, the natural breath, or could it be that visually, the longer line appeals to you?

EB: Nice image, "crawls." The iambic as a sort of quintipede. I could hardly have escaped the iambic, brought up as I was on English poetry. But I have to explain something here. The arrangement of the poems in *Rainforest* may be misleading in that the poems aren't dated. A poem like "Brown Girl," and one or two others with a pronounced iambic or related beat, belongs to my "crawling period." They are among the earliest poems in the book, as far as the chronology of composition goes. Wayne Brown more or less spotted this in his review of *Rainforest,* referring to them as the poems in which I was going through the stage of showing that I too could "suffer in accurate iambics," to borrow a phrase from Walcott. I suspect that I have a prejudice against "the staccato of single-word lines"—it somehow seems too easy and theatrical. Yes, I believe that the rhythmic principle which I've favored does have to do with natural breathing patterns, or with natural phrases as the rhythmic unit. At the same time, this principle sometimes works along with, or in counterpoint to a more imposed, but I hope shadowy, pattern in which all the lines will have, say, four stressed syllables each, although you can't scan the line into traditional metrical feet.

KD: What is your editing process like? Mervyn Morris speaks of letting it all out, and then trimming down to the poem. Kendel Hippolyte suggests that he constructs each line with care and attention. The shape is almost constructed as he writes. Most people argue that both patterns characterize their work, but every poet appears to have a system, a way developed from years of knowing one's cheap tricks, one's bad habits.

EB: I don't know that I have a system, or any editing process. One always has to edit, but sometimes the editing is so simultaneous with the first coming into being of the poem that one might not even be aware of any editing as such—you know, as if the poem comes whole and virtually finished from the beginning. "Nigger Sweat" was a poem that came like that; but that rarely happens. The editing may sometimes be a matter of rearranging the sequence of lines or sentences, but more than anything else it's a matter of cutting back, paring down, knowing what to leave out. There's a lot of stuff that keeps wanting to be included, but you have to be ruthless. One principle I think I've arrived at through experience is that whenever you're in any doubt about a line, about whether it's really working, leave it out, or change it.

KD: The female is a dominant figure in your collection *A Tale from the Rainforest*. Whether it is in the sensitive and moving poems about your mother, or in the pieces about the female muse, the "she" is consistently present. No doubt, this is not a self-conscious pattern, but are there ways to respond to this observation? To what extent do you think this pattern can be tied to your own biography, your own experience?

EB: I wouldn't know. I guess you ought to ask a psychoanalyst to have a go at me and answer that question. But how could I not write about women? They're central to everything, aren't they?

KD: I would like you to talk a bit about influences in your work. Of course, there are the sort of British classics, but even as you speak of those influences and how they work in shaping your poetic character, could you talk also about other West Indian writers and their influences? Invariably, because of your fluent line, your gentle wit and the strong elements of introspection, people will link you with a poet like Walcott. Is there something in this?

EB: It's difficult for anyone to be aware of all his influences. Some influences may be of so deep and diffused a kind that one may hardly even be aware of them as influences. For instance, the English Romantics must have influenced me in some general way, because that was the poetry that turned me on when I was at the age where the idea of writing poetry myself must have first been taking hold in me. That was what I was taught most at school, especially in the sixth form. Then there was a time when I, like a lot of other people, was very impressed by a modern Romantic, so to speak, Dylan Thomas. But then, there was my Eliot period. Perhaps the very fact that I am conscious of having to be on guard, in my own writing, against the too mellifluous or too sonorous is an indication of how deep the Romantic kind of influence was. One has to resist the seductions of eloquence. But then, what's wrong with eloquence and "the mighty line"? I suppose I work within that tension, between the seduction and the resistance. I have no problem with being thought to have some link with Walcott. One of the landmark moments of my life with poetry occurred on the afternoon when, in the periodical stacks of the Mona Library, I came upon Walcott's just-published "Tales of the Islands" in *Bim*. The next, about four years later, was when *In a Green Night* came out, in 1962.

KD: A sequence of poems in *Rainforest* chart memories of childhood characters that were important to you with some fondness and pleasure. But these poems are also about the pain of growing up, of becoming distanced from the past through a process of growing into the complications of class, education, and economic progress. There is a quality of loss, and a resultant process which leaves the poet outside the memory, somewhat alienated. Do you find this to be an inevitable condition of the poet, the writer? Is there, as is suggested in "Small-Town Story," a suggestion of guilt and regret that underlies the emotions evoked by these memories?

EB: Yes. Your reading of some of the childhood poems is spot on. Memory, or rather nostalgia, is another of the dangerous seductions. The challenge is to exploit memory without wallowing in nostalgia. There's another childhood-memory poem, "Responsibility," which is post-*Rainforest*, and which also moves in nostalgia, but which also, I hope, does something more, including being a recognition, belatedly no doubt, of all the taken-for-granted responsibility that parents exercise on behalf of their children.

KD: When I heard you read "Nigger Sweat" some years ago, it struck me at the time that many non-Jamaicans would read this as a poem exploring the difficulties of working-class Jamaicans to get a visa to the U.S. Apart from the allegorical and symbolic implications of the poems, I was impressed by how well I could identify with the fellow waiting to have his passport and papers checked—the sense of dignity abused, of vulnerability, of shame—a condition that transcends class in the Jamaican context. Here, then, I found that the narrative amounted to more than a poet scavenging on the vicissitudes of the suffering. I was impressed by your ability to become that man largely because I was that man in many ways. I have found this true in a number of your poems that assume the dialect voice. Is this a difficult balancing act—the act of trying not to be condescending, not be a poetic anthropologist, if you will, while constructing deeply felt poems—that you are conscious of as you work?

EB: Again, I have to congratulate you — this is becoming tedious — on your reading of my work. That's how I should like the reader to receive "Nigger Sweat." But I never thought of it as any special achievement in crossing the class line. I just wrote what I felt. I suppose the identification in this case was easy, because the simple fact is that I was in that queue and *my* palms too, clutching my passport, were sweating. But the validity of the poem, or the voice, ought not to depend on the reader's knowing or thinking that I was actually there. The poem ought to work essentially as an act of *imagination*. Yes, I suppose it is a difficult balancing act to write across class lines, but the big thing is to find just the right voice, and the poem will follow. Besides, one ought to be able to feel when one is being condescending, and if you feel condescending, don't proceed with the poem, unless what the poem is going to be about is that you were feeling condescending.

KD: I think your poem "A Rain-Washed Town by the Sea" offers a refreshing way of seeing the place of memory in verse: "These memories define me. I keep them / against that morning when my eyes / no longer turn to greet the sun." How much of your poetry could be called a mission to excavate the defining quality of memory — a kind of ordering of the self?

EB: For me, at any rate, memory is elemental to poetry. There are two lines by Walcott, from *Another Life,* that are inscribed on the wall inside my head: "a man lives half of life. / The other half is memory." "To excavate the defining quality of memory" sounds good. I don't mind identifying with that. I think that self-definition is one of the motives of my work. Apart from the childhood-memory poems, there are a few others which would also seem to be about defining the self, e.g., "Mistaken Identity," "Capricorn," and "The Poet Bemused." Beyond that, there may be a lot of truth in the idea that a poet's true autobiography is his or her poetry.

KD: One of your clearest and more amusing poems is "Truth and Consequence" in which you philosophize about the myth of the "apolitical." It is a deeply ironic poem that smacks of a kind of cynicism about the place of the artist in society. Placed beside the equally amusing lines, "why, as you'll note / he never even wrote / a Rodney poem. Can you / blame me for leaving / the creep?" in "The Poet Bemused," one gets the impression that you are not entirely comfortable with the notion of the poet as self-defined political voice, at least it is not a role you assume for yourself. Is this true? Have you sensed a shift in West Indian writing, from the politically charged writing of the seventies, where there was always hope of an answer, to the more introspective posture of the nineties? Has this happened with your own writing, your own engagement with politics in your poetry?

EB: Yes, it's just not in me to set myself up as some great political spokesman for "the people." But you're likely to be more popular if you do just that. So I'm cynical about that presumption, and cynical about my inability to undertake it. I guess my problem is that my cynicism is total. There's a line in "Capricorn" which indicates something of that: "the weakness in everything leaps immediately to my eyes." Cynicism never changes the world. It's the people with great pretensions and ideals, the fanatics who do. So, alas, I'm not likely to change the world. The great achievement would be to write a great poem about the passion of good sense, which is a contradiction in terms. However, cynicism is neither nihilism nor despair. There's always life and living and loving and people and pain and food and the sun and human effort and the beauty of human weakness, and in writing about any of these things one may touch responsive chords in people and may, in effect, speak for people—give thanks.

KD: As an artist, what is your response to the question: "Where are we (Jamaica) going as a nation now?" Kamau Brathwaite's *Trench Town Rock* is a frightening charting of the descent into violence and a certain anarchy in the country; it is also a piece about the debilitating effects of fear and loss. A friend responded to the book by saying, "Jamaica always seems worse when you are away." And yet there seems to be an overwhelming sense of decay in the fabric of the society, an almost absurdly exaggerated manifestation of the notorious Jamaican strong-will and no-nonsense way. When you look at Jamaica, what do you see, hear, feel? Do you feel compelled, as a writer, to write about all of this?

EB: Man, that's exactly the kind of grand public question that needs a guru, not me. No doubt there are all sorts of signs that things are falling apart; but the trouble with things is that they are always falling apart. If you are a mythopoeic poet with a large, apocalyptic vision, then Jamaica now will lend itself to that vision. It will have great symbolic potential. I guess I just work away at little corners of the canvas. A poem such as "Lignum Vitae" would fit the picture your question paints, except, of course, the lignum vitae is used as an assurance of resilience and survival and beauty. As a poet I've never had any agenda. Perhaps one might be discovered in retrospect.

KD: Related to that question, can you talk a little about what it means to live and write in Jamaica (as against living abroad)? Are there challenges here that can have an impact on the material you produce?

EB: Living in Jamaica for the past thirty years or so has been a challenge. It can be frustrating and infuriating, but it's also always exciting. In any case, it's where I am. I've never lived and written anywhere else long enough to be able to make any useful comparison. I don't have any complaint about writing here. In an earlier period I would no doubt have complained about the difficulty of getting published. I couldn't complain now about my work not being known or appreciated, at least among an appreciable few whose opinion I value. The Jamaican language situation, which is now more than ever a burning, divisive issue, is also a special source of energy and possibility for me as a writer.

BORN 1937

MERVYN MORRIS WAS born in Jamaica. He attended the University of the West Indies and then was a Rhodes Scholar at Oxford University where he read English. He returned to Jamaica in the mid-1960s to teach at the University of the West Indies. He has been teaching there since.

For many years few Caribbean writers wrote with candor and wit about subjects of everyday living—family, marriage, fatherhood, and lust. But from the publication of his first collection, *The Pond*, in 1973, Mervyn Morris bucked the trend toward overly politicized verse devoted entirely to a postcolonialist discourse. It is hardly that Morris was a confessional poet intent on playing out the details of private life in his poetry—in fact, Morris's poetry is a study in the business of counter-confession, a kind of poetry of sophisticated masking and distancing that is devoted to the singular thesis of the poem as the artifact—the moment of craft that takes second place to nothing.

Yet his poetry charts with sensitivity the details of being a father, a husband, a son, a friend in a Jamaican middle-class society. In many ways, there appears to be an inherent contradiction here—the poet whose subject is invariably autobiographical, and yet who eschews verse that gives too much away, that indulges in sentiment, and that lacks the enigma of brevity. However, once the quality of irony as a poetic and character trait is stirred into the mix, Morris the poet begins to make absolute sense. Ultimately, this ironic eye is what distinguishes Morris from most of his contemporaries.

He is a professor in West Indian literature at the University of the

West Indies, in Jamaica. He coedited *Jamaica Woman* (Heinemann, 1980) and *Voiceprint* (Longman, 1989), and edited *The Faber Book of Contemporary Caribbean Short Stories* (Faber, 1990). His own collections of poetry include *The Pond* and *Shadowboxing* (New Beacon, 1973), *On Holy Week* (Dangaroo, 1993), and *Examination Centre* (New Beacon, 1992).

KWAME DAWES: In a poem in your most recent collection, *Examination Centre,* you speak of irony as a cancer—a kind of ailment, if you will. And yet, there is a sense in which irony is at the heart of your persona as poet. Indeed, I think it was Bill Carr who found, in your early work, a refreshing capacity for irony that he felt was missing from much of Jamaican literature. Can you talk a little about the Janus-headedness of irony in your poetry?

MERVYN MORRIS: Well, I have to agree that there is a lot of irony in my poetry. I guess there is a lot of irony in the way I see the world. It's not just a craft thing, it's a thing of my personal viewpoint. But, I suppose, it's also in a sense a thing that connects with literary antecedents. Some of the poetry with which I was in contact at a crucially formative stage, like in the early years of university, was by the Metaphysical poets of English literature—John Donne, George Herbert, Andrew Marvell—and, of course, that was the period when the influence of Eliot in criticism (through various others, Leavis and so on) was dominant, and where one of the critical buzzwords was irony—if you think about Cleanth Brooks's *The Well-Wrought Urn,* for example, where one was being taught that a poem that is most successful is likely to contain a criticism of its own main contentions. So that, in literary terms, one was encouraged towards irony. But I don't think that's where it comes from. I think it's probably something out of my own personal and family formation. My father was a great humorist, a very witty man, and my whole family was very verbal, so that one is always alert to the ironic implication of statements which people might make innocently.

KD: Critics often describe your poetry as representing the "finished thought," as distinct from the thought-in-process. The idea is that your brevity and conciseness constitute a most acute self-consciousness about your ideas—a distillation, if you will, that has been so carefully honed that only the essence remains. While the critics express admiration for this, there is a certain quality of uncertainty about the satisfaction felt by the reader. Perhaps an uneasiness about the intense intelligence of your presence in the verse. Does all this make sense to you as you think about your poetry?

MM: It makes sense, but it's something I'd like to resist, contradict, argue against. In fact, I have done some of this in print. In *Hinterland*, that anthology edited by E. A. Markham, when Archie asked me for a statement on some of my work, I thought through and wrote some of the things I felt, and those have become the basis of what is now an article in *The Journal of West Indian Literature* called "Behind the Poems." And essentially, what I'm saying there is "Yes, I am trying to move towards essentials" which may be like the "finished thought" (as you say). The process of my own work is to start with the stimulus experience and to keep working and working and working until what I have seems to me to be the essential significance; hopefully, with enough to make it believable. But my tendency now is to remove a lot of the detail which is not essential to the central story or the central images. So that there is a sense in which the poem is somewhat like what you call "the finished thought." I think one of the first people to say something along these lines was Pam Mordecai in Daryl Dance's *Fifty Caribbean Writers*. Pam Mordecai's piece seems to me to be very sensitive and very accurate in many, many details. And she may even be accurate in that, but I disagree—in fact I mock a little her position that she wants to be a pillion rider and be taken right through the experience. Well, fine, but my work these days doesn't offer many pleasures to the pillion rider. I don't see any reason why you have to be taken on the trip. I can give you a report or a snapshot that is complex enough, I hope.

KD: I know that you have a preference for the terse and fatless poem. In your editing process, what are the elements that tend to go first? Where is the fat located in your poetry?

MM: The "fat" is mostly in the early drafts, which I would think must be pretty normal. When you think you have a poem arriving, you tend to have minimal censorship of the flow; and certainly when I am teaching or when I am trying to help people to produce poems, this is one of the most important things. Let it happen, and if you let it happen, if you're lucky, then there may be something there which you will recognize as possibly either more or less interesting as it is or there may be a few lines that tell you where it is you should be trying to go. The process moves from just rolling into trying to shape. And when yuh rolling, you're just spilling your guts. That is the raw material, and if yuh lucky, you begin to see where something else might begin to happen. I guess one other way of trying to answer your question would be that sometimes, one has published a poem or, at any rate, let it out of one's tight fist, and then realized that there are chunks of it that didn't need to be there. I often remove things, not because I think they are "fat," but because I think they are unnecessary. It's not quite the same thing. There are various poems in various published versions which would make that sort of point fairly clear. One of them would be a poem which started as "A Drowning" and was published in at least two forms, one of them in *Bim*. The poem was provoked by the actual response of various people to a drowning, and the way the boarding-school community was kind of shaken by this, to be quite literal about it. And quite a lot of the texture of those moments is in an early poem. I'm not really embarrassed by the early poem. But in *The Pond*, the poem "Outing" is a lot shorter, and in my view better. Not because I've removed "fat," but because removing some of the very specific details of where the poem was coming from allowed the central images, the crucially more important images, more space to shine, I hope. That is the kind of process that I use. I keep trying to rescue the center—not only the experience center, but the image center—of the poem. That's one of the reasons why the poems are so short. If I think that the image can sustain itself, I'm likely to just leave it.

KD: In titling one of your poems "My Rodney Poem" and dedicating it in part to Eddie Baugh, you demonstrate a certain dialogue and banter between poets that *seems* rare in Caribbean writing. But this willingness to take on issues and critics appears to be something that you gladly do in your verse. Indeed much of your commentary on the Black Power movement of the '60s is contained in both *Shadowboxing* and *The Pond*. The persona in some of those poems struggles against the pigeonholing of the poet along political lines. In at least one of those poems you appear to make ironic commentary that seeks to champion the independence of the poet; the need for a Caribbean poet who is black to not be expected to be a Brathwaite, for instance. Is that pressure still there for you or for other Caribbean poets?

MM: I don't know about other Caribbean poets, but that's not a considerable pressure for me at this time. It was a great pressure in the late '60s and early '70s. It really was something quite disturbing and some of the poems that come out of it are really poems that are trying to claim a space. A lot of people that you would think would be alert enough to understand the silliness of some of what they were doing and saying, were saying things that struck me as overstatement to the point of silliness. I think one of the poems of that period was originally meant as a kind of joke to annoy a friend who had invited me to help in a poetry reading. "For Consciousness" is talking about some of the silliness of some of the positions. One of the idiocies of the late '60s and early '70s was the prevailing suspicion that the CIA types were those who were openly opposing the left. Whereas, of course, if you really want to think about where the really dangerous people might be, they were probably very near the top of the organizational structures that were supposedly pushing the left. That's why that poem says, "Is who and who to tackle when the call to backle blow." Wherever you have a strong political movement or group, people who are moderately alert soon learn what it is they are being asked to say, and it's very foolish to assume that the people who are refusing to say what they are bright enough to know they are being asked to say are the real enemy. They often are not. The really dangerous people are very often the ones who are saying, "Lord, Lord." But that was a very special period. I don't seem to write many poems out of that context anymore. Not really. And that madness passed. You, know, we are all free-enterprisers now. And they don't press that quite so hard that it sort of worries people.

You mentioned "My Rodney Poem" and you know the Eddie Baugh poem it refers to. That Eddie Baugh poem ["The Poet Bemused" in *A Tale from the Rainforest*] genuinely, I mean those two and a half lines, long before the poem was published, were among my favorite lines, because they, in a very, very short space, made a very, very fine critical comment on a whole period of madness: "why, as you'll note / he never even wrote / a Rodney poem." I mean it was just so accurate about the period, you know. Anyway, that time has passed.

KD: In terms of writing technique, while we talk a great deal about your terseness of verse, we talk less about the careful use of meter, the precise play with line breaks which allows you to be ironic and ambiguous at the same time, and about the use of the playfully conceived rhyme and meter of the ditty. You use these tools with the same kind of dexterity that I associate a great deal with a poet like Kamau Brathwaite. Some would call this an unlikely comparison, but I think not. Is it? Can you talk a bit more about the way you use those "tools" in your work?

MM: I think line breaks are fundamental to the crafting of verse. Teaching workshops now, there's a certain stage at which one feels that if you can sensitize people who have some talent and are practicing to the crucial importance of the line break, they move forward a lot faster. Because that is really the main thing that separates prose from verse. The ability to decide when the line will break is one of the most crucial options available. So I concentrate a lot on that. One of the things that the line break often does is create syntactic ambiguity, which allows you to read the thing two or three different ways and still make sense. And that, I think, is one of the ways of making what could seem quite simple become quite tensely complex, so I use that quite a lot. I am very conscious of rhyme and I use a lot of rhyme irregularly. With me it's often associated with some sort of "closure." But one of the things I try to teach is that rhyme should seem inevitable, or almost invisible, sometimes almost inaudible, hardly heard sometimes. It's a thing I get a lot of in one of the poets who I greatly admire, Philip Larkin, where all the stuff is rhyming virtually and a lot of the rhymes are not making the kind of loud sounds that mean you are aware that they are there all the time. And of course in Walcott's *Omeros,* some of the rhyming is outrageously emphatic and some of it just quietly disappears and it's not until you start looking closely down the page that you realize that this stuff is rhyming.

KD: A distinction of your poetry has been an almost systematic commitment to exploring a series of themes. In fact, each of your collections, apart from *On Holy Week,* can be broken down into very distinct sections: poems about writing and the writing process, political poems, love/family poems, and what I can only term cryptic philosophical poems. Your family poems are often intimate, even as they betray a poet who is intent on avoiding the sentimental and the maudlin. At times, these often self-deprecating intimacies are marked by a controlled tone which creates distance and less vulnerability. I have two questions related to all this: firstly, to what extent is the process of writing poems about "domestic existence: family, love, etc." one of working through your own emotions and ideas, and secondly, how intense (because I suspect it is there) is this urge to maintain a certain control of the emotions in such intimate poetry?

MM: I'm not sure I am going to give you an answer which is clearly enough defined for you, given the way in which you have asked the question. I believe that, in relation to what you call domestic existence, family/love, etc., the recurring thing in my work is the presentation, often in a celebratory way as well, of moments of tension, moments where one is recognizing a pull in different directions at the same time, and I suppose I have become so accustomed to that as a kind of fact of existence that I am inclined to believe that this is centrally what human experience is about. So that a lot of my poems are really very much about dramatizing moments of choice or dramatizing the very interesting moments where one refuses to choose and therefore does choose. "Working through my emotions and ideas" —very much so. But I like to think that these are very often common experiences in a sense. That poem "Love Is," which ends the "the torsion / balance in my life" is one of the ones which would, I think, in capsule form, make the point. I don't know where that image came from. What I know is that by the time I finally let it go, I had looked it up very carefully. I mean when the image arrived, I really had to check and find out how that functions and why, but I just don't know, in a sense, where it came from. I mean, I don't have much to do with physics and I have never seen a torsion balance. Obviously it was a part of my passive vocabulary, but why it arrived, I don't know. But the fundamental tension that is settled by the line break in "torsion" and the twisting, etc., and "balance," is absolutely central to me in terms of most relationships. There is both a kind of calm and a kind of disturbance, a kind of freedom and a kind of almost imprisonment. But I think this is a very common human experience. In "torsion / balance" partly I'm talking about the kind of opposition Derek Walcott talks about at the beginning of *Sea Grapes*, in the poem mentioning "The ancient war / between obsession and responsibility." It's the same kind of thing. And of course a "torsion balance" is an instrument for measuring. I do believe that the capacity for love is often the measure of who the person is. You can discover who someone is if you learn what it is they are capable of loving in the broader sense—admiring, really. But then when you split it up with the line break into "torsion / balance" you also get two elements in tension.

But you asked also about "controlled tone that creates distance and less vulnerability." Yeah, I work towards that. I really feel that sometimes people might be able to look at something and deduce where it is coming from, but I am not anxious to assist them. I would sooner create something that has its own energy and which would be harder to place in terms of the simple biographical detail. So that insofar as the removal, or the transformation, of the biographical detail may be a defensive maneuver to make oneself less vulnerable: guilty. But one hopes that whatever tension one is exploring remains built into the verse.

KD: Can you talk a little bit about some of the important poetic influences that you have had?

MM: This answer may seem a little pat because this is something I have been asked before; I think my formation is comparatively unusual, and I have sorted out the answers a few times. Perhaps the most important thing to say is when I was in sixth form at Munro, when most other people in Jamaica were doing as their special subject in A-level English either the Romantics or in some instances the moderns, early twentieth century, my English master happened to choose the age of Johnson. So that I had early contact with verse which made itself available to readers, which believed in a discourse which was fundamentally public no matter what the pain inside (and there was a lot of madness in the eighteenth century). So that that was a kind of model of balance and rationality—on the surface, anyway. Another thing was my interest, again at Munro, in reading weekly magazines which came to our library usually a month or so after they were published in England. Things like *Punch*, and *The New Statesman, Spectator*, and *The Listener*. I was attracted by and amused by some of the competitions that used to be run—usually competitions in literary cleverness. And also, the prevailing verse being published in those journals at the time (my sixth-form years would have been '52 to '54) was verse influenced by (or a part of what was called in England) The Movement, which reacted against some of the wilder excesses of Dylan Thomas and a kind of grand Romantic verbal gesture and insisted that a plain speaking which was nevertheless subtle might be one of the ways to go. One of the things that's often quoted is a line by Donald Davie, "a neutral tone is nowadays preferred." A lot of the verse that one saw was carefully shaped, more or less accessible, more or less interpretable by prose standards, but usually with resonances going beyond that. Then when I went to the University College of the West Indies, the main thing that we were introduced to, that we had to work at, was Metaphysical poetry. Partly because the stocks of the Metaphysical poets had gone up with the influence of Eliot, and it was really a very convenient classroom way of teaching people to pay attention to verbal texture. So, a lot of my formation came out of that.

Then there is the other thing—that I had a great interest in light verse. I used to devour anthologies of light verse or comic verse and I used to write light verse in school, lampoons of the masters and that sort of stuff. And I continued that when I was on campus. At that stage, I didn't even think that I wished to write poetry seriously. I was writing some prose fiction, short stories, most of it not very serious, entertainment written for pocket money. I may have written one or two poems that I hoped were serious before I left Jamaica. But they were really awful. I started writing more seriously in England in one of the summers, I think it was the summer of '59. I wrote a hell of a lot. I remember I used to sometimes go off to a residential library on the edge of Wales, just across from Chester. It was a convenient place to go; it wasn't very expensive, it was residential, it had enough books for me to get on with work and I did a lot of writing. Most of it hasn't seen the light of day, but properly so. I think the earliest poems in any of my books dates from 1960. Those poems would be "The Day My Father Died" which was sometime in '60, and "West Indian Love Song (from England)."

I remember the first time I ever bought a book by an individual poet whom I had never heard of was when I walked into a bookshop in Oxford and I picked up a book called *Poetry for Supper* by R. S. Thomas, who at that time I didn't know anything about. I think few people did, by the way, because it was only his second book. But I liked that and I bought it, and I still care for Thomas. His stuff is hard-edged, it tends to be very short, nicely controlled work—it fitted in with the kind of thing I was reading and admiring. One of the people I used to read quite a lot of at that time was Robert Graves. Again, you see, poetry which seems on the surface quite accessible but, in Graves's case, of course, is constantly linked with myth. I guess, those are some of the influences I am aware of.

Then of course, to come nearer home—I don't know why it's taken me this long—I always knew I liked, for example, Louise Bennett, which is very much the same kind of sensibility, in a sense. Most of my family loved her work, we used to read it aloud at home. And eventually, as one started writing about Louise Bennett as an artist, I suppose one became much more aware of her specific skills, skills which are very easily related to the central skills of metaphysical poetry. She focuses a lot of meaning through being alert to the way in which words talk out of two sides of the mouth. Then, of course, I admired Walcott—though he was not a very strong influence on me. I have always loved Walcott but always resisted him, especially the early Walcott. Resisted him in the sense that I never wanted to write like Walcott because the early Walcott, particularly, had a lot of that grandness which is related very much to the kind of thing Dylan Thomas might have been doing: "Choc Bay." But there were some things I loved. I loved "Tales of the Islands" all along. The kind of Walcott I most admire is very much related to the other things that I admire; you know: like a line from "A Letter from Brooklyn:" "He is dead, Miss Rawlins, but God bless your tense." A language where the simplicity on the surface is actually containing quite a range of complex feeling. Then at a later stage, I was much influenced by Brathwaite, without ever writing like him. Certainly, he made a lot of sense to me. His whole thing of continuities out of Africa, which had not been part of the way I was brought up. At the same time, I have always resisted a certain kind of political claiming of Brathwaite, because Brathwaite has always been and, I suspect, still is very, very much more complicated than they used to say. He became the focus of a set of extreme positions which I certainly wished to resist. But he himself was nearly always carefully more complex. He never dismissed parts of his heritage.

Then there are poet friends. I guess the closest poet friend I have had would be Dennis Scott, who helped me a lot, but a lot less than Wayne Brown. I'll explain. The thing about Dennis is that Dennis— being a very good reader and incredibly swift—didn't challenge very much. He tended to understand what it was I was doing, and that wasn't quite as helpful as not understanding, which Wayne Brown was very good at—in a challenging kind of way. Wayne Brown would sort of wipe out whole areas of what one was trying to do, but he nudged me towards taking on the visceral. I guess that coming out of the light verse thing, I was very much inclined to head verse, and Wayne's contribution was to keep insisting that the only verse worth anything was belly verse. You know "The Forest" in *The Pond*? It was provoked by Wayne. Now Dennis was enormously helpful to some of us, however, in one area. He didn't challenge where you were starting from but he was very, very good at tactfully saying, "Can you get away with that?" and above all, many of us gained from him insights into lineation, alertness to the way in which the fundamental unit of verse (which is of course the line) can be used to modify rhythm and meaning—Scott was teaching us all that constantly.

KD: *On Holy Week* does speak to a certain agnostic quality to your expressed religious position. In the poem "Thomas," arguably one of the more realized of the pieces, the Christ narrative and the tenets of Christianity are challenged by the inclusion of a doubting voice—a certain skepticism. Still, there are pieces in the collection that appear to celebrate the faith. Is this ambivalence imagined on my part, or is there a real tension in these poems on the question of religious faith?

MM: In the sequence as a whole there is a real tension on the question of religious faith. But I read Thomas as one of God's ways of validating doubt if it is honest. But a friend of mine who is a minister insists on Thomas's inadequacy. He quotes a bit which I don't quote, "Blessed are they who have not seen and yet have believed." Which is clearly a part of the picture, okay? I think Thomas is a very important figure in the gospel story. But it's extremely important to recognize that the ending of *On Holy Week* with apparent skepticism is also an ending with the submerged acknowledgment that Thomas is open to criticism. I tried, however briefly, to draw attention to some of this in the author's notes, where I say "the skeptic Thomas recalls a parable commending faithful obedience." You see, Thomas says somewhere, "Sand seems more honest than rock," and he says that only three lines from the end of the whole book. And everybody who is aware of the gospel narrative is supposed to hear that irony, which is a very important part of Thomas's statement. So that while you say there's a certain skepticism, and that is true, it is the skepticism which is also acknowledging the criticism of its skepticism, and in fact, the last lines are very religious: "If my Lord lives he will meet the needs of those who question those who mock, of us who wanting faith...."—"wanting," lacking or eager to have—"... faith will stand aloof." If you believe in a loving personal God, then presumably you may believe that he accommodates the range of human experience. Thomas is a crucial part of this. Thomas is an honest man.

KD: "Help thou my unbelief..."

MM: Yes, yes...

KD: You return to the question of religion briefly in *Examination Centre* in the poems "Version" and "Recreation." The former is, of course, a variation on the Adam and Eve theme—this time treating the question of infidelity and faithfulness. At the same time, it has grander implications about sin and punishment. It is appropriate that the Adam and Eve motif be employed to explore this moral issue. Yet Eve is really nonexistent except as symbolized in the eaten otaheite [apple] in this poem. The doctrine here is fairly conservative and traditional despite the "version" it represents. "Recreation" is a little different. God and the creation are employed as metaphors for the creative process. At the same time, the poem plays on the sometimes popular doctrinal question "how could God make us the way we are, intentionally?" There is a playful suggestion that this divine being is somewhat jovially observing the world from an ironic distance. Is this simply a poetic conceit or does this perception of the divinity dominate your thinking about faith and religion?

MM: I will answer your last question first. I think, insofar as I am aware of it, the truth is that it's a poetic conceit. But also I believe that God must have a sense of humor. There are all sorts of theological ways in which one could play around with that. I believe I am persuaded by the way in which you have read "Recreation," but it's not where I thought I was at. You've given it a weight which I wasn't conscious of. It was a poetic conceit, really, at its conception, which as you know, does not mean it can't bear the weight. But I was far more conscious of having shaped a tightly rhyming poem that I hoped might sound unforced.

Your other question was about "Version." And again, I think it can bear the weight of what you are saying—sin and punishment, that's always been there—but that wasn't my emphasis. My emphasis, I guess, was on playing with the myth and the Jamaicanizing of it—the otaheite apple.

KD: Have you ever considered writing another long, connected movement of poems like *On Holy Week* with a parallel allusive thread, whether it be the bible, some classical narrative, or a folk cycle? I ask this as a way to determine how comfortable you felt writing a sustained series of poems around the same theme or derived from the same basic source. That is what I meant by "the sense of departure," because that sustained theme for a whole book—well, I see your usual work as these tight pieces, and then there is this larger narrative thing.

MM: Yes, I have thought of doing another connected movement or sequence and I'm still thinking of doing it. But the other thing: there is a sense in which *The Pond* is a collection of poems, but it is also, in a way that some collections are not, one book. *Shadowboxing* is a collection of poems and also one book. *Examination Centre* is perhaps a little looser, but not much, because the whole thing is connected by that opening poem. So there is a sense in which each of my books is a long poem.

KD: You were born in Jamaica and grew up here. Your poetry, however, does not celebrate, in any overt way, landscape—except in a poem like "The Pond" which has some references to nature. Is landscape important to you as a poet?

MM: No, there's not a lot of it in my poetry. In recent days I have had reason to reflect on that same thing. In a colloquium here in Miami recently, there was a passage of discussion talking about exile and somebody made the point that sometimes you move from one country to another and you do not even know the names of the trees and so on. And the person was saying, "I know the names of the trees where I live," etc., etc. I don't know the names of all the trees where I live. There are plenty of trees I recognize, but I never really internalized the names. But I care about landscape. I certainly care a lot about light. But no, I am not very much into references to nature.

KD: This question has to do with your love poems. These are "male" poems—poems about male sexuality: from "The Stripper" to the defining "Love Is." In *Shadowboxing* and *The Pond* the muse is often personified as a female (a classical carryover, of course), but the relationship between poet and the muse is consistently one of tension, and a profound need to take control. The muse is often diabolic, manipulative, and antagonistic. It all represents a curious tension-filled relationship between male and female. Does this brief analysis seem reflective of what you are trying to achieve or have achieved in your work? Because it does raise troubling questions about gender and the portrayal of women in your poetry.

MM: I suspect "Guilty as charged" might be the short answer. Very few of my poems, except, like in *On Holy Week*, attempt to create a female persona. The one I can think of, and I don't know if it's the only one—there's a poem called "Womansong" in *Shadowboxing* which is very much the voice of the woman. But that doesn't protect me against the particular angle of your charge because that woman is still speaking about her vulnerability and of oppression by the male. When I say "Guilty as charged," I am not just joking, really. I think I often write from the point of view of a man who is thinking about the man's own situation. You mention the muse. I make a connection with some traditional images of the muse, in particular, Robert Graves's white goddess. That the muse should be both equivocal and malevolent and attractive, equivocally dangerous and so on, is quite, as you know, traditional.

Claire Harris

BORN 1937

CLAIRE HARRIS WAS born in Trinidad, where she attended high school during the waning years of Trinidad's colonial era. Like many of her generation, Claire Harris left Trinidad to study abroad, completing her bachelor's degree at the National University of Ireland in Dublin. She returned to the Caribbean to obtain a diploma in education at the University of the West Indies in 1966, after which she emigrated to Canada to teach English and drama at the secondary school level in Calgary, Alberta, where she has primarily lived since that time. In 1974–75, she traveled to Lagos, Nigeria, to complete a diploma in mass communications at the University of Nigeria. She credits this time spent in Africa as pivotal in her movement toward professional writing.

After returning to Canada, she became involved in several projects aimed at developing a greater appreciation of Canadian writing among Canadians. She served as editor of *Dandelion,* a Canadian literary journal, and was managing editor of *blue buffalo,* an "all-Alberta" literary journal. She is recognized as one of the more distinguished poetic voices from both the Caribbean and Canada, having managed to locate herself as a writer devoted to exploring the landscape and culture of a Canada that is decidedly transcultural in its makeup and as a writer who remains rooted in the Caribbean landscape.

Her poetry collection *Fables from the Women's Quarters* (Williams-Wallace, 1984) won the Commonwealth Poetry Prize for the Americas Region. Her poetry collections include *Dipped in Shadow* (Goose Lane, 1996), *Drawing Down a Daughter* (Goose Lane, 1992), *The Conception of Winter* (Goose Lane, 1995), *Translation into Fiction* (Goose Lane, 1984), and *Travelling to Find a Remedy* (Goose Lane, 1986). She was nominated for the Governor's General Award for *Drawing Down a Daughter*. Both *The Conception of Winter* and *Travelling to Find a Remedy* won Alberta Poetry Awards. *Dipped in Shadow* was nominated for the Writer's Guild of Alberta Award.

Now retired from teaching, Harris continues to live in Calgary, which serves as the base for her many travels throughout the world to give readings and lectures on writing, the politics of writing, and the way writing relates to culture and identity.

KWAME DAWES: I will begin with a question that is most obvious to anyone who has looked at your work. It has to do with form. Your work shifts from the standard line break formatting of free verse to what is commonly described as poetic prose, in which the margins are justified and the line breaks are not pronounced. Can you talk a bit about the kind of technical decisions that go into how a work appears on the page?

CLAIRE HARRIS: I suppose I have a very visual view of poetry, but I think the page by its very nature is important. It is the place where oral literature parts company with print. There is also that essentially modern notion of a frame against which/within which the line and the word jostle and mean. Anyway, when I begin a poem/piece there is a very clear image of what the poem will look like on the page. This means that content and form, as has been said before, are not merely indivisible but the same thing. Unlike other writers, poets have the gift of the page, which is space and form; the gift of compression; and the gifts of rhythm, that is, the movement of sound in time. We have as well those strategies of modernism and postmodernism which test/stretch/stress both form and word. However one chooses to write, it is one's determination to master these, press them into service without destroying meaning, that makes the work. In a book-length poem, I'll have the tale in prose/prose-poetry, narrative verse of some kind, the big themes ... love, death, whatever I'm on about, in lyric form, and pure social comment, philosophy, fooling around, filler, connections, etc., in both prose and a form of verse which, like a jazz solo, allows a level of spontaneity. In such a space I can examine the word, think, stretch form to idea, use clippings, quotations, whatever comes to mind. Like any other artist working seriously over a length of time, there is on the whole a personal grammar of form, rhythms, etc., evolving. Luckily, I still have "and miles to go before I sleep, / And miles and to go before I sleep."

KD: Clearly, this eclecticism, or nonpredictable use of prose and verse, represents an ideological statement founded on the notion of breaking convention. Are you constantly working at formal questions in your work, and to what extent do these formal considerations define your writing process?

CH: I don't see how one can write poetry without taking formal decisions all the time. I mean each word is chosen precisely because it can be mined for sound, rhythm, sense, each line broken or begun, placed just so on the page, for the same reason. One has to craft the stuff. There is a kind of order particular to an idea/form and one must cleave to this order to maintain the "truth/passion" of one's idea.

The work is not about form, that's just the poet's material; it's about idea. I'm not painting paint, as distinct from color/light/society/nature/rudimentary philosophy, etc.

I don't stick to established hierarchies of form and genre, because I know that there is more than one "corpus of ideas" within which/part of which one can be "human" and "enlightened" in the world; that all forms of human culture are, in the final analysis, equal. My work must illustrate that—self-respect and so on.

In societies/"civilizations," in which status *as a human being* is based on consumption, race and/or a specific idea of God, the idea above is, of course, ridiculous. Barbarisms are rife in our relations in and with the modern world precisely because "consumption equals humanity"/"ours is the *true* religion"/"my race or no place" is at the very heart of vulgar use of "civilized." In contrast, or in counterpoint to the notion of a civilization, a society, essential questions are about the individual. Why intelligent, self-reflective life? What is one to make of the fact that one *is*, and *here*? What does it mean to be human, given one's particular place and moment? I began writing at the very time when the European male in all his/her variety, and his/her hangers-on, first began to proclaim the "victory" of "Western civilization"—the "end of history." The hubris!

It seems obvious to me that the worst catastrophe to have befallen the human race, and Earth, was the movement of the West out of

Europe. Apart from the terrible loss of "ways of being," of knowledge, art, and myth, total victory over other human societies and the environment can only be accomplished by devaluing the individual human being. To be reductive but accurate, the simple barbaric arrogance involved in "your life is worth my reelection" is unbelievable. What continues to amaze me is the obvious disbelief in the truism: essentially, what can happen/be done to any individual can befall any other human being.

All in all I cyaan imagine risking me-self paying mind to anything I ain't work out for me myself. An' is these things I thinking through in my writing what determine the form mi work take.

KD: You are clearly committed to the long poem, which in most instances amounts to a narrative piece. Consequently, your volumes are often hard to label, to "nail down." You like this?

CH: Of course, I don't wish to be labeled. Labels as the human race uses them are extremely dangerous things. On one hand they veil all that is there, tamping down the furious, conflicting energies underlying the surface of any art; on the other they leave one a sitting duck for the vagaries of a criticism that often amounts to little more than comment on fashion.

They convenient, eh, these movement, school, etc., an' is politically astute they astute in the short run. But not for no artist. Even when she take it up she-self so, as a way she work out an' proclaim up a new vision an' ting. Makin' you'self a writer, a poet, whatever it 'bout, it ent 'bout cage, and it ent 'bout group-think.

KD: Would you say that the poetic impulse for you is driven by the metaphor; the image, if you will, or the narrative—the story? My question implies a dichotomy which may not really be there. But can you talk about how your works germinate and gestate and finally burst forth in glorious birth?

CH: Knock off "glorious birth." Nearly everything can be seen as a metaphor for something else. I spend a deal of working time letting the idea germinate. I need two things in my work: first narrative, because that is clearly how our brains allow us to perceive time and make sense of it in our lives, and also because the rhythms conducive to narrative can thrust one headlong through the long poem; secondly, there must also be a relatively "original" concept, a metaphor for dramatically conveying an idea. Usually I examine what it means to be "human"; that is, how we might deal with whatever hi(S)tory has handed us . . . and I mean hi(S)tory, not simply the physical working of bits of DNA/chemistry/time. This sounds very "determined," but in fact, I work very slowly, and with a blindfold. Over two years or more I write bits and pieces, all of which seem to have their own energy, but all of which tend to converge on the same idea, the same metaphor. Finally, I figure out some of what is going on. That's when I really begin to write a book and have some fun exploring, not only metaphor/rhythm/form, but also the ways in which whatever is going on in the world I'm living in at the time of writing would affect both my character, and the techniques I can use on the page to highlight that other reality.

KD: The woman is consistently at the center of your poems—her body is celebrated and relied upon for metaphors and symbols. This "use" of the female body is not unusual in Western poetry, but the gaze appears to have shifted—the female gaze appears to be less engrossed in objectifying and more in constructing a new language of metaphors and images. Is this at the core of your rendering of the female in your verse? I think especially of the volume *Drawing Down a Daughter*.

CH: If the poetry of black women going be truly different, surely it have to be discarding the male gaze. Which for we African woman what to write amount to moving from the traditional posture Europe, in particular, lay down for we. A change o' content ent mean nothing. Perceptions/prescriptions have to change . . . the woman body have to belong to woman she-self. No easy thing. We got to reach down into we womb an' pull weself out. (An' this we gotta do in the face o' hellfire, gunfire, fire off the job. In the face of all the dismissing/animalistic metaphors what the West think up and spread everywhere 'bout we, and which everywhere we seem to internalize.)

This moving, this turning inside out ent no pure or line-up process, an' it have to be catch in the act o'changing. If there wasn't all this shifting and mixing o' new insight, plus insight what old, plus what we just kinda beginnin' to tease out; if we weren't all trap-up together, man and women, in these barb wires what they does call "history" and "circumstance," is how you and I so could talk to each other?

A book finally have to be a kinda conversation with the reader, and so with history. So it have always three character what present all the time. The story of s/he in the book, the story of s/he who write the book, and, important as them two, the story of s/he who reading. Is how you manage these; is how you leave space for them three, and still play these spaces off each other, what interesting to me. And is this what makes new images possible.

Besides, why on earth should I waste time doing what has been done before? And why would a woman, black woman in the Americas, want to repeat without putting her mark on them the insidious, death-dealing approaches of the West?

KD: Can you talk a little about the very ideas of "influences," because in many ways, the act of naming influences becomes a political and ideological one which sometimes obscures the more fascinating question of how we "use" these influences; how they emerge in the writing. You dip freely into multiple palettes; how then do you arrive at your own voice?

CH: Influences. My father used to sing Latin hymns, accompanying himself on the piano. His favorite was "Dies Irae" sung in the most mournful tones one can imagine. At his funeral, my brother made sure the choir sang that hymn in the "correct," upbeat fashion which was entirely new to me. That, he said, was the correct rhythm for those words. I think my father liked the heavy roll of the long Latin syllables, understood the hymn as part of the funeral service, and sang to suit his feeling about death. I do much the same thing. What I take from anything I read is often quite the opposite of what the authors, African, or otherwise, intend.

As a child I read poetry for sound and rhythm. As an adult I read for technique. No African can read European Lit after Shakespeare without a certain amazement at the culture which could so diminish inquiry with the naiveté of racism. My truly literary influences are so only in the sense that the work is passionately political, or they wrote prose poetry, or they developed metaphor in intriguing ways, etc., or they can genuinely use rhyme, or something. As a West Indian how could one read Aimé Césaire without spluttering and sadness? As a woman how listen to calypsonians without Bobbit-think?

Usually, when I'm asked to talk about influences, I pay tribute to the grandparents, the aunts, great-aunts and godmothers, the cousin-family who told me the myths and tales of Africa-Trinidad, and had an endless fund of Wise Words for all Occasions. In *Drawing*, it's possible to hear those voices very clearly.

It is, I suspect, a mistake to focus only on the books, myths, music, and celebrations of a culture, oral or otherwise, in a discussion of influences. The attitudes, the notions of proper behavior, of self-respect, the expectations forced on one, the levels and ceremonies of faith-practice, the color of the sky, earth, sea, the particular green of trees, the shapes, colors, sizes of houses, the ceremonies of the table, the cuisine, all matter profoundly. There remains a terrible dichotomy between what was/is taught at school (for my generation taught by white people), and the world of most books available to Dia-African children in the Americas on one hand, and what one was/is, what was taught and expected of one at home on the other. It is in the necessary reconciliation of these worldviews that the influences become clear. It is important to note that this is not a static process. Assuming that one continues to grow, what surfaces will change as one's experience, knowledge, and mood/attitude shifts are to be discovered. Yet the voice is not a patchwork quilt. It's born out of what one has to say, and the passion with which one needs to say it. It comes whole with the idea/form of the poetry. It's everything one has lived, and is what one is at that moment in place and time.

KD: There is a classicist learning in some of your influences — classical in a modernist sense. Your own poetry reflects the classical engagement with the philosophy of the present; however, there is a more compelling energy, a breaking of structure and form that is postmodern. Do you, like Walcott, declare that the classics satisfy only so much . . . and then? What happens after the influences have lost their satisfaction?

CH: Like Huxley's "There comes a time when one asks, even of Shakespeare, even of Beethoven, is this all?" You will, of course, notice that it is difficult to chart my reading from my books. I don't imitate my influences; the poems are poor things but mine own. Perhaps what you are asking is what propels me into poetry. I continue to be mystified by human beings. I continue to hope. I want to know how people get from calling a greeting to the neighbors to walking down the street with those neighbors' dripping heads in casual hand. How does it happen that we who boast about bombing Iraqi women and children "back to the middle ages" can describe machete killings as "savage"? Is this because we can kill faster and many more without getting our hands wet? Is that it? Clean = Civilization! And if one can bomb Panamanian slums, can one bomb (pinpoint of course) inner-city ghettos? Does Dubois's "double consciousness" really exist? How is it manifested in real life? Eventually, you begin to desperately hope there is a God. If only because He ought to be asked to explain Himself . . . I feel that, like the griots, my business is to record the age. "Living in interesting times" is very helpful.

KD: In your essay "Why Do I Write" there is a clarity about what you set out to do in your work. The first points to your strong African consciousness; a need to be a part of "the re-inscription of Africa on the Western consciousness." What does that translate into for a West Indian living in Canada? Is this an extension of Fanon; a kind of crusade that is founded on a construction of Africa as not simply a geographical space, but an intensely consuming culture?

CH: On the simplest level, anything I write is Diasporic African writing inasmuch as I am descended from Africans brought here before the abolition of slavery. To inscribe myself on the consciousness of Canada is to directly challenge everything Europeans of the Americas expect of/believe of the Dia-African, and therefore much of what they believe of themselves. One has to change the concept of "civilized," of "discovery," one has to challenge the uses and purposes of history, of the literary "canon." One has to challenge the society's common sense. After I'd been in Canada about three months in 1966, a young teacher exploded, apropos of nothing, "There has to be something wrong with blacks otherwise we wouldn't treat them so!" It isn't particularly difficult to cause unease. It is difficult to create change. White people have so much to lose. While Canada is aware of the dangers, it does not see them as unmanageable, so it tries to preserve the status quo. I think it's worth noting that in a racist society one first has to inscribe the "I." I do it by the angle from which I observe, by my choice of topics, my readings, and in talks, panels, etc. By the way I dress, walk, talk. And by my insistence that this too is Canadian.

Until Europe, both here and there, accepts its cultural/economic debt to Africa nothing will change either. It is not merely that I am African; it is that they are African in much of the culture of their daily lives. No other minority group has been able to so impose themselves on the culture of an alien nation. (See music, slang, dress styles, dance, food, etc., cultural norms like "cool." Notice how more and more white singers sound "black"?) Moreover Canada, like all Diasporic nations, is in the throes of negotiating its culture. We must have a seat, and it must be at the center. We are a long way from that. My work, like the work of other Dia-African writers, indeed of all writers of color, is perceived here as satellite. (This is also true of African American writing in the U.S.) Until this changes our children remain stateless in their own country.

So an extension of Fanon . . . yes. But it has to be seen as different, we have moved on from 1952. Fanon sees us, in some dreadful sense, as doomed to be "mimics" denying Africa, because he thinks we have no choice but to accept Europe as it is. Culture is the ground where one truly exists; to be capable in the world one must draw from it all the time. What is happening in Canada is the deliberate negotiation of our status as Canadian–Dia-Africans. What we have done, continue to do as we move around in the West, is shrug the world around us, and in making it fit we have become something new. Look, you take sixteenth-century Africa, you season it a tiny bit with Indian and Chinese, you marinate it in the West, turn it into a pot mark "slavery." After, you put on the burner mark "power," turn up the heat mark "pride," throw in courage and religion, then cover it with "need to show who is who." Is so you get Trinidad. You take that cookup, you bring it here, marinate in Canada. Use the same burner only fiercer. You don't have much choice.

KD: Forgive me for returning constantly to your essay, but it introduces elements of your "posture" as a writer that elicit questions from me. You talk about writing characters who fight against the reductionist inclinations of white Canada, by being "real." I would like you to expound on this concept of "realness" and the attendant notion of invisibility or "unrealness" that you appear to be writing against. How does it function in the Canadian context?

CH: There is a very one-dimensional view of Dia-Africans in Canada. We are uneducated; we don't work; we are dirty; we are good entertainment, sports, etc.; we are lazy; we are stupid; we are angry; we want too much, and we want it for nothing; we are violent; we are thieves and drug addicts, prostitutes and pimps; criminal behavior of every sort is natural to us; we are ungrateful, since we don't recognize how lucky we are to be in Canada; we are exotic, but never beautiful; we are victims, and helpless in our Darwinian victimization. More important than any of this, *we are different in kind.* Europeans on the other hand are everything we are not. These extreme views are supported in papers as "prestigious" as the *Globe and Mail,* and by that segment of Upper Canada and its wannabes who would like the country to return to the 1950s. This in spite of the fact that in 1983 the Canadian Historical Society used Statscan as authority for the fact that Caribbean peoples were the most highly educated "ethnic" group in Canada. None of these people, of course, see themselves as racists. They are "realists." Such a view means that I and the majority of Africans working and living here are invisible. We can't be seen for the fog of malicious ignorance.

Any writer who draws characters from life; who describes Canada as it is; who examines, not only those topics like racism which are narrowly deemed our only area of expertise, but ideas; whose steel is merely the natural human response to the situation described; who is prepared to turn news stories into poetry as realistic as the stories: such a writer stands in denial of all the myths of non-black Canada. By refusing to dance to their tune, by insisting on who and what we are, as well as who and what they are, by claiming the full range of human interest and experience for our own, we force attention to the width and depth of African reality in Canada. In practical terms, all my books are different in content and, therefore, style, precisely because I'm dealing with the full range. This is why there are people of all races in my work. This is why the "myth" underlying some of my work reflects the theories of the new physicists.

KD: Also in your essay, you define yourself as a West African who is writing in a tradition derived from European literature. Tongue-in-cheek, you seem to be suggesting that the labels that place at the fore the "southernness" of your writing may be misguided. In light of your declared influences, this notion of your being a descendant of Shakespeare (literary descendant, that is) makes absolute sense to me, but it must be a problematic articulation to make. Surely, this is the very basis of the arguments against the notion of postcolonial literature. And yet, only the naive writer who has been educated on the European classics would deny that their work derives from that tradition. How do you respond to the inevitable question that your claim of lineage to European literature amounts to a privileging of your writerly or *literary* influences over your oral or nonliterary influences which are founded in the South?

CH: The "truth" is seldom problematic for the speaker. (Let's hope I can say this clearly.) I suspect that a Dia-African has four possible stances available: the victim, the celebrant of myth, the Bad John, the observer. There are problems with each stance. And few people stick completely to one. However, the first three all have as their *essential, deep* subject the dominant culture. Worse, in many instances this subject is unspoken, and therefore twice as powerfully present. One cannot complain about McDonald's, without calling attention to McDonald's. (Mcjobs, etc.) Moreover, if the language is standard English with a scattering of West-Indianisms, the language itself (handled by a real poet) and the rhythms of modern poetry are powerfully present in all their transatlantic insistence on European civilization. The observer stance leaves one open to attack from both sides, but at least it is inherently "true" to the facts. Moreover one can uncover the language and its assumptions. And one can ensure that Dia-Africans become the deep subject, simply by contrasting one's own skin color, and one's take on the subject, with that of the character. My new book, *Dipped in Shadow,* does this and does it deliberately. I will be told that this book is not about my people, but it is. It questions assumptions Europeans maintain about themselves, in the teeth of the evidence, and thus questions their assumptions about us. I know from critical reviews of one of the poems that people get it.

Now for Shakespeare. As I said before, I read for style. My Shakespeare is not Canada's or even England's. When I taught high school in 1971, apart from the usual ideas attached to these plays, I taught *The Tempest* as colonialism, *Merchant of Venice* as self-congratulatory racism, *Hamlet* could show what happens to people who don't respect their elders, ghosts, etc. I'm quite sure this is not what comes to mind when H. Bloom picks up Shakespeare. Most European "classics" can be read with the reality of Euro-savagery in mind. A Caribbean person only has to know who she is when she picks up the text.

We both know that our education, and our survival in the world, depends (1) on our having an education based on the whole range of human knowledge, however Caribbeanized, (2) on our ability to manipulate the language. What we are discussing here in respect to "privileging" is politics. A proper reading of my work, all/any of it would indicate a writer not at all impressed by Europe. Language is a tool. I use it as I use a car. Culture is the way one sees. One has no choice, if one is to avoid falseness.

Olive Senior

BORN 1941

OLIVE SENIOR WAS born and grew up in rural Jamaica. She lived and worked in Jamaica until recently, almost always in publishing and editing. She is best known for her short fiction, which has garnered for her a strong international reputation. Her poetry has been compared to Derek Walcott's for its clarity of metaphor and its dynamic use of image throughout, but this relationship may be somewhat exaggerated. Senior's poetic contribution is distinctive; her verse consistently explores the role of landscape in the quest for identity and a place of belonging. In her verse her fascination with the Jamaican landscape, its vegetation and topography, is inextricably linked to her search for a way to speak of her own spiritual sensibility. She is rooted to the earth and the earth brings with it the complexities of history, social realities, and the metaphor of cultivation, which becomes a kind of metonymic reading of the business of writing and creativity.

Her first collection of short stories, *Summer Lightning and Other Stories* (Longman, 1986), won the Commonwealth Literature Prize. She has published three subsequent collections of short stories, including *Arrival of the Snake-Woman* (Longman, 1989) and *Discerner of Hearts* (McClelland and Stewart, 1995). She has published two collections of poems, *Talking of Trees* (Calabash, 1985) and *Gardening in the Tropics* (McClelland and Stewart, 1994). She was for some time the editor of *Jamaica Journal*.

Senior now lives in Toronto, Canada, but maintains her Caribbean connections.

KWAME DAWES: While this is not the most striking feature of your collection *Gardening in the Tropics,* it does stand out as a departure from your first book, *Talking of Trees:* I speak of a greater willingness to offer a political posture of we an' dem—an almost Manichean praxis that is at times quite polemical. Is this a conscious decision on your part to tackle issues of history and politics from this confrontational position?

OLIVE SENIOR: No, I wasn't aware that I was being confrontational or polemical; rather, what I think I'm doing is engaging "The Other" in a dialogue. I'm providing the means by which people who have been voiceless in the pages of history can now engage in dialogue with those people who formerly had control of the word. So, they might choose to take a confrontational position, but I, myself, as a poet, am not engaged in a confrontational position. That's not where I'm coming from, at all. I just want to open up the dialogue and have people talking in a different kind of way. We haven't had dialogue; what we have had is texts—historical text, anthropological text, etc., and I just want those people who have been written out to start talking about their own lives, their own experiences.

KD: What is striking about *Gardening in the Tropics,* particularly in the sequence thus titled, is not only the deliberate use of that phrase ("gardening in the tropics") to open each poem (suggesting, of course, that they are all one long poem), but the historicity of the allusions and references in the movement. I am curious about how much research went into the writing of this movement, and what kind of research was involved? Is it important for you to locate your poetry in a distinctive historical context?

OS: Before I can answer the question in a specific kind of way, perhaps I should explain how I see myself and what I am doing. I haven't done research for any specific poem, but my writing is not separate from my life; and I have spent my entire life doing research (if you want to put it that way) in order to answer all the fundamental questions we ask about ourselves in the first place, starting with the existential questions like "who am I?" But that, of course, inevitably leads into "who are we?" And that, in turn, leads into "where are we coming from?" And it seems to me that this is my engagement, which is an engagement with history—both a personal and an ancestral history, but also with a wider notion of history: the history of the Caribbean, and indeed of the so-called New World. So because I've spent a lot of time doing all kinds of research, when I come to write creatively, I think, all of that knowledge that I have, which is the knowledge of all my years, comes out in the work. But I didn't deliberately set out to do research for a particular poem, although I might check facts and so on. I think each represents a coming together in my unconscious of a lot of thoughts and observations and knowledge about different things. Somebody, I forget who it was, said that I was like a literary archeologist, which pleased me because that is how I look at it myself.

KD: There is far more lyricism, far more of this person called Olive Senior (as defined in the discourse of autobiography) in *Talking of Trees* than in *Gardening in the Tropics*. I mean that the confessional posture, so clear in such poems as "Nature Studies I" and "Nature Studies II" and in the seemingly autobiographical "Cockpit Country Dreams," "Ancestral Poems," "Eighth Birthday" and "Colonial Girls School," rarely appears in *Gardening in the Tropics*. There is, instead, a far greater sense of distancing. One senses the same engagement with the past, but the "I" narrator becomes more diffuse, less definable about a single individual (this is true about the Hurricane Story poems especially). The use of multiple voices enhances this sense of distance and creates a discourse that is far less involved with the discovery of a poetic self than with discovery of a community. Two questions, then: (1) does the assumption of these multiple voices result in a certain distancing, a reduction of the so-called poetic angst, and (2) is there something larger taking place here — something related to the realization of the poet in a non-Western context — that is the poet as griot who is defined vis-à-vis the community?

OS: Perhaps I should point out that we are comparing two books that were written almost thirty years apart. *Talking of Trees* represents my very earliest adult poetry. I think, then, that it is natural that it would be autobiographical, it would be confessional, because it was very much a part of me finding myself, finding my own voice as a human being — not just as a poet. Whereas by the time I came to write *Gardening in the Tropics* I was much more confident about who I was. I had dealt with all these questions in the intervening years, so I think that explains in some ways the kind of difference that exists between the two books. And I did set out to distance myself in *Gardening in the Tropics*. In other words, I wanted to take away the author as much as possible and create characters that speak for themselves. I am doing the same in my fiction. So that there is virtually no Olive Senior in the book, at least not consciously so. In fact, I think Olive Senior only appears in the Jean Rhys poem, because that arose out of a very specific occasion, my visit to her grave. So to answer your questions about the assumption of these multiple voices, I can only say that I am very conscious as a writer of removing myself and my personal concerns from what is going on in the text. I try to become these people that I am writing about; I assume various personas.

The other question is whether or not I see myself a griot. I see myself as making things possible for my characters, like setting the stage and giving these unknown people from history the chance to speak to the other world. But I, personally, do not assume any roles for myself; that is not what I want to be. I want to be the archeologist, to dig and to bring up these things and say to the world, "Here they are." And let people draw whatever conclusion they want from it. But I don't see myself taking an activist role or playing or assuming a role that is mystical or ordained or anything like that.

KD: But you are, I am sure, aware that the construction of this North/South discourse which explores issues of colonialism, tourism, environmental exploitation, slavery, and a history of exploitation, provides fodder for many "postcolonial" scholars in their critical analysis. The Manichean relationship between the North and the South that you explore in your work, in some ways, slots quite easily into somewhat stereotyped appraisals of colonial history. Here the politics of struggle defines societies along lines that employ terms like postcolonial, Commonwealth, Third World, etc., to contain. Does this bother you, and do you ever seek to write against such seemingly easy stereotyping of the ideological content of your work? Or is this a complete non-issue for you, in that you write the poem first and grapple with its politics after?

OS: This is a very important question. It's a non-issue in the sense that I'm not writing to please critics. I'm writing what I feel I truthfully want to write. I have the sense that some critics are not reading so much as pouncing on the work and this bothers me, because they are not reading the work, they are reading *into* the work, and they're reading into the work their own biases, prejudices, and also what they need to fulfill their own agendas. I think there is a dangerous new form of colonization going on, and I think it is very important to resist this; you know, to just not fall into the trap of conforming to what people want you to be. And since I have spent my life in a posture of resistance, as a woman and coming from where I come from and so on, I don't have a problem continuing to resist. In terms of writing the poem first and grappling with the politics after—I don't grapple with the politics in a conscious way. What I grapple with is telling my story, forming my characters, finding the voice. Those are the issues for me. Obviously, my work is going to reflect the worldview of Olive Senior. But I don't do it in a deliberate kind of way. So, the way I function as a creative artist is far more important to me.

KD: To what extent are you aware that readers come to both your fiction and your poetry with an intense desire to find out what is happening in the Caribbean and especially in Jamaica, today, and how much does this affect what you write and how you write?

OS: I have no awareness of this as I write, absolutely not. And I am not sure it would affect me. There is a certain imperative about what I write and how I write, and I'm going to follow that imperative regardless.

KD: And that imperative is prompted by . . .

OS: . . . the desire to explain. It's the why, the who and the why. I am driven by those issues. I enjoy playing around with time—going backwards in time, dealing with long time spans and all of that. I am a journalist by training, but I am not practicing journalism, so I am not here to fulfill people's intense desire to know what's happening today, so much as to understand the forces that shaped what is happening.

KD: You appear to be unfettered by restriction about what poetic voices you can assume and what peoples you can identify with. This pattern began in *Talking of Trees,* in which you make the telling comment: "My spirit ancestors are those / I choose to worship and that / includes an I that existed / long before me. . . ." In that context, you are in the process of justifying your affinity with Arawak ancestors to which you are unlikely to have a "natural" linkage. You speak of the connection emerging through the "whisper of clay fragments," an anthropological and historical connection that evolves into a profound spiritual link. *Gardening in the Tropics* takes this theme up and really runs with it. Does writing poetry allow you this kind of freedom, and to what extent has this ability to explore a spiritual affinity with the Arawaks, for instance, been a critical influence in your writing?

OS: I would say I feel much freer now writing poetry than I do fiction. Freer in the sense that I feel I can transcend time and space much more easily. I'd like to do it in the fiction, too, but I just haven't found a satisfactory way of doing it. I have always felt a spiritual affinity with the Arawaks, because when we were growing up in school, our textbooks gave us this image of these simple people that existed when Columbus arrived and then suddenly they were no longer there. Since childhood, I have been haunted by their presence, or perhaps I should say by their absence. And for the last ten years or so of my life, I have devoted a great deal of time to studying island Arawaks, whom we now call Tainos, because I feel that they are very much a part of our inheritance and we've totally ignored them. I don't feel that they just vanished from the pages of history; we now recognize that some cultural transmission took place that we can see in elements of our culture even today. I also am interested in the meeting between the red man and the black man in the New World. I'm fascinated by the notion that the worldview and spiritual values of these two people were so similar—not just values, but practices—that there might have been a more profound connection between these two races of people than between, say, the European and the African or the European and the Taino. So it's an area that's engaging me a lot right now. In order to understand the Taino, I have been looking at the religion of the native peoples of South America (because of course that is where the Tainos originally came from), and I think all of this has really infused *Gardening in the Tropics*. This mythological element is very strong in this book. I feel that this link has enabled me to open to a much wider world than I have been able to do, for instance, in my fiction, which is still very much rooted in Jamaican realities.

KD: One of the obvious connections that I can observe in your interest in native societies and native voices is the intense fascination with vegetation—or to put it more politically, with the earth. You have always had a strong interest in nature and nature images have played a pivotal part in both your collections. The thematic interest is clearly related to your own history as a rural Jamaican, a person who grew up with a dependence on the land. Can you talk a little about how this agrarian childhood has shaped your own poetic sensibility?

OS: I suppose the main thing about me is that I don't feel or see any disjunction between life and land or between living and landscape; I don't make those separations at all. I imagine that I'm like that because I grew up in deep rural Jamaica and I was conscious from earliest childhood about the power of plants. I mean, we didn't have easy access to doctors and medicines in pill form or anything like that. If you had a bellyache you would go out and boil mint and if you had a cut you'd pick a bush to wrap around it. We knew there were plants that were good and trees that were good and trees that were bad that we stayed away from; because either they were the abode of ghosts or they were used in *obeah,* and so on and so forth. At that age I didn't understand the meaning of all of this, but I grew up with this awareness of plants being an integral part of our lives. I have a poem, "My Father's Blue Plantation," which talks about bananas feeding us and sending us to school, but the banana plantation was not over there, it was right in our faces and at night, around the house was so dark because there is nothing darker than a banana plantation. So, as I said, there is just no separation in my mind between myself and that world out there. I also think that one of the things that has shaped my sensibilities as a writer is the intense beauty of the country in which I grew up. I have internalized this landscape; the mountains, in particular, the valleys ... Those are the profound elements that have shaped me: the fact that we lived with trees as a part of the social fabric of our lives—with plants—and the fact that we lived in this intensely beautiful landscape. Not lost on me as a child was the fact that it masked a lot of hardship and pain and so on.

KD: The environmental concerns do become, as I have said earlier, somewhat political. You refer to the destruction of the South American landscape by the collective "You" and "Them" of exploitative Western societies, for instance, and the tourism inspired rape of Caribbean islands and the people who live on these islands. You pull very few punches here. But your polemic is tempered by irony and a certain pragmatism that undercuts easy idealism. I think especially of the poem "Tree of Life" in which the persona/Adam/farmer figure extols the virtue (even divinely determined validity) of diversified farming over the cash-crop mentality of single-crop farming. The diversified farming approach, he argues, is more practical, and will lead to self-sufficiency. This is clearly an economic discussion, and yet you handle it with the sweet palatability of a folk tale. How much of your writing involves this kind of acrobatic feat—this "juggling of words / on your shoulder"? Can you also talk a bit about your own environmental concerns? Do you still have any connections with the rural farm life of Jamaica?

OS: Gosh, there are many, many questions in this. Let me try and break them down. My family lived in rural Jamaica up till last year when my father died at age ninety-four. The land is still there so I don't know what will happen in the future. But I have those connections. What I do in these poems? Well, I would like to address the specific poems that you're talking about. I don't agree, for instance, that "Seeing the Light" is political and polemic—at least my intention was not polemics. But I think it might appear so because of something I said earlier. In writing that poem, I assumed the persona of a native South American, and I said, if that man (somehow it seems like it's a man to me) had the chance to talk to a European, how would he talk? And what he would be doing is expressing his own worldview, not just his worldview, but talking about the physical world; and that is what I'm describing in this poem. It's simply that we are getting it from the perspective of the other in that sense, and we are not used to that; we are not used to hearing these voices put forth another viewpoint. This speaker is contrasting how native peoples have dealt with the land, the environment, and the world around them, with how the incoming Europeans dealt with the land. I think the ending of this poem subverts the notion that it is polemical because it's ending on a very philosophical speculation. You might not agree with this, but I am just trying to explain where I'm coming from with this particular poem.

The other poem is "Tree of Life." There is a very deep mythological element in many of these poems and "The Tree of Life" is one because it is going back to the notion of the first garden that was ever planted. We grew up with the notion of the Edenic garden and I don't see why the Carib notion of the first garden should not be celebrated. And again, when I started writing this poem, I just started writing about the tree of life. I had no agenda, and I think it ended the way it did because of who I am. I'm a country girl and I know how country farmers feel about government people in their white shirts coming down and telling them what to do, and that the small farmer still regards it as dangerous to get into mono-crop cultivation because if something happens he can't feed his family, and that is the bottom line. So again, it's a combination of mythology and my own practical knowledge. I think that explains the juggling of worlds, because I think that I know a lot about all these different worlds and they come together in my mind. What happened with these poems is that a lot of knowledge just came together—bang!—once I found the gardening metaphor which has enabled me to do all of this digging and planting. So while I suspect that most people will be inclined to say that the work is polemic, the intention is not polemic. The intention is to engage in dialogue and say, "Hey man, why don't you ask me how I feel about this?" This is not just *a* voice—this is a voice that's representing all these people stretching back from the first time of the European conquest, and speculating about a lot of things that they see happening that they just don't understand, even the notion of a savior that is crucified on a cross. So I was trying to capture the puzzlement of someone about another's culture.

KD: In *Gardening in the Tropics* there seems to be a certain resolution of what appears to be in *Talking of Trees* a tension between an Afrocentric and a Eurocentric series of paradigms. In *Gardening in the Tropics* you do celebrate Africa in a direct way in the "mystery" poems. You celebrate non-Western belief systems and you celebrate traditional folk practices in direct opposition to a western Christian ethos. Is the tension, clear in *Talking of Trees,* still extant in *Gardening in the Tropics,* and how does it manifest itself in your mind and in your poetry? At the end of *Gardening in the Tropics* one is left with celebration of Africa that recalls Langston Hughes, Kamau Brathwaite, Wole Soyinka, Aimé Césaire, and Grace Nichols. Is this a progression, a conscious movement? And could you comment a bit about your connection as a poet with Africa?

OS: Let me address the question about the tension first. As I explained earlier, *Talking of Trees* was very much a part of my working out some of these tensions and answering the questions of who am I and where do I stand. I mean, I am a person of many races; I am racially mixed, so that was an important question. I really think, though, that I have resolved these tensions in the sense that now I affirm myself as a Caribbean person, and the way I define that is as somebody who, precisely like me, embodies, if not different races, different cultures. So I identify myself with the Caribbean—as belonging to this particular place in the world. So once I was able to do that I no longer worried about questions of personal identity that relate to race and so on. I mean, people just have to take me or leave me. To talk a bit about the connection with Africa: I have spent a lot of time doing research on African religions and so on. I grew up in a small village that, though I did not know it at the time, was like a West African village in the sense that most of the people were of African origin and the way of life reflected African values. There was a strong sense of community which expressed itself in systems like "day-work," all the women going down the river to wash, music accompanying everything, storytelling at night, communal activities like corn-shelling, wakes and so on, in which African-Jamaican cultural elements were expressed; elements like stories, ring-games, etc. But at the same time, when I went away, first to live with other members of my family and then to high school, I was being socialized quite differently. European values were important then. And we were taught that, of course, anything that smacked of the folk or Africa was pure superstition and something that we needed to rid ourselves of. So I think that all of us, whether black or white or in between, grew up with that conflict once we got into the educational system, and it wasn't until much later that I realized, "Hey, we're talking about Africa here!" That these things weren't just superstitions or fragments of anything; they represented a real culture, the culture of the majority of the people. I have continued that kind of research and have extended my thinking to the point where today I'm working on a dictionary of Jamaican folklore, because I think it is very important for us to acknowledge all the elements in our culture including the African. So learning about Africa has been very much a part of my personal education. I grew up learning about Europe, I did that research into Africa, and then I turned to the Amerindians. And I feel all of us need to be engaged in these different aspects of our culture. I wrote the poem "Mystery" because I was really thrilled to discover Yoruba culture, in particular, because, of course, I grew up learning a lot about Greek and Roman myths—it was part of the curriculum. The African Orishas are much more fascinating, because, as I keep saying to people, they are still alive. Their histories and personalities are just as interesting as those of the Greek gods, but we have never been told anything about them. I am not Afrocentric in the sense that it would be absurd of me, looking the way that I do, to say I am only affirming the African part of my being, but I think it's important simply because Africa has more profoundly affected all of us, regardless of our race, than we realize. The way Africa has shaped us as a people is something that I would like to explore.

KD: When I finished reading *Gardening in the Tropics,* I had a reaction not unlike the one I had upon the completion of *Talking of Trees.* It was the word "clean." The word "clean" is my best description of your line. Especially in the earlier poems of the collection, the lines are pared down without being minimalist — just this cleanness, this economy. And yet these are layered lines that resonate with ironies, ambiguities, double entendres, puns, etc.:

> My mother sought a sign
> in the basin.
>
> She said: sky's so clear
> nothing's given back here.
>
> I said: Agué Lord of the Sea
> rules over me.
>
> You can't keep
> a good man down,
>
> if you born to hang
> you can't drown

This brief quote alone draws from me a number of questions. One has to do with the shift in language registers. It is something you do a lot. Is this the outworking of your natural voice — that Jamaican middle-class voice; both schooled in standard English and in Patois? And yet, this dialect voice which sounds Jamaican is spoken in the context of a poem about Haiti. What is going on here?

OS: First of all, I find it very natural to switch. That's how I speak so I don't have a problem writing like this. So I'm not being facetious when I say that there is nothing extraordinary going on in the use of language. It just seems very natural to me to write this way. It doesn't matter whether it's somebody from Haiti or Martinique or Guyana or what have you, I'm just enabling somebody to express him or herself in a particular way. Do you have a problem with it?

KD: No, no . . . I really like it for what it does for Patois—for the dialect. Well, the second part of the question then: There is a certain architecture inherent in the line allowing it to be held together, sustained if you will, by a rhyme and rhythm pattern that does not announce itself. It simply makes its logic felt by the rightness of the phrase. Suddenly the cliché "you can't keep a good man down" has an arresting quality derived both from the context of the poem, and the shape of the line. I am playing critical analyst here, but is any of this conscious — this sophisticated shaping of the line? I know how much craft means to you, this is why I ask.

OS: Craft is very important to me. Somebody said that poetry is the art which most aspires to music, because in music form and content are one, and this is what I aspired to do consciously in these poems. I found it easy to write this book in the sense that the poems came very easily to me. I didn't do a lot of rewriting or restructuring (some less than others). But what I spent a lot of time on was finding the exact, right shape to express each poem and of course that has to do with line lengths and so on. For some, it took me a long, long time before I hit upon what I intuitively felt was the right shape. I can give you as an example the "Stowaway" poem. The words came easily but I was very unhappy with it because of its graphic shape; it was too dense. So I spent a lot of time playing around with it in terms of line length, breaks and so on, and eventually I hit on this idea of putting the short second line to the right margin. Normally, you'd indent it to the left. So I put it to the right, and suddenly I realized that this is how this poem was meant to be written. Because I was signifying the ebb and flow of the sea and the movement of the boat, and I was also pulling back each time. There is no openness in this poem; it is signifying this enclosure, this closed space, and also this person who is trying to escape but may not. So that's a good example of how I think the form and the content cohere. I try to do this in virtually everything. I haven't always succeeded, but this is why there are so many different shapes in this book. For instance, "The Immovable Tenant" also gave me a lot of problems because it is a very, very long poem. How to divide up the line? Eventually I hit on the form that's there. So a lot of time and effort goes into the shaping.

KD: I would describe your verse as free—you eschew the Eurocentric formal poetic modes—at least in part. But your verse is very carefully organized around rhythms, whether they be the tumbling cadence of many of the poems in the suite "Gardening in the Tropics" or the complex rhyme and rhythm games in the nature poems and a number of the Traveler's Tales; or the heavily drum-inspired sounds in the suite of poems "Mystery" which celebrate "African Gods in the New World." I am describing a fairly eclectic range of styles which makes sense together; but I am curious about what kinds of influences have helped generate that kind of writing. Can you talk a bit about influences in your work?

OS: I think that there are three major influences on my work. One is that I had what would have been called a classical English education, which it was at the time I went to school. So, of course, I grew up on this diet of Wordsworth and Keats and Shelley and, you know, the great English classics. So I think that has influenced my work. I also grew up on the bible, and I regard the oral tradition as having played a very important part in shaping my work. And when I talk about the oral tradition I'm talking about not just the content but the rhythms, because a lot of our games in school, for instance, were based on rhythm and physical dexterity—you know, clapping and all this kind of thing. Everything was performed to rhythm: the floor was cleaned to rhythm, the clothes were washed to rhythm—you just couldn't escape this. Therefore, I feel that all of these things are coming together in my writing, because I am very conscious of rhythm in my prose as well. I think I have a good ear. It's all there in my head, all these sounds. And of course, I've read, and read, and read, and read, all my life.

Cyril Dabydeen
BORN 1945

CYRIL DABYDEEN WAS born in Guyana in 1945. He grew up in a largely rural environment, but one that was acutely familiar with the values of education, of literature, and of cricket. A gold medalist in poetry in his native country, in 1970 he traveled to Canada to undertake studies at Queen's University, where he received postgraduate degrees in English literature and public administration.

In the space of almost two decades, Dabydeen has published more than a dozen books, including several collections of poetry, an impressive selected works, three novels, and several collections of short stories. His verse is controlled and carefully rendered; his capacity for irony is profound, but so is his conviction that love in its many forms is what sustains us. Writers of Dabydeen's generation have often been overshadowed by the two "big guns" Walcott and Brathwaite. His departure from the Caribbean in 1970; to Canada rather than Britain or America, did for a time relegate him to "peripheral-poet" status in the echelons of West Indian literature by limiting the exposure that his work has received.

Cyril Dabydeen lives and works in Ottawa, where he was, for a number of years, the poet laureate of the Canadian capital. After teaching for many years at Algonquin College and the University of Ottawa, he now works in race relations in Canada and as a consultant to the Federal Government on cultural policy.

His published poetry includes *Poems in Recession* (Sheik Sadeek, 1972), *Goatsong* (Mosaic, 1977), *Distances* (Fiddlehead, 1977), *Heart's Frame* (Vesta Publications, 1980), *Islands Lovelier than a Vision* (Peepal Tree, 1986), *Coastland: New and Selected Poems* (Mosaic, 1989), *Stoning the

Wind: Poems (TSAR, 1994), *Born in Amazonia* (Mosaic, 1995), and *Discussing Columbus* (Peepal Tree, 1997).

KWAME DAWES: Constantly, in articles and essays written about your writing, the point has been made that you are primarily a poet, despite your obvious production as a fiction writer. The perception is that you are a poetic fiction writer with a profound propensity to poetic brevity and imagism in your fiction. Do you struggle with the apparent dichotomy that could be found in working in these two distinct genres?

CYRIL DABYDEEN: Strangely enough, I began, if I recall correctly, writing fiction first. One of my first short stories, called "A Tide at Beachhead," won a prize and was published in the *Sunday Chronicle* in Guyana, I think appearing in 1970, even though it was written before 1970. So, even though I am better known as a poet, especially in Canada, and perhaps in the Caribbean as well, I have been working in both genres, side by side so to speak. Having said that, though, I must say that I've spent more time during most of my writing career in the early years writing poetry. Only within the last six years have I been giving more attention to fiction (novels and short stories, of course). Currently, I do spend far more time on fiction than poetry. I can't recall when last I have written a poem, to be honest, though I might be revising poems continually, mind you. I suppose revising is a form of writing poetry—and you are a poet yourself so you know how the process works. The writing of a poem is never finished until one revises and revises endlessly. The question of brevity is an interesting one. Some critics have made reference to the brevity in the writing, and I suppose I grew up with the notion that excess fat in writing is always a harmful thing; you know, less is more—to use that cliché. And I've always been influenced by condensed writing, even though there are so many different schools, but at this stage it seems to me that brevity is indeed one of the things I bear in mind continually.

KD: In your editing process where do you find that the fat is usually located?

CD: When I do edit, it comes to me instinctively, what has to be taken out, or what has to be left in. I am a great believer in the power of the metaphor; and the simile and metaphor are, of course, close cousins. The power of the metaphor seems to be all, and sometimes

I sacrifice logic just to give energy to the metaphor or the various figures of speech that I use in my poems. Aesthetic energy in a work of art or fiction (short fiction especially) seems to be uppermost in my mind very often. With long fiction, the approach is different. You have more room, it seems to me, for self-indulgence, where qualifiers can appear here and there and perhaps not affect the personal style that much.

KD: Your first collection of verse was written at a very tender age. You were in your teens, I believe?

CD: Yes, I wrote many of my earliest poems in my teens, some of which appeared in a small collection called *Poems in Recession*, published in Guyana. They were poems concerned with nationalism. Guyana and the other Caribbean states were trying to wrest their independence from the European powers. The idea of forming a nation, of national self-identity, seems to have been paramount in these poems. There was also a strong social commitment, and the sense of history, combined with lyricism. Technically, they might have verged on density, a profusion of imagery, seen in some of the poems I wrote in my early twenties.

KD: Critics have suggested that even at that point you had a voice that had a very distinctive quality and perspective that is usually expected of more mature poets. Do you think that you did evolve a poetic voice at that age (your teenage years) and can you talk a bit about the question of voice? Is it a myth of critical analysis or is there, in your experience, such a concept as "finding one's voice"?

CD: I am a bit flattered that critics have said that I discovered a voice or found a voice at that age, because sometimes it seems to me one takes an entire lifetime in writing to discover a voice. This is especially so considering that the kind of voice I may envision for myself might not be what comes out on the page; it might even be a different kind of voice one senses in the imagination. Growing up in the Caribbean, of course, and the kind of context in which I wrote — the context of struggle and especially in the '60s and '70s (primarily in the '60s when I was living there; I left Guyana in 1970) — a context which involved us taking part in the struggle for freedom; maybe the politics in this social milieu as a whole might have generated in me as a writer, a sense of energy vis-a-vis voice. I was focused very early, perhaps compared to and in contrast with many Canadian writers in whom that sense of "voice" might not have been as focused as mine was and still is. That voice, though it has evolved over the years, is still with me.

KD: Would you say, then, that voice is tied in that sense to the context and to the content, or is voice a question of style? I ask this because in your work I can identify some kinds of stylistic patterns that are sustained through your various evolutions. Where is voice located? Is it tied, as some poets have argued, to the "spirit" of what one is doing?

CD: What you say is something I often wrestle with. And as we are speaking here, I am really thinking out loud about "voice." I see voice, no doubt, as all-embracing, encompassing style. I agree with those poets who argue that it is the "spirit"—spirit of the place, for instance (although a cliché, it has relevance to this discussion). Voice is also closely integrated to language: the way you express something —a sensation or feeling—because you just can't separate language from the vision. I think it is Walcott who says that when he is writing a poem, he is not sure what he will be saying next, but the writing itself—the ideas, the voice, the spirit, everything—evolved during the actual writing process. I am a believer of that, in many respects, that the spirit, the philosophy evolves in the actual process of writing. And perhaps it's a sense of presence in one's self, or inspiration that really becomes voice also, all that the "ubiquitous unconscious" forces you into imagining and becoming.

KD: Your nonfiction writing is decidedly political, often polemic. The pieces that I have read so far reflect this. Your early poetry appears to have this quality of political advocacy, like you've mentioned, but such easy labeling cannot be done without reference to your later poetry. Indeed one critic has declared you an "apolitical" poet, while another has argued that your Canadian voice is distinctly political. How do you react to these varied reactions to your poetry, and what place does the political have in your poetic and creative experience?

CD: When I set out to write, I don't think specifically of writing a polemical piece or a political piece. If I did, I think I would produce very bad art. I tend to work, as I've said before, with a sense of the energy of the metaphor. Now that metaphor itself can suggest, implicitly, some level of the politics that is already there. But, perhaps, the polemic of the nonliterary pieces does exist even though it has been toned down in many respects in the poems and prose. But one does not necessarily feed the other in any linear fashion. It is there subliminally, I feel, because the politics that I express—human rights concerns that I have (and I work in the field in a day job that deals directly with race relations and community aspirations)—are a part of my psyche, my mold of mind as it were. The mettle of experience that one may have is all part of one's mental makeup feeding the art when I get down to writing. Now, having said that, let me be honest: there is one poem I wrote called "Racism" which hasn't been published yet, and there it was a tongue-in-cheek poking fun at the whole question of racism through art. So I can play games with the social question as well, but in some way it seems that the concerns that I have—politics and so on—are there, even though some critics tend to see only political elements in my work. I feel they may be doing some injustice to my work because I deal with many other feelings and emotions. In my novel *Dark Swirl*, for instance, I deal with elements of depth psychology, mythology, the hinter-landscape, the hinterland mind as against the metropole mind. I feel the metropole mind perhaps is equivalent to what you find in organized societies: that is, it is perhaps too much of the intellectual side and not enough of the affective. It is the cognitive versus the emotional and the intuitive and spiritual that I dwell on. Writers from the so-called "Third World" (the Caribbean and elsewhere) have a tremendous contribution to make when their works get published because of the insight they bring to bear because of this experience—the way of looking at the world. Maybe it is a very Guyanese thing also: the sense of mysticism in the work. In *Dark Swirl* it is there and it is there also in some of the poems, because I grew up in a region that is broadly speaking a part of the whole Amazon area. I want to say, too, to get back to the politics per se, that we are all going through this difficult time of getting our works published, and it is thanks to publishers like Jeremy Poynting of Peepal Tree Press that we are getting a chance to express that hinterland voice in us with its particular truth, which has been suppressed because the Eurocentric art forms have dominated the world for so long.

KD: Your poems clearly draw from a multiplicity of landscapes and language registers. What is the rooting of your language sensibility? In other words, what language rhythms drive your poetry? And do you find any of the tensions of multiple voices competing with each other affecting your poetry at all?

CD: I grew up speaking a dialect in Guyana, the so-called Nation Language, to use Kamau Brathwaite's phrase. In Guyana, and no doubt in the other Caribbean islands (but I haven't lived for any length of time in the other Caribbean islands to speak confidently about this), you have different rhythms working within the dialect. I find this in Janice Shinebourne, who, even though we lived in the same district, has an ear for the local dialect and argot that is somewhat different from mine. She was one of the editors of my book *Dark Swirl*, and some of the dialogue in that book might have been closer to her ears, though no less convincing or authentic in the novel. My ear for the local dialect is closer to someone like M. R. Monar's, the Guyanese poet. It is essentially the sugar plantation ear, as it were, in my rhythms, because I grew up in the heart of a sugar plantation. What I am saying, in summary, is that there are gradations of dialect throughout the Caribbean, a multiplicity of voices, in my work at times which might have become more manifest when I moved to Canada. Frank Birbalsingh, the critic, once suggested to me that some of my poetry, for instance, is now more Canadian than Caribbean. Now, I haven't written a great deal in what is accepted to be dialect—a few poems here and there—but in some of my best poetry reflected in *Coastland: New and Selected Poems* there is one poem called "Sir James Douglas." Whenever I read this poem in dialect to Canadian audiences, I do get a warm response; usually the audience would say I should read this poem more often. It is also my signature piece more or less, because in it the energy and "voice" that we talked about earlier are really coming out. I suspect also that my Canadian audience might perhaps be enamored of the "exoticism" of the language, and not see this language or dialect as the result of fractured experience—the experience of oppression, slavery, and indentured labor, and what results from it. And it is good that writers are seeking to legitimize dialect through literature, more or less, that it is no longer seen as inferior but that it is integral to art, literary art. Dialect is a language of the people, and we give it the stature of art when we use it in this way.

KD: Despite your obvious prolific output and quality production there has still been a relative failure to acknowledge your work by West Indian and Canadian critics alike. How has this situation affected your writing and your own critical evaluation of your work; do you think that there is a movement away from this trend currently?

CD: Well, it is an important question, and it is something that I have as part of my angst. I am getting on in years, I am not a teenage writer any more. The problem, really, is that of getting a big publisher to accept one's work, and when you do get a big publisher, you can make quick leaps because of the latter's tremendous resources in promoting the work. Big publishers will call up the *Globe and Mail,* and or have lunch with the book-review page editor; they might call upon people to organize readings or even organize readings themselves, and in short vigorously promote your work. With my novel, *Sometimes Hard,* published by Longman in England, I can see the difference. I have dealt all along with relatively small publishers: Mosaic Press, Fiddlehead (now Goose Lane Editions) and so on. They are good presses, but the only problem is that they do not always have the resources, for example publicists, to promote one's work. Of course, publishing is a very competitive business, as you well know, Kwame. Also, sometimes reviewers in Canada tend not to treat small-sized publishers' books seriously. As a critic myself I could sense that bias in my own responses, and I would quickly come to my senses and say "No, you can't think like that." Back to the reception of my work, let me say that there are writers in the Caribbean, for instance, who could have been as big as T. S. Eliot but did not have the exposure that the power brokers of art and taste in metropolitan societies have; it is the entire cultural apparatus spawning its own establishment perhaps. And so, those writers, while writing brilliant work, never have the exposure due to the promotion that Eliot and others have had, and therefore remained relatively obscure. I am thinking of someone like the Guyanese writer Martin Carter, for instance.

KD: I am always fascinated by how poets "discover" their poems. How do you define "the poem"? Is yours a definition derived from a Eurocentric conception of poetry, a non-Western perspective, or a perceived universal understanding of what verse is? I am talking about the identification of what makes the poem "the poem," and I am talking about influences as well.

CD: Of course, I grew up with the notion of universality. I heard Edward Said talk about this in Canterbury, Kent, in 1989, challenging what is universal—who defines what is universal, and so on. Growing up in the Caribbean, one sees the Eurocentric influence is palpably there, being in one's consciousness to an extent. So one has to go through a process of unlearning and it is very difficult to unlearn things, of course. I spent a great deal of time unlearning during the first few years of my writing career, and I am still doing this. Maybe it is simply coming to grips with one's own voice, the inner self. And over the past couple of years I've been quoting Eldridge Cleaver's definition of literature: as "the combination of the alphabet with volatile elements of the soul," and so on. Now take the whole business of dialect, for instance, and what the dub poets in Canada and England are doing; they have shaken things up, have really challenged the powers that be with their whole notion of the canon (who controls the canon, you know?), which they have shown to be essentially Eurocentric and not universal. My own sense of what is a poem, of course, is much more inclusive at this stage in my writing career. I like what the Russian poets say of poetry, and perhaps Robert Lowell's definition, that a poem is "a magical orange grove in the midst of a nightmare"; or Sylvia Plath's view, that a poem is simply "a moment's movement." For a while I used to read a lot of the American confessional poets like Plath, Sexton, Roethke, and others. Although I still listen to rhythm, I do not go so far as measure meter in the Tennysonian sense when I write. But even as I write "free verse" I know that there is no such thing as "free verse," for there is always my internal ear at work for language; all that one slowly develops and which is continually there. No doubt I have developed my own sense of the aesthetic stemming from my inner sense of what is art. And every writer, I am quite sure, no matter how one defines these things, has his or her own sense of aesthetic—the aesthetic line, the perfect line, for instance.

KD: What/who are some of the greatest influences on your poetry?

CD: In an essay I wrote, I made reference to the fact that as a young man I would go to the British Council Library in Guyana and read the "famous" writers: Eliot, Spender, Louis MacNeice, Auden, and so on, coming to an understanding and appreciation of the "tradition." And using the word "tradition" in itself can be very troublesome, but I don't necessarily mean it in the sense of Eliot's. But the other influences, because of my Indian ancestry, included Tagore, even though I did not read a great deal of his work because I, like many Indians in the Caribbean, had become creolized. The influences of African-Caribbean writers, Derek Walcott (a major influence), Kamau Brathwaite, MacKay, and all the other well-known

Caribbean writers, I have been reading continually, especially Martin Carter and A. J. Seymour. I used to listen religiously to the programs broadcast on "Calling the Caribbean" and "Caribbean Voices" from the U.K. on the BBC. So the Caribbean influences have been significant. V. S. Naipaul, especially the early V. S. Naipaul, has been an influence. My short novel *The Wizard Swami* was influenced to some extent by V. S. Naipaul. The poetry is a different matter. Martin Carter was really one of the more important voices because of the political elements as he had been involved in local politics to a greater degree than, say, Seymour. Carter's *Poems of Resistance*, for instance, was a classic work for us, and in fact, as I have said before, my very first book, *Poems of Recession* (a chapbook) is perhaps derived from Martin Carter's influence. Other influences came from America, because don't forget that one got one's culture also from listening to the radio, and I listened to a lot of things that came across on *Voice of America,* for instance. When I came to Canada, of course, I was curious about Canadian art and Canadian literature in particular, and there again there were some "influences." I quickly became aware of what the Canadian writers were doing. I formally studied Canadian literature and became quite immersed in E. J. Pratt, A. M. Klein, Earle Birney, and a whole host of contemporary Canadian poets, especially when I was a relatively active member of the League of Canadian Poets. It was at this time that I met the distinguished socialist poet F. R. Scott and exchanged books with him. Later, too, I would meet in Ottawa, when I became the city's poet laureate, the Russian poet Andrei Voznesensky, and chatted with him about the then-changing Soviet Union. I do read a lot of Russian poetry also, poets like Akhmatova and Yevtushenko. Now, a point I have made has been that in the Caribbean, my writing was very thickly layered, metaphorically dense; and one of the things I learnt here was to lighten up, and make the poems more accessible. When I look back at some of the stuff I wrote in Guyana, I realize that in many respects they were difficult poems because the average reader in the Caribbean could not easily understand some of those poems. The same is true of the work of Derek Walcott, I would say. In Canada I began to lighten up, making the poems more accessible as reflected in my *Coastland,* for instance. As a creative writing teacher, I have placed emphasis on tightness, on form.

KD: As for most Guyanese writers, the complex and dynamic Guyanese landscape is a place of deep mystery and spiritual density for you. It is impossible to miss this in your works. What is it about this landscape that has such an impact on the content of your work? Is it sustained even having arrived in Canada and having lived here for so many years?

CD: Actually, there's Wilson Harris's influence also, in my response to your earlier question. I recall reading Harris's *Palace of the Peacock* about a dozen times; I was drawn to it primarily because of its sense of landscape and the spirit of place which are so resonant in the works of Harris and Jan Carew. I remember listening to Jan Carew when I met him on our way to Havana, Cuba (there is a reference to Carew, by the way, in my short story "Jogging in Havana") — the raconteur that he is — and his works have been a marvelous influence. Carew grew up in the Courentyne, a place he might have romanticized, symbolic of the idyllic tropics, though the Courentyne can be a very daunting place also. Wilson Harris, of course, traveled a lot as a land surveyor, up the Canje River, and I grew up in the Canje. So the landscape in Guyana really does HAUNT you; it is imbedded in the psyche. Sometimes I juxtapose in an unconscious way the Guyanese landscape and mysticism with my Canadian life experiences. When I first came to Canada, I lived in northern Ontario and I worked my way through university in the forest as a tree planter. I might have planted one quarter of a million trees in the region, where I saw black flies fat as fists and mosquitoes long as fingers, if you pardon my hyperbole. Now I thought we had large insects in the tropics, but you should see those in northern Ontario. Northern Ontario also has its elements of mysticism, the sense of the Native Great Spirit which I became imbued with. I lived in bush camps with Crees and Ojibways, and wrote a short story called "Methuselah," and dedicated it to Jan Carew, as part of that juxtaposition and seeking correspondences. Here I deal with what I have argued in my introduction to *A Shapely Fire* [an anthology of Canadian/Caribbean prose and poems edited by Dabydeen] about the kind of pendulum-swing of the imagination that the transplanted Caribbean writer like myself experiences. In actuality it is not contrived, but is a kind of symbiosis. But place, landscape, the Guyanese hinterland are very much prominent in my psyche and imagination, and to use the Joycean phrase, "memory is the imagination," indeed the "kingdom of the imagination," as Elie Wiesel calls it.

KD: You deal very movingly with issues about immigration and being away from the Caribbean in poems like "Absences" and "Offspring." These are both touching expressions because of their honesty. Now how critical is this process of articulating or discovering "truth" to your own work?

CD: I think there are two broad themes unfolding in my writing. One is the genuine sense of mysticism stemming from the hinterland landscape as well as living so close to the Atlantic Ocean in Guyana. This might be reflective of the deep inner self, the sense of the "dream" perhaps. And then there is the other—the social consciousness deriving from history and living conditions. And maybe a third has to do with immigration; the upheaval resulting from the movement, a sense of placelessness. Self-revelation, of course, is also true in the poem "Offspring". And immigration is important in the context of Caribbean writing as a whole, since all Caribbean writers, because of where we come from, experience this so-called "sense of void," which is part of the way of life in the Caribbean—a feeling that we don't belong there. Now many writers have wrestled with reestablishing a sense of roots, and I speak here of someone like Kamau Brathwaite, whose work is essentially focused on that kind of exploration. We could posit that we do belong there even though we might have African or Indian and subcontinental and other Asian backgrounds, origins, and contexts. Yet immigration is still a palpable thing in the imagination. I was the eldest child of my family. And it's a great responsibility—you see what I am getting at, in terms of the economic thing. What I am saying, too, is that immigration is also separateness. It separates you from one's roots. But it is also a way of finding one's self, the search for one's roots because as a result of distance, you may see more clearly where you came from, perhaps, in a more interesting way. The poem "Offspring," even though it has some pathos in it (I have been told), speaks to the sense of the link with that which I have left behind, and the fact that I have not cut off that connection but am always longing to be part of it, longing to still be a part of the "tribe" through symbiosis, again. Eliot has said that the aim of the poet is "to purify the dialect of the tribe."

KD: I found it moving because there is that honesty and yet that wonderful capacity for irony.

CD: The reason that the irony is there is so that you don't fall into too much sentimentality, which can, to some extent, work against the poem.

KD: Mervyn Morris, of course, speaks of irony in his last collection, *Examination Centre,* as a "cancer"—a disease that he thinks he has. Bill Carr has argued that part of the problem with West Indian literature was twofold. One was the lack of tradition, and the second was related—that without that sense of tradition, there was little basis upon which to be ironic, thus limiting the capacity for irony in West Indian literature. Implicit in his comment is the notion of irony as a luxury, a tool of distancing that belongs to privileged society. How is irony played in your own work?

CD: Irony, it seems to me, has always been present in West Indian writing. It is integral to West Indian life as a whole. Survival itself is ironic. When you look at calypso, which is a form of oral literature, it is chock full with irony, and it's been there from the very beginning. Just to survive in the Caribbean, you have to be ironic, and it becomes part of one's range of expression, including humor. It is the tragicomedy of someone like Samuel Selvon (another important influence), a capacity for irony that was in Selvon's work from the very beginning, even before he moved to London to write *Lonely Londoners,* for instance. In my writing, I wouldn't say I deliberately set out to write irony, but it is there, implicit in the possibilities of language and place, and coping with movement from one place to another. No doubt irony can be variously defined, and not only in the sense of "gentle raillery," as Dryden calls it. I think the very harsh conditions we come from provide the background for ironic intent, for simply coping; yet it is also a British thing carried to its extreme in satire. We see it a lot in Naipaul. Writing or creating literature becomes one of the positive ways of using the elements of irony purposefully. A few Canadian critics have seen elements of romanticism also in my work, which is different from irony, romanticism perhaps in the way I have embraced the hinterland landscape and dealt with the whole notion of innocence as seen in *Dark Swirl.* Maybe in my book of poems, *Discussing Columbus,* irony is seen at its best in grappling with the instinct and impulse to override what is romantic, especially in the title poem in *Discovering Columbus.* Here, the assumed innocence is really not innocence at all, and this is expressed in the experience of the indigenous inhabitants of the Caribbean region.

KD: Can you talk a little bit about popular East Indian culture and the way that it may have affected your own writing?

CD: I have used the word "creolized" to describe what I have become. Interestingly, a certain anglicizing too has taken place; a genuine mixture. I taught in a school, St. Patrick's Anglican in the Rose Hall sugar plantation in Guyana, for a number of years. The East Indian music I heard was the commercial type, and on the sugar plantation, growing up with my grandmother (my parents were separated very early), the music was everywhere alongside other African and Western influences. At my grandmother's cake shop, which was a kind of mini-community center where the workers would come in the afternoons and play dominoes and cards and argue about politics, cricket scores, and boxing matches and so on, I would watch closely and listen keenly to what some of the older men would say. They would talk, too, of an Indian past, of Mahatma Gandhi and Nehru, and especially about the character in great Indian lore and tradition: about the *Bhagavada Gita*. My own taste was already becoming very cosmopolitan, for I was listening keenly, avidly, to Mahalia Jackson and Aretha Franklin—not just Hemant Kumar or Asha Bosle. I was never a great fan of commercial Indian music. It may be because I don't know Hindi, even though my grandmother spoke a little of it. You see, we were so busy, and my grandmother sent me to become a Christian by making me attend a Lutheran church. Now, I am more eclectic. I respect all faiths. The impact of Indian culture was changing, impacting more on my mother and my grandmother than on me. I would go and watch American western movies, which are also commercial, but would not watch the traditional Indian films because of the language barrier perhaps, the fact that you couldn't understand the dialogues. Also, the Indian commercial movies were terribly sentimental, though I was aware of the Indian tradition and I'd read Tagore. And when some of the old men at the cake shop talked about Indian cricketers and juxtaposed them with the West Indian ones, it was clear that there was a sense of tradition; whether they be Indian or West Indian (Gupte or Kanhai, for instance), they were forming in our memories and consciousness.

KD: Thanks Cyril. This has been good.

CD: A pleasure and a delight.

Lorna Goodison

BORN 1947

LORNA GOODISON'S UNQUESTIONABLE accomplishment as a poet rests in the sheer originality and distinction of her voice. Goodison was born in Jamaica and grew up during a time of social and political upheaval; the late 1950s, '60s, and '70s in Jamaica saw complex and shifting attitudes toward race, gender, and politics. While she began writing with some seriousness in the 1970s, her main creative focus was initially as a painter. In 1980, her first collection, *Tamarind Season,* was published by the Institute of Jamaica Publications. It was the beginning of what has been a remarkably successful career, especially striking because her first book demonstrated a fairly realized poetic sensibility, a voice fascinated by the social complexities of her world, but at the same time one deeply seduced by the magic of words and by the sheer lyrical indulgence of art and the artist. Her poems also offer a daring articulation of faith and spiritual hope.

Goodison has published five collections of verse and a collection of short stories. Her other verse publications are *I Am Becoming My Mother* (New Beacon Books, 1986), *Heartease* (New Beacon Books, 1988), *Selected Poems* (University of Michigan, 1993), *To Us, All Flowers Are Roses* (University of Illinois, 1995), and *Turn Thanks: Poems* (University of Illinois, 1999).

Goodison divides her time between Jamaica and the United States, where she teaches at the University of Michigan, Ann Arbor.

KWAME DAWES: What does it mean to be a woman writer in Jamaica in 1996? Do you see yourself as somehow guided by a role that your status as a writer has created for you?

LORNA GOODISON: It's not something I give a lot of thought to on a daily basis, so when someone like you wants an answer to a question like that I have a hard time to come up with a suitable answer. Because really I am just going about my business. I have been going about my business, that is, doing my writing, for a long time, for over thirty years. I never felt that I was doing anything for anybody. I would have written all the things I have written even if nobody else had read them, because I had to write them. I never felt any particular sense of destiny or a sense that I was charged to speak for anybody or anything. I write because I have to write. As you know, I started out life as a visual artist but I always wrote, too. And then there came a time when I began to write more than I painted. I believe I started to write because I wanted to read what I was writing. When I was growing up there were no images of me in the literature I read. I didn't see myself or people like me in any of the literature of my youth. I certainly never saw them in any of the books I read at St. Hughes High School. The closest I ever came to seeing anybody reflected in literature who could possibly have been any kind of role model for me was Selena in Paule Marshall's novel *Brown Girl Brownstone*. I really liked her. I really liked that character; but I read that book when I was a teenager. I spent a lot of time before that trying to find a character with whom I could fully identify.

In truth there's nothing tough about being a woman writer in Jamaica in 1996, but I do not make my living from writing poetry when I'm in Jamaica, so I do all kinds of *jobs* in order to do my *work*. I've worked in radio and television, advertising, and written speeches in order to buy time to write my poetry. So I have a pretty ordinary existence as a mother, daughter, sister, priest, and worker. I like the fact that a lot people I don't expect to know about my work seem to know about my work. That is truly rewarding. The work has had some kind of use, had some kind of meaning to people. People use my poems at weddings and funerals and state occasions. I would say all in all, in terms of being recognized and appreciated for what you're trying to do, I have no complaints. I just don't earn my living in Jamaica.

KD: Do you see yourself as a product of the earlier writers—a product that has been shaped and guided by their work? I suppose I am speaking here of influences—the influence, that is, of other Caribbean poets.

LG: Sure. I remember as a teenager being very excited the first time I got and read one of the very first books I ever read by a Caribbean writer. It was *Miguel Street* by V. S. Naipaul, and I still love that book. I then developed a kind of greed, an insatiable appetite to just read anything that anybody, any Caribbean person had ever written. I found *In a Green Night* [Derek Walcott] when I was sixteen years old and it changed my life. I've read that book over and over almost to my detriment. I abandoned every other book I was supposed to read and I just read *In a Green Night* over and over. So of course, I am shaped by all of those things. I'm shaped by the voice of Vic Reid, George Campbell, Una Mason, Louise Bennett, Philip Sherlock, Samuel Selvon and Neville Dawes and Derek Walcott. But as I said, these writers were not taught in the schools that I attended. I found them on my own. So my earliest readings were by writers like Wordsworth, John Donne, John Keats, Rupert Brooke, and Edna St. Vincent Millay. I also received *The Oxford Book of Modern Verse*, edited by William Butler Yeats, as an English prize in high school. My voice was also shaped by the poems in that book.

I'm very lucky that I grew up in a household where my sister worked at the *Daily Gleaner* and she loved books. My mother loved books. So we always had books in my house. I read most of those books and magazines that my sister brought home. So from a very early age, I read. I read very eclectically. I would read magazines. I would read anything from *Reader's Digest* to the *Saturday Evening Post* and the *Daily Mirror*. Then I would read my sister's books. Anything she brought home, I read it. So from the time I was four years old, I remember reading all the time. I didn't like everything that I read. I felt very uncomfortable with some of the books, the voices in there, the way black people were represented in some books. But I also recall reading (and it turned out I didn't even know it then because I was too young) from *Go Tell It on the Mountain* by James Baldwin. And I remember being affected by its kind of strange beauty and power. There was this fine poetic language and there was also this great empathy that he had for the people in the story. It was an insider's voice. He was writing about people in a way that meant he was not standing outside of them, judging them, or feeling embarrassed by them, and I liked that. That has certainly influenced my writing. So I think all of that reading had an impact on me. I developed my own critical sense. I knew what I didn't like. And certainly

I liked Baldwin, and Paule Marshall, and Walcott. And I also had a real fondness for the British writers like Alan Sillitoe, John Braine, and Stan Barston. I like those writers very much, mainly because they were very concerned with British working-class life. And I don't have any illusions about where I come from and where my loyalties lie. So I loved those stories about British working-class life. And I'm sure that had a lot of influence on me. On my voice, you know.

KD: The majority of the early writers in the Caribbean are male . . .

LG: That's true. And maybe one of the reasons that I felt compelled to write was due in part to the sort of overabundance of male voices in Caribbean literature—where were the women? I was able to see that the female point of view wasn't very much in evidence. So I ended up writing what I wanted to read (i.e., the half that had never been told).

KD: You are postcolonial because you have written after colonialism (official colonialism, anyway). Do you see yourself as belonging to a wave, another kind of writing movement that has certain commonalties? If the political context of the writing of the '30s, '40s, and '50s was colonialism, what is the political and social context of your writing?

LG: Okay, what are my politics? My father was a very passionate member of the People's National Party. He wasn't a card-carrying member, but his sympathies, his political sympathies were definitely PNP. I used to go with him to political meetings and rallies. And growing up in Kingston in the '50s and the '60s I developed a strong sense of what constituted "progressive" politics as opposed to a more reactionary kind of politics. I don't think that distinction is very clear anymore. I came from a background where people wanted to believe in education and in forward thinking, and that people should not just want "a little more bread and a little more butter." I think I grew up thinking that people deserved more than that. And so that definitely shaped my view of the world. Rastafari was also beginning to have a very strong impact on urban life then. That was something else too; I had no idea until I started to think about it not too long ago, how strongly Rastafarian thinking has influenced my work. I have six brothers and they had friends who became Rastafarians and sometimes I would listen to them "reason." And so the radical views which Rastafarians embraced, the way that subverted the English language, certainly influenced me. The way that they thought it was okay to look just the way you were as a natural black person. That it was okay to be yourself was quite significant to me. But the most important thing I got from listening to Rastafarians was the sense that you could define yourself for yourself. You can say that what Rasta did for me was to show me that they had "seen through" the game being played by the Establishment. It was a given that we as ex-slaves were battling with all the old rules. And then there were certain rules by which you played, but no matter how clever you were, no matter how faithfully you played by those rules, *you couldn't win.* No matter how you tried you couldn't look the way that they wanted you to look. No matter how you tried you couldn't *sound* a certain way. Because if you imitated the way they spoke all you ended up sounding like was a weak imitation of them. You just couldn't win. So I think that what Rasta did was really refuse to play the game at all, and they made up their own game and their own rules. I didn't think you could do that. And the business of subverting the language, of course, was not anything that I heard about or learned from anybody about, or read anywhere. I heard it was being done down on Studley Park Road. There was a Rasta camp just below that All Saints School, which I attended. I wasn't able to go down there; my parents would not have allowed that. But as I said we had friends who became Rastas. I listened a lot when I was a child, and, you know, heard things which found their way into my writing. So I like the fact that a banana became a "freenana," 'cause black people had been banned long enough. That we "overstand" instead of *understand* because to be under means you are in an inferior position. Those things that I used to laugh about, but didn't realize it was a very real need to call attention, it was an extreme way of calling attention to things which are taken for granted and things which in fact worked against us, undermining our self-confidence. So, you know, I had those things to feed into my work, to inform my work.

KD: The decade of the '70s in Jamaica has not been fully documented and understood in terms of its impact on writing, art, and music in the island. Your first collection emerged at the tail end of that period, but I know you were writing seriously in the '70s. What did the '70s mean for you as a young black woman in Jamaica, an artist, and a Jamaican? How have the '70s shaped your writing?

LG: In the '70s, I worked for a time with the Jamaica Broadcasting Corporation, and I worked with the Jamaica Information Service, and I also worked on various projects which I'm very proud of. For example, I did several public education campaigns, and on energy conservation, and on self-reliance—tun yu hand, mek fashion. We were teaching people to conserve energy because there was a serious problem with fuel shortages, due to the rise in oil prices, as you remember. But the thing about the '70s is that I know for a fact that one day people will recognize some of the positive effects of the changes that were made then. We will have to be very honest and say that some very good things happened. The way in which black Jamaicans, poor black Jamaicans perceived of themselves underwent a big change. In Jamaica there were a lot of leftover nagging, terrible, reductive kinds of attitudes towards poor black people. People were still telling domestic helpers that they couldn't come through the front door, that they had no rights, you know. I believe that the children who came up during that time have the sense that they're much different from children who came before them. They have a kind of self-confidence that a lot of us never had. A lot of Jamaicans were made to feel very marginalized in their own country before the 1970s. I am very saddened by the leaders of that time who now declare that it was all a mistake. A lot of good things happened. And culturally, it was a really wonderful blooming forth, in the music, with the emergence of dub poets. The music from that period was absolutely brilliant; it was the golden time of Mr. Bob Marley and the Wailers. The '70s were a time of necessary social experiments. I maintain that a lot of good, and lot of change came at a high price, but it would be very unfair to say that it was all bad and it was all foolishness.

KD: I see in much of your work odes to popular musicians: Drummond, Ibo Cooper, Keith Jarret, Miles Davis, etc. Many of your poems are structured around the discourse and cadence of reggae music and you, like many poets writing in the '70s, have incorporated Rasta-speak into your poetry. What is going on here? What is the significance of the emerging reggae presence and the multiple prophetic voices of Marley, Tosh, Spear, Third World, etc. on your own writing? I would love you to talk a bit about reggae and your work, and about music and your work.

LG: I grew up in a house where there was a lot of music. My brother, Bunny Goodison, is now a kind of recognized authority on Jamaican music, jazz, and popular music in general. My brother, Keith, even more than my brother Bunny, the truth be told, always had a very keen interest in Jamaican music from the very beginning and he always bought Jamaican records. I remember there was a tailor shop near where we used to live, owned by a man called L. L. Lowe. Some of the earliest "local artists," as they were called then, used to come over to the tailor shop to get their suits made, and my brother Nigel and I used to go over there and ask them for their autographs. My brothers and I used to go to stage shows of visiting American performers and saw a lot of rhythm and blues performers like Frankie Lyman and the Teenagers, the Cherrelles, Jackie Wilson, and the Drifters. Orange Street, where I was born, is unofficially known as "Beat Street." Music of all kinds is a thing I grew up with, it's very much integrated in my work.

KD: Many people who have heard Kamau Brathwaite read like to say, "You have not heard the poems until you have heard them read by Brathwaite himself." In a sense, Brathwaite has suffered for that. People have argued that his reading skills have made what is rather pedestrian appear poetic, eloquent. It has to do, they say, with performance. I suspect that embedded in many such comments which have also been directed at you is a suggestion that your performance of your poetry becomes a kind of spell-weaving that seduces the hearer, that allows you to "get away" with a lot. How do you deal with such responses to your work?

LG: I do not deal with it! People should realize that there is not a finite amount of opportunities for writers or for artists, you know. I think if you're good, you're good. I myself have always had the attitude that I just do my work, and I do what I'm doing, and if I get recognized, good. But I'm perfectly willing to just go about my life and if some big things happen, that's wonderful, and if they don't, I am still going to be Lorna Goodison. I will continue to just be myself. Listen, to be able to read well, to be able to read your work well is an added blessing. People like Dylan Thomas, who was a wonderful writer and reader. Kamau is a great writer and reader. Nobody can take that away.

KD: Is there something very conscious about the choice of language registers in your poems, or is your task as a poet largely to reproduce your own natural voice and language registers in your poetry?

LG: I write what I hear in my head. I put things together in English, in Standard English, and in Jamaican dialect — Nation Language. The answer is simple, the answer to that is yes, I am merely attempting to reproduce my own voice. I write the way I speak and the way I hear things.

KD: What are some of the challenges you face as a writer and how do you cope with them?

LG: Time. Time. I don't have enough time to do all the work I want to do. I'm not able to. I'm a mother and a teacher and up until two years ago I was a daughter to an ailing mother. I just do the best I can with the time I have. Because I don't have that kind of luxury. These days, for the past year or so, I have been trying to write for a couple of hours at least, a week. Because I began to go for like months without writing anything. I don't write every day, but I like to write more often. I find myself blocking off two hours here and two hours there. That's as close as I have come in the past few years to doing any kind of regular writing. Because I love words, I really love the pleasure and consolation you get from words. Words can be nourishing or medicinal or at their worst, poisonous.

KD: When do you know that the poem is finished?

LG: Well, you just know. There are some things I don't think anybody can teach you. If you don't know, you're not really a poet. Some people can write so eloquently about the process of writing a poem, I don't do that. But I do know when a poem is finished. And I also know when it's not finished, because I'm very aware sometimes that I have stand-in words, words that are kind of holding up space until I can find a more fitting word, that nicest, most perfect word. And when I find it, I know it. I just know it.

KD: You are passionately a stay-home poet. I mean that you tend to stay based in Jamaica and when you leave you appear to be thinking about the return as much as you do about being where you are. Has this reality had a great impact on your work?

LG: I've written poems about being in Jamaica when I'm away, and about being away when I'm at home. I live in the country of the imagination so much that a lot of the times it doesn't really matter where I am. The only thing that matters is I'm greatly affected by the cold — but I have come to love the rebirth I experience every spring. As I grow older, I live more and more inside myself, so if I am well inside myself, if I'm praying and recollected within myself, I'm okay where I am.

KD: We have seen the emergence of a remarkable cadre of women writers in the Caribbean. You represent a part of a significant development in Caribbean writing.

LG: It's terrific that there are these women writers, Caribbean writers, emerging. They're emerging the same way that the men emerged. It's just their time, nobody can stop it. They are the ones that have to tell the half that has never been told, and they will tell it.

Ramabai Espinet

BORN 1948

RAMABAI ESPINET WAS born in Trinidad, where she grew up in San Fernando in a Christian-Indian community that was largely creolized. However, she grew up acutely aware of the notion of difference in a society and culture that, for years, effectively rendered the large Indian population a marginalized subcommunity in a country politically dominated by people of African descent. Espinet has lived in Toronto since her late teens and has established herself as an important scholar in the areas of literature from the Indian Diaspora and literature of the Caribbean. She has collaborated with other artists on dramatic renditions of her poetry and has been a strong advocate for the principles of multiculturalism in an increasingly diverse Canadian culture.

Ramabai Espinet is primarily a poet, but she has published children's fiction and is now completing a novel. Her short stories, criticism, and academic research have been published in various journals in North America and the Caribbean. In 1989, Espinet edited one of the most ambitious anthologies of Caribbean poetry: *Creation Fire* (Sister Vision, 1990) contained the work of an impressive range of Caribbean women poets — both established and previously unknown — writing not only in English, but in French, Dutch, and Spanish. Her poems are collected in *Nuclear Seasons* (Sister Vision, 1991).

Ramabai Espinet lives in Toronto with her family, and is a professor of English at Seneca College. She also teaches in the English Department at York University, and in Caribbean Studies and Women's Studies at the University of Toronto.

KWAME DAWES: Dislocation and displacement/misplacement are themes that recur in your work. In fact the position of the alien, the exile—"I am a stranger / Everywhere"—has become a poetic trope for you, offering you metaphors of uprootedness and being untethered. This is clearly a manifestation of your multiple "homes" or lack of "homes." Brathwaite's "rootless/habourless" Caribbean person comes to mind. Is this a peculiar condition for you as a Caribbean woman in Canada, or does it extend to that earlier displacement, the Indian "memory"?

RAMABAI ESPINET: No, I don't particularly write with a sense of interrogating "Displacement," although I see why that can be read into my work. In a profound way, I belong to the Caribbean and don't see myself as "belonging" anywhere else. This does not mean that I won't choose to live elsewhere, but the Caribbean archipelago is my home, the primary "landscape of my heart," to quote Angela Carter. I am there not through real choice, but through indentureship, an event described as "a new system of slavery." No matter, this is where I situate myself psychically, wherever I may happen to live.

There are, however, particularities about my condition as a Caribbean woman that I do want to tackle. One is the fact that we, collectively, are only now beginning to view the Caribbean as also an "Indian" place. I grew up with what Lloyd Best has described as a sense of "cultural insurgency" regarding the Indian presence in the Caribbean. The reasons may be mainly sociopolitical, but also important is the fact that Caribbean intellectual thought positioned Indians outside of what was normative in Caribbean reality. Not to mention the Indian population's own sense of distance from what was Caribbean. Those of us Indians who moved towards greater integration were oddities whose task was to cut and paste and achieve some kind of fit into a Caribbean rapidly defining itself after Independence out of a colonial reality into something else. A not-Indian self. This was perhaps my first realization of being an outsider. The sense of outsiderhood from India came later as I groped through writing, mainly, to understand the place of India and things Indian in my imagination.

I think that V. S. Naipaul's sense of "misplacement," which is perhaps best explored in *The Mimic Men*, is connected with an acute sense of loss for a magical Indian place with its own mythological history, peopled by heroic figures such as Arjuna. There is in this novel a young man's anger at being deprived of a rich heritage which is his birthright and being fed scraps of Western thought instead. A wonderful, intriguing way to experience the inferiorizing intent of a colonial education.

But this acute sense of loss was not my experience of being Trinidadian. I believed, in 1962, along with many other Indians after Independence, that we were building a new society and inventing a place where we could all experience full growth in a new nation. And only slowly over the next few years did I become aware of the place that being Indian assigned me in a society that was being developed in an unequal way. Yet it is difficult to define this in all of its subtle contradictions. I mean there was and there was not room enough for everyone at the same time. I adored the Creole culture which I experienced as "Trinidadian" culture. I participated fully in it and did not participate as an outsider. But I think it was the very fact that I felt so integrated into Trinidadianness that left me acutely sensitive to the slightest signal of unbelonging. I would not, could not, tolerate it. And as my analysis of the sociopolitical realities of the Caribbean and of Trinidad and Guyana especially, deepened, I was able to understand more objectively how *Indianness* functioned as *otherness* in the Caribbean even as assimilation was taking place. As otherness and as invisibility in the equation Caribbean-African/black identity. And this was the case until fairly recently.

So intellectually, I had to reckon with belonging to a place that did not allow me a real sense of belonging, while navigating life as an immigrant in a social and cultural milieu (Canada) in which every bit of space had to be earned, as it were. Not to mention the fact that I had refused, from an early age, the traditional role of an Indian woman in an Indian community setting, even though my own segment of this community, the Indo-Presbyterian-Naparima community, perceived itself as having reformulated that role into something more progressive and less constrained. But I found it difficult to live with the contradictions within that "re-formulation." To be frank, I experienced all of it (Indianness in Trinidad) as "not me" and left all of it at once on one level, while maintaining my strong links to our large extended family. Reintegration is still a part of my current project.

As for "home" and "homing," yes, I do feel as if I do not now and never will have a home that is not a site of contestation. And this is underlined by the fact that I am an Indian woman engaged in contesting that very identity.

KD: In "Hosay Night" you declare: "This land is home to me / Now homeless a true refugee...." Yet you try to distance yourself from Naipaul's sense of alienation and uprootedness: "And silks, the dhows of Naipaul's / Yearning, not mine." What is it about the Naipaulean take on displacement that bothers you?

RE: I am not really bothered by it; I think it was a brave and necessary thing for Naipaul to do at the time and it constitutes part of his monumental achievement. I am an admirer of V. S. Naipaul and I read his work with great care. He has told me more about myself than almost any other writer I can think of. He has also, by the gaps in his writing, pointed me to areas concerning my own sense of self that force investigation. And this is what "Hosay Night" is registering—that my yearnings are different, and also perhaps as necessary. The romance of "elephants and silks . . . the dhows" were not mine. These were several layers removed from me and I saw a different version of what being Indian was.

When I learned more about the women who had migrated, the early lives of women on the estates, and the "lot" of Indian women in general, this difference was reemphasized. More by instinct than by knowledge, I understood that in such a setting mine would not have been a position of privilege. Not that privilege would have been necessarily more palatable, but the deep inequities dormant in that cameo of romantic India were definitely not palatable. Understand that I am not forgetting Naipaul's later treatment of India which is definitely not romantic. Nonetheless, the "elephants and silks" function as a part of his imaginary worlds in a significantly different way from my own. The distance from Naipaul signals "difference," and not, as one might read it, "hostility."

KD: One of your most striking lines for me, and one that I think is worth quoting again and again (especially out of context) is in "In the Jungle": "It is not for nothing / That we inherited a massive / Unknown and unknowable presence." There is something daunting and disturbing about that declaration. Yet there is a quest in your poetry to fathom that unknowable presence, not necessarily in the sense of trying to retrieve a history, but certainly in the sense of retrieving a culture, a sense of self. Is this not part of what is being intoned in "Lost Cargoes"?

> The message said: Take
> These ragged sights
> Bone and weed dipped in the sea's
> Long washing and make a whole,
> A life,
> Lighten the water, plant flowers
> Gather the sea, lace the land...

RE: We were unknown — even to ourselves, or particularly to ourselves, I'm not sure which. We largely chose to be "unknowable" in an alien and hostile environment and so ensured our survival on our own terms to a significant degree. I'm convinced that this is what really happened and that Indian survival in these islands depended upon a tacit communal guerrilla formation whereby we kept our selves intact. Customs, rituals, food, ways of coping, religion, etc. We kept them by a series of strategies that did not open them up to public view. Women were the key keepers of this, and obviously the most "unknowable." Needless to say, this system also kept hidden its abuses and its systems of containment. The tight-lippedness preserved many things of value; its excessive deployment in an alien environment negated many others, such as the passing on of information from woman to woman.

Much has been made of the institution of the *matikor* and its preservation, and I think that it is indeed a signal of women's strength over the long haul that this form of initiation survived. But the *matikor* is a ritualized form of communication, and on an everyday basis women continued to be isolated from each other. In my view, the stories of our lives have been repressed within our communities and continue to be repressed by the patriarchal order of things, within which women themselves are socialized and are also committed to maintaining. Opening our mouths and saying our words, breaking the cycle of the "unknowable," seems to me right now an essential tool for our survival, on our own terms, and for that of our daughters and granddaughters. We can only become stronger as we build upon each other's experiences and strengthen that repository of woman-knowledge (also community-knowledge) of which we are the rightful inheritors.

Your question about the lines in "Lost Cargoes" — yes, that is what is being intoned in the poem, but it is not a borrowing from a grand past in order to bolster a wounded sense of self. It is more like taking the small, the ragged and the insignificant, the discarded, the output of beggars, of those cast out of the community, and yes, of those cast out of the community's "official story," i.e. its women, and making a whole out of those outlawed consciousnesses as well as those of the "patriarchs" whose story hides all of the suppressions and filth and abuse inside of what really happened. There is a need to fit it all together and to begin to fill out the picture—a more complex picture than the one we have at present.

KD: But I sense, also, a certain attraction in your capacity, and by extension, the Caribbean person's capacity, to create "from nothing." Is this part of what is happening?

RE: Yes—and here I do take issue with Naipaul. That famous sentence of his that nothing was created in the West Indies is not a sentiment I share. But by now, with so many of his other sentences registering different perceptions, it's amazing how people cling to this early thought as embodying his entire opus! But yes, I do think with Senghor, "Hurrah for those who have never invented anything." I think that as Caribbean people we have accomplished the supreme act of creativity. Out of "nothing," we have invented ourselves. "From him who hath nothing, even that little shall be taken away." It is impossible to be alive and have nothing.

Elsewhere Naipaul has said, at the beginning of *A Bend in the River*, "THE WORLD is what it is; men who are nothing, who allow themselves to become nothing, have no place in it." This statement is the absolute opposite of his former youthful dismissal of the Caribbean. And I understand and appreciate his rage. *Biswas* is also the book of an angry young man who sees too sharply not to confront his homelessness. The "Caribbean" that was being constructed in the imaginations of thinkers in England and in the West Indies in the '50s was a Pan-African Caribbean place, and this is indeed what it became later. How could a person like Naipaul navigate such terrain? Yet, and I view this as a testament to the single-mindedness of the nationalist intent to create the nation out of all the disparate elements that constituted the Caribbean, he was not seen by intellectuals of the day (C. L. R. James, for example) in the category of "Indian writer." There was at the time no articulated notion of an "Indo-Caribbean" consciousness, so if he had been perceived as "different" he would have been labeled as an Indian writer but this was not the case. And it was as a Caribbean writer that he was assessed and found to be lacking by not joining the project of building a common nationhood.

In the early '80s Walcott wrote in an article about *The Enigma of Arrival* that Naipaul never embraced the "community" of the Caribbean but chose to distance himself from it. Here Walcott seems to be echoing the common belief that Naipaul bought into the white man's agenda by disdaining his Caribbean roots. I don't agree with this view at all. I would argue that he was registering accurately his deep sense of outsiderhood from that notion of community that was developing in the Caribbean without reference to its Indian population. He had no place in it and was unwilling (or unable) to contest that outsiderhood. By his silence about this, he too, bought into the undifferentiated colonial construct. Now, at a distance of twenty years or so, and grappling with those deep issues of authenticity in my own writing, I can see this rupture in a different way.

It is also much clearer to me, also, why Sam Selvon's writing took the direction it did and perhaps why, too, it did not develop after a certain point. In the early Tiger books, there is a sensitive and even painful probing of the Indian sense of self. *An Island Is a World* is an even more searing treatment. One values the impishness of the Moses books and, of course, the grand "federation" experiment of the all-ah-we-is-one Caribbean reality executed, most appropriately by language, in *The Lonely Londoners*. It is around this point in Sam's writing that he begins to veer away from the particular in favor of a "Pan-Caribbean perspective." He only returns to the *Tiger* motif at the end of his life through an unfinished novel, a fragment of which deals with "free paper"—the pass that Indians had to carry when they left the estates of their indenture. This is published as the short story "Turning Christian."

My point is that here was Sam, almost at the end of his life, struggling to reopen that vein in his writing which probed the Indian sensibility, and invoking the humiliation of the pass-system that existed as a condition of Indian serfdom. This was not standard in all the territories of indenture, but it did occur in Trinidad. I can't help but wonder about what would have happened if he had not been waylaid by the simplistic falsehood of the all-ah-we-is-one agenda and had continued to explore the Tiger-type character. Or even integrated both —because Sam really belonged, unlike Naipaul, to both worlds. Yet ideologically, as "Three into Two Won't Go" so eloquently expresses, he positioned himself within the "progressive" agenda of mixing and merging and inventing a true-true Caribbean *creolized* self, and my question really is, at what cost to his writing? Or how did this facilitate his writer's agenda?

The other thing to remember also is that Sam Selvon was not taken up hotly by those in the "international" world who make writers (partially) by giving them opportunities to work, and to be seen. So whereas in the early period black studies departments at major universities in the U.S., for example, began to invite black Caribbean writers to sojourn there, Sam never quite got on to that circuit. The Afrocentric direction of these departments has to be understood in context—after all, this was not the multicultural Caribbean. All the same, it left him out in the cold. So what I'm really asking here is how is the Indo-Caribbean writer situated within the world of Caribbean (black) arts and letters, and by extension, the white or Chinese or Lebanese writer? How are these categories invoked and how do they falsify our realities?

KD: Part of what makes Trinidad such a fascinating and fecund place of the imagination is its almost impossible eclecticism, its multicultural condition that is elemental to its nature. The tensions of this multicultural world are part of what give meaning and depth to much of the writing that comes out of Trinidad. You bring another dimension, that of the Indo-Trinidadian female poet writing from Canada. You hate categories, I know, but these elements are clearly important ones in your own work. Are you writing your way through conflicting identities or is this merely a fiction of theorists?

RE: Trinidad is the most interesting, improbable, wonderful place one can imagine. I sometimes think that it's because we're placed at the bottom of the Caribbean Sea and we function as a rich alluvial delta—collecting centuries of accumulated silt and turning it into improbable black gold. Being part of this alluvial accumulation is central to my identity. But living in Canada has obviously shaped me in different ways as well.

My perspective on issues of race clarified itself in Canada. I lived through the '70s here in Toronto when the black Caribbean community was giving voice to its concerns and carving out its place. Racism was named and therefore had to be reckoned with. I was very much a part of this struggle and did not perceive myself as "other" within it. But returning to the Caribbean in the '80s and living there for a number of years as an adult gave me another take on race and racism.

For example, one of the popular jokes in the Trinidad workplace of the '80s was "Ride ah Indian or walk." Its usage was primarily sexual with the Indian woman as the sexual beast of burden. But this joke also resonated with a societal awareness of growing Indian economic ascendancy and the anxiety about keeping Eric Williams's "recalcitrant minority" in check. Second-classness for Indians in the mainstream order of things (politics, culture, etc.) was assumed and had to be maintained by the mainstream. The seeming acquiescence of Indians in the face of all of this was puzzling unless one began to read it as one in a series of strategies being deployed by this group without recourse to organized strategizing. It also became clear that any analysis of phenomena such as these had to take on the politics of the society in order to make sense of it. The complexity of the situation remains baffling, to say the least.

All the same, if my category is that of the "Indo-Trinidadian female poet writing from Canada" I have to confess that I do not have a handle on what that really means. I agree that categories are important, and it is important to problematize them and see them as dynamic and fluid even as we use the convenient shortcut of classifying. Categories also help us to think through identity issues even though by the end of the process we may decide to throw them out. It is the fixedness of these divisions that essentialize that I am wary of.

As for writing myself out of conflicting identities, no, I don't believe that's what I'm doing. There is a wonderful hybridity to life in Trinidad that one can experience positively, without running into the danger of romanticizing it. In my own case, I don't experience a sense of conflicting identities although I find myself in constant negotiation with the question of identity. And of course, it is almost never possible to be fully oneself externally as one is constituted internally. I find that prospect exciting especially because of the way it opens up the possibilities of narrative. I don't think my writing is particularly (or mainly) autobiographical, although that raises a series of other, perhaps stickier, questions. As for the theoretical aspects of this issue, I do think that theorizing about conflicting/opposed/erased identities is essential to the common Caribbean intellectual project. There is work to be done — major work — and we have been slow in doing it.

KD: Your poetry relies on a certain compacting of images. The narrative line comes second to the metaphor, the image, it seems. I am especially drawn to the chiseled quality of your first lines, or first stanzas. It is as if you work very hard on that opening image. Is this my imagination or is there something about the first lines that epitomizes your intensity as a crafter of the word?

RE: I like your comment about "the chiseled quality of your first lines." I'll remember that.

Yes, the image is very important to me in the crafting of a poem. As a young person the imagist school appealed to me very much. It's hard to comment about the patterning that you notice because I am not especially aware of a method that I employ. Different works emerge differently and I pay no real attention to the external process. Internally I think there is an identifiable process which can be captured by one word: obsession. The thought, the line, the image, the one word: whatever is the germ of that particular poem stays and stays until it reaches its needed form on the page. And once I begin work on a poem I stay with it until it feels right. Sometimes this may mean reworking a single line over and over. Other times I hardly rework the poem at all.

In *Nuclear Seasons,* you are right, the narrative line, for the most part, comes second to the metaphor. But I find myself writing a series of narrative poems more directly, now.

KD: In "City Blues" you invoke Tiresias, the blind prophet who sees all, and who, you add, "feels all." Is this how you perceive the condition of the poet? I use the word "condition" although I want to say "role," but that seems to be a related question — that is, do you think the word "role" is appropriate to describe the relationship between the artist and the community? Certainly, there is a certain advocacy role that you celebrate in mothers, "night mothers," but how have you addressed the question of your function as an artist?

RE: The seeing all and feeling all is the special burden of the poet's condition. I like "condition" better than "role" because I can't imagine the relationship between the artist and the community as anything less than fluid. I think that the artist lives in a place of indeterminate boundaries. It is an unlikely, perilous, difficult-to-define place.

I suppose I invoke the figure of Tiresias because he is a blind old man, "with aging female breasts," and is overcome with grief for his burdensome seeing and feeling. Being blind he sees all; having reached the age of androgyny, as it were, he feels all from both gender perspectives. I am deeply interested in the implications of androgyny in terms of sexuality and gender politics.

Here gender becomes crucial again. In writing (poetry, fiction, plays, etc.) I am aware of functioning as an Indian woman from the Caribbean in dialogue with the world. The world may choose to ignore that dialogue; all the same this is what I am doing. And at a primal level, I and my kind (Indo-Caribbean women) are prohibited by the full weight of patriarchal law and authority from having dialogue with the world outside the home. The negotiations that occur when this prohibition is defied or even modified are very interesting to watch. There are Indo-Caribbean women who function in the world as skilled professionals but very few of them who operate in arenas of self-investigation. They may have careers in law, medicine, science, to some degree in the social sciences, but always, it seems to me, the inquiry stops short of creating knowledge by focusing upon ourselves. For example, in Trinidad, in recent times, a fairly sizable array of excellent Indo-Caribbean women journalists has emerged. I think this is positive but a question lingers. Why is there development in journalism and not much in creative writing?

I will speculate that it's because journalism invokes the passive voice. Reporting puts the writing agenda at the service of an investigation that avoids putting the home into the world. The world is investigated, the home remains sacred and veiled. Perhaps I would have no problem with this if I could buy into the idea of the Indo-Caribbean family as providing a safe haven for its female members. But I don't think it does this, any more than other family walls do. As more and more examples of dysfunction surface it is becoming increasingly clear that the idea of family needs careful scrutiny and redefinition. And in the Indo-Caribbean community, in the Caribbean as well as in the Diaspora, the price paid by women and girls for acts of noncompliance or transgression within the family walls is very steep indeed. So the question is really to whom do we owe our primal loyalty? Is it to group and family solidarity or to our (i.e., our woman selves and that of our community's women) own well-being and achievement of potential? Is there an enforcement of silence? I think that there is.

Back to Tiresias, then. Who is the female artist functioning in a community such as ours? She speaks but her speaking drives her into a place of otherness when she speaks her truth. She is an outsider. She is subject to unbearable strain, from within and without, and she functions largely without supports.

Now more Indo-Caribbean women are beginning to speak "themselves." There are poets such as Mahadai Das, Shana Yardan, Niala Maharaj, Asha Radjkoemar, Chitra Gajadin. They are writing themselves out of the family walls—breaking them down so that they can stare fully, unveiled, at the world outside. The act of writing calls for breaking faith with service—family service. Beginning the difficult task of consolidating a self—outside of family servitude. Finding out that to write what one sees one must live what one sees. The anchorage of the model Indo-Caribbean family, that self-fortifying myth, is disappearing. When writers like these register this change, who are they addressing? So far they are largely ignored within their own community. Are they addressing the outside? Does the outside care?

Such a writer must be prepared for the community to lash back in anger because in the first place she is breaking the laws of censorship by speaking and secondly she is performing a fundamental act of disloyalty—exposing the insides, in a shameful way perhaps; at any rate she is inviting the alien world into the inner courtyard and therefore committing a most profane act.

I think that primal and archetypal though these structures might seem, they are the ones operating in our unconscious as we, Indo-Caribbean women, acquiesce in silence to the dictates of the community's patriarchal law. Never mind that the questions and challenges that face us as modern, urban, women with complexly constructed hybrid identities are not met by adherence to this law. Our coping strategies are negotiated individually and never reach a place of community knowledge and growth because we are forbidden to speak to each other except in approved family constructs. If I have a function as an artist it is to open my mouth and speak. But I refuse to be alone. I would like to work with those others who are beginning to speak too and to receive the answers that come from the community at large.

KD: It is my wont to try and discern influences that have shaped a poet by close scrutiny of their work. You are more difficult because you seem to feed off a wide range of poets, but most critically, you have evolved a poetic language that seems rather distinct, fresh. The influences that come to mind may not even be accurate, but they are good connections: Olive Senior, the chant/song of praise and possibility of Lorna Goodison, and the metaphorical flights of Derek Walcott. Can you talk about influences that may have helped to shape your writing?

RE: I don't myself recognize other poets' influences in my writing. I think it's always difficult to do that even as it's often impossible to see the resemblances between oneself and one's own family members.

But I'll try another angle. I loved poetry and read it widely from the time that I first began reading. As a child, when we got our new reading books at the end of the long school holidays I would always turn to the back and memorize all the poems. We had numerous anthologies at home and I read the Romantics, Tennyson, Longfellow, etc. at an early age. But the two poets whose work I read in totality as far as was possible for me in my late teens were William Butler Yeats and Derek Walcott. I was enamored of Yeats, one of the prescribed poets for A-levels, and part of my interest was the political cause of Irish independence, the battle for an authentic language, the research into Irish folklore that informed so much of his work, and the sheer beauty of the poetry. It was easy to make the connection between the aesthetic struggles of the Irish Renaissance and the emerging efforts in the Caribbean to produce our own literature.

Derek Walcott struck me as *the* artist launched upon this endeavor. I read his poems and plays (*In a Green Night, Twenty Poems* and *The Sea at Dauphin*) and was aware of the innovative work he was doing at the Basement Theatre Workshop in Port-of-Spain. One of Walcott's early metaphors that made a lasting impression on me was that of the gradual saturation of corncake with rich Creole gravy to evoke the light sweeping a country church at evening. Most important of all, Derek Walcott was writing about us, our lives, our place, performing the political act of turning the tourist camera back out to sea to sweep the horizon, while simultaneously using the finest brushstrokes to capture how we lived beyond the tourist brochure with its sea and sand and limbo. Of course, there were other artists doing this at the time but Walcott's work was what resonated for me. Where I think Walcott has really extended Caribbean poetics is in *The Star-Apple Kingdom*. I really admire in that poem his seamless transitions between Creole and Standard English, giving them equal valences.

The two other notable poetic events that mattered to me in my teens was reading the work of Barbara Jones and Gabriela Mistral. Both of these poets brought home to me the issue of women's poetics in different ways. At the time there was no access to feminist literary criticism or analysis of women's issues. If you experienced gender inequity as I did, very sharply, you ranted about it aloud or in your mind, you resisted it, but you couldn't bring it to a place where women were collectively sorting these issues out and exchanging ideas. This was the '60s and feminist discourse was just emerging. In Trinidad this came to us in jokes about bra-burning militancy.

The collection by Barbara Jones, *Among the Potatoes,* was stocked in the San Fernando Public Library, but it was locked in the West Indian collection at the back of the reference stacks, a veritable holy of holies. I only found it because I worked in the library at that time and spent most of my spare time in this little room reading. It was the first time I had read erotic poetry on the subject of a black woman's sexuality. It was an inspiring read because its liberatory intent leapt off the page. More arresting than this, though, was the unspeakable loneliness experienced by the poetic persona of the text. She was locked in isolation. Why? Was it because she was saying the unsayable?

The other event was reading Gabriela Mistral. She had been awarded the Nobel Prize for Literature in 1959 and her books were part of the library's small Latin American collection. Up to then I had not read any work at all which railed against women being forced to take on the "shame" of reproduction, pregnancy, sexuality. I read these poems with immense relief. Finding that you are not alone in anger at "immutable" laws inscribed by an overarching patriarchy assuages anxiety to a degree that's hard to describe. I've never forgotten these two moments when the shock of recognition really happened to me.

Later I studied Wallace Stevens and Pound very closely. Emily Dickinson and Edna St. Vincent Millay were also favorites in my teens. In the mid-'60s one of my cousins gave me a record by Bob

Dylan and it was a mind-blowing experience. I loved the beat of it, the folk concerns, the pulse of the people in Dylan's music. I moved to North America and became a person of the late, late '60s. The hippie culture was already turning into something else, but for me, it still embodied that idea of freedom from constraint that I was searching for, especially in thinking about ideas. The all-night conversations, the arguments about art and poetry and wine and revolution, these were the passions of the day and they happened to be mine.

It's hard to measure influence. I read a lot of poetry. Connections or influences, I don't know. As a child I went to bed every night in the months before Carnival, listening to calypso broadcast straight from the tents. My father was a calypso peong [fanatic] and the first person to awaken my interest in the piquancy and wit of calypso lyrics. He would quote calypso or utilize it in ordinary conversation in very funny ways. The word-music of calypso and the beat of Trinidad creole — those are deep influences.

Recent poetry by women that I really respond to are Adrienne Rich's work and Audre Lorde's. The American poet Ai is doing interesting things with poetry — writing poised at the edge. I like her work a lot, especially *Cruelty/Killing Floor*. Sujata Bhatt, Chitra Devakaruni, and Mahadai Das are of special interest, of course, since our poetics have common elements.

KD: The spirituality in your work betrays a catholic or perhaps a Hindu-centric embrace of various religious and mythological worlds. Can you speak a bit about religion and faith and how they emerge in your work? In some poems you invoke Kali, in another Gethsemane, in another the spirit of the ancestors and so on . . .

RE: Spirituality matters a lot to me and your use of "betray" to describe the emergence of varying strands of religious and mythological thought in my poetry is intriguing. "Catholic" in the sense of "universal" is probably right, but like every clean, twice-blessed postmodernist these days, I am afraid to employ the "u" word. The spiritual in human experience is what I am interested in exploring — how we manifest this spirituality, how we derive a multileveled faith in the face of adversity from this source, how every spiritual act connects with another beyond the narrow boundaries of organized religion. The mythological world within which we function in the Caribbean is one such potent example. In Trinidad it is compounded out of a dense array of beliefs from Asia, Africa, Europe, and the

Amerindian world. This syncretic spiritual world then produces secular insights which we utilize in our everyday life. I am fascinated by this; it's one of the areas of Caribbean life where there is a real possibility of give-and-take and respect, even if only out of the anxiety to avoid angering an alien jumbie.

The references I use belong to the spiritual and mythological world that I inhabit, with no organized religion as its particular motivator. I did not grow up in a Hindu world; my family have been Christians for several generations and I was brought up as a Presbyterian. The bible is such a potent source of myth and symbol within the English language that Christian myth would be part of my lexicon even if I had not deliberately invoked it. The same is true of a mythological Hindu world—it's hard to recognize how it emerges in syntax, in form or even in a general worldview, because it's largely taken for granted. But I find myself returning to Indian sacred texts and Indian literature as referential points, constantly.

I think that the mythic dimensions of our beings reside in that unchallengeable domain of the psyche from which we are informed about our surface reality. We live these beliefs; in the contemporary world we hardly have occasion to affirm, or even acquaint ourselves with our worldviews. They just are. It is the syncretism, and the concomitant strength in syncretism of the Caribbean worldview that I access for my own spirituality. It consists of all of these elements—Islam, Christianity, Hinduism, African religious practice, and folk beliefs that are peculiar to our geography and circumstance. Underpinning my desire to draw from this source is my very real intention to unearth the female mythos by which we live as well, and which, embedded within the patriarchal overlay of our official spiritual discourse, appears to be hidden and even absent. And so part of my project here is the invention or the renewal of lost myths, especially Caribbean feminist myth. The *matikor*, a Hindu women's ritual which takes place on the night before a wedding, is one such example; folk figures like Mama Glo or the diablesse are another. It's all part of my opening my mouth and speaking the words that we already own.

John Robert Lee

BORN 1948

JOHN ROBERT ("ROBERT") LEE was born in St. Lucia, where he grew up and now lives. Lee began writing at a young age but did not seriously consider himself a writer until he had traveled to Barbados to complete his bachelor's degree at the University of the West Indies in the early '70s. Lee became involved in the Rastafarian faith on his return to St. Lucia and was drawn into the group of cultural artists and advocates who sought to discover a language that spoke to the experience of the Caribbean people.

Lee has published six volumes of poetry since his first collection in 1975. His poetry has evolved with him, moving from the strident advocacy of the early poems in *Vocation and Other Poems* (St. Lucia, 1975) and *Dread Season* (St. Lucia, 1978) to the ethos of spiritual Christianity (a faith he now strongly embraces) in later collections such as *The Prodigal* (St. Lucia, 1983), *Possessions* (St. Lucia, 1984), and *Clearing Ground* (New Life Fellowship, 1991). He has collected his poetry in *Saint Lucian* (St. Lucia, 1988) and *Translations* (Sunshine Bookshop, 1993), which feature poems from earlier collections that have been revised and reworked for the new volumes. He is also busy working on a long sequence of poems of memory and transformation.

Robert Lee lives in Castries, St. Lucia, and works as St. Lucia's Director of Information Services at the Sir Arthur Lewis College; he also preaches in local churches. He remains involved in the celebration of the work of his fellow artists in St. Lucia and the organization of various arts-based projects on the island.

KWAME DAWES: I want to begin with your Christian faith and its impact on your poetry. There is often, especially in the traditions of evangelical Christianity, a tendency to regard the singular pursuit of poetry as an act of vanity. Working against that seems to be a distinct source of poetic and moral tension in your work. Is this a fair statement? Is there anything to reconcile between your vocation as poet and your Christian faith?

ROBERT LEE: I think, yes, for the Christian poet, so called, the tension is always there between the Christian beliefs, Christian doctrines, in a sense, and the world in which one lives. And the poetry reflects that. Poetry is a vehicle, the form, the means, the instrument that the poet uses to examine experience, to deal with his experience as a Christian in the society. And I think the tensions come within the content of the poetry. The Christian poet, at best, tries to show the reality of being a man, a person, human being in the society coping with what the New Testament would call the world, the flesh, and the devil; coping with that and making sense of it through the poetry. And I think the tensions come as one tries to be honest about the struggle there, and tries to show how one travels as a pilgrim — as one tries to show honestly and clearly what one is dealing with and how one tries to cope with one's life using one's perspective of Christian belief. And the same would be true of whatever ideology one holds, whether it be Marxist ideology or Muslim ideology or whatever. The tensions in the poetry come from all of those things. I am a Christian trying to find what I call New Testament biblical Christianity by going back to the roots there for myself. There is always the tension of trying to live those truths, and yet facing up to my own weaknesses and limitations as a human being. Another tension comes from the fact that I'm very aware that it is not very politically correct (to use the politically correct term) to be even an evangelical Christian, today. I think the temptation will always be there to avoid, as a Christian, writing about personal relationships and that kind of thing; but as the Christian poet, I think I have to deal with them. In fact, what's the point if I cannot show, as a Christian, as a poet, what happens when the faith and the world connect and collide? The best Christian poets are those who don't write just tracts (I mean there is a place for tracts) or sentimental, postcard greeting-card types of things. But the greatest of Christian writing comes from where the Christian writer confronts issues honestly and realistically.

KD: You are a lyrical poet—a poet inscribed in the process of personalizing the image. Caribbean poetry displays, more clearly than any other tradition of verse, two distinct instincts: the lyrical, and the griot-centered posture of the poet—the poet political. Where do you place yourself in this clearly artificial equation? Do you buy the equation, anyway?

RL: A question like this, I sort of translate into terms of the scribal and the oral, "private" and "public" poet, the poet's "personal" concerns and the poet's "public," "political" concerns. I'm moving towards a sort of synthesis or resolution of these things. Okay, maybe there is a larger question behind all of that. For whom do I write? And it's a question I have tried to answer this way: in a sense, I write first for myself, and secondly, I write for those who will read. This means that when I write for myself—and any writer writes for himself *and* for an audience—I may not know who that audience is. Some writers know who their audience is. For many of us living at home in the Caribbean, I think after a while you can't really say who you are writing for because your books are still there on the shelf; you're not sure who will pick it up. Maybe they will slowly disappear, but you don't have a kind of feedback like you do in countries where people write reviews and people talk about you on the radio, and so on. The challenge of not knowing kind of frees me up. If I was in the States, I know I would have certain critics looking out for my head; and the more famous you become, you know, you begin to write for the critics—which is a trap. So we are left free to say, "To hell with you all, I go write what I want." So in a sense, I'm writing for myself. It means that I can now sit down and say, "Now what do I want to say about this situation?" Whether it be a personal situation, or whether it be a public situation. I am saying that the lyrical poet, the griot, the historian and the storyteller all come together in the sense that one tries to make one's private concerns and private perceptions and personal perceptions accessible. I think one must be careful, especially since the more one writes the more one tends to move away from obscurity. When you're young you are deliberately obscure, but the older you get, I think you do try to be more accessible. So, you have your private working out of things but what is your public statement? In a sense one leads to another and one cannot do without the other. There should be a balance between the two. The poet is sort of the mouth of the community, and the hands and the feet of the community sort of expect us to produce for them what the mind of the community is thinking, and so at best, we reflect and we echo the very heart of our community.

A thought occurred to me as you were asking me this. If we don't have a good critical audience and you don't have critics waiting for you, then in fact, you may give up and not write as well as you could. It throws you back on yourself, that you have to be personally self-critical, which I think may be very good, but I think very few of us are self-critical. I think a few of us who are really dedicated to this thing of writing poetry will remain, quite independent of everything else — it's almost a personal vocation to remain self-critical. And the majority of people probably won't and because there isn't that kind of pressure outside, they may produce less than their best. Where you don't have informed critics, you don't have a real recognizable audience, a lot of us subtly give up, or don't work as hard as we should. I think that is true because when I go to another country for a while, and enter an artistic milieu, immediately, I am aware of a certain kind of stimulation which I've been missing at home. Or if you're among writers for a while, or you are in a place where there are a lot of libraries, a lot of bookshops, something else in me begins to come out and I find I am writing more, writing stuff I know is better. So I think the isolation does tell after a while. I don't know how we resolve that.

KD: You clearly have a meaningful relationship with the poet Derek Walcott. The density of sea imagery and the image of the poet walking the streets of Castries both echo patterns established by Walcott and which have been taken up by people like Kendel Hippolyte and Jane King. Can you talk a bit about what it means to be a poet associated with as significant a poet as Walcott, and about how you feel your respective visions differ? Is it a generational thing?

RL: Well, I think we can start with the last part of the question; the generational thing rather obviously. I mean Walcott is eighteen years older than I, he was born in '30, I was born in '48. When I was born, his first book was just out. And he grew up in the very heart of the colonial period even though it wasn't too long after he was born that the whole colonialization thing began to fall apart in the '50s and '60s with independence in Africa and so on. But certainly, for at least the first thirty years of his life, he was under colonial rule. I didn't have that. I grew up here. I knew the colonial administrator, but I also was a schoolboy when the administrators left. I have known independence. And so I am aware of what colonialism can do to us, and more and more I've come to realize how great a disease colonialism is. Even the problems for us as writers, as creative people in our society as people, the kinds of political problems that surround us today, the mindset of the politicians still in power, a lot of ingrained things in society, the attitudes towards the arts and to readings and to libraries and cultural things, are all part of the disease of colonialism. And yet, for me, the view of colonialism and what it has done is definitely different from that of Walcott. You look at Walcott's plays, you look at his poetry, and it's like the central battle for him is that fight against the colonial master. It's the old dilemma of "divided to the vein." I don't think that for my generation, and for those coming after me, that that has been our battle or struggle. I think that our battle and struggle has been more of a personal one. Sometimes I think of myself as being a transitional figure between colonialism and independence. There are others who have come after me who have never known the red, white, and blue Union Jack. And they've known nothing but independence. Walcott's fight against colonialism and of course his own mixed-raced thing (a lot of his plays deal with sort of white central characters, which is valid, which is okay), those have not been my concerns at all. So the difference is generational.

I have said this several times already, but I have certainly learnt from him how to write poetry; he still remains to me the major poet whom I keep going back to, I keep learning from him in terms of his metaphor. He's helped me to see St. Lucia—he's written about everything around us already. I always remember sometime in the '70s, mid-'70s in Barbados, I was in a room with Timmy Callender and Eddie [Kamau] Brathwaite, one evening late after a show talking. Eddie Brathwaite said that when he came back from Africa he came first to St. Lucia. He had already been writing poetry, but he began to write even more in-depth poetry that resulted in things like *Rights of Passage* and so on. And he said a very interesting thing that I have never forgotten. He said whatever he turned to write about, Derek had already written about it. And that was Kamau Brathwaite, the next major poet alongside Derek Walcott! So imagine when we, as younger poets, come to write. I must say of Kendel Hippolyte, he is the most modern of us in this younger generation, and the minute I say this, I say, but you know, Kendel is doing this, that is true, and yet I go back to Walcott and I find that Walcott has already outstripped all of us. In fact he's already passed Whitman and Ginsberg, he's writing Lowell and some of us probably don't even know who Lowell is. So no matter how you look at Walcott, Walcott is a major figure; he is a Miltonic figure, a Shakespearean figure, a Chaucer figure. He stands in Caribbean literature like those figures: Chaucer, maybe Spenser, Shakespeare, Milton—those major, major massive figures who have already covered generations of work. And others come along who have their own value, their own work, but these guys have always already done more than anybody else. You look into the past, they've already done the past; you look into the future, they've already done things in the future. So he's a significant poet because he is *the* major poet, in terms of form and style, concerns, themes, and so on. And I very much look to him for form and so on. In terms of the ideology and the content, as I say, I think there is certainly a difference, as I move more and more into Christian poetry. You couldn't really describe Walcott as a Christian poet—not in that strict sense of the term. Our concerns have been independence, how we deal with the politics of the situation and so on. More and more, my own personal thematic concern has been as a Christian believer; how to live this faith and make sense in the midst of my culture? He has done his work and I think those of us coming after have to do our own work. We can't repeat him. We should not. We should learn from him and move on.

KD: Of all your collections, I find *Translations* to be the most realized movement in treating the metaphysics of faith and the confessions of the poet/prophet in a veritable wilderness of society. Is there a sense, for you, that *Translations* is the beginning of a clarity of vision, a place where the poem is finally speaking the faith?

RL: I don't know if *Translations* is the *beginning* of the clarity of vision. I think from my collection I did called *Clearing Ground* some time before . . . even before that, I think *The Prodigal* was my first movement into what I would call "Christian poetry." It wasn't as direct as the later books, *Possessions* and *Clearing Ground*, and *Translations*, but I think the sort of Christian influence was beginning to appear certainly by the book *Prodigal* which was done in Jamaica in 1983. I wrote a long poem called "Sighting" in which I was working out a lot of questions about Christian theology. And even then, it was tied into the politics of the Caribbean: Walter Rodney, Bob Marley, and so on. Certainly, no doubt, it's got clearer. Even the title *Clearing Ground*, that was a pun in about three ways: the clearing, and a clearing ground, a ground cleared for building, which is one of the ideas of the poem. And I wrote a poem called "Ground," which may not even have been in *Clearing Ground*, I can't remember now, but the idea was about ground being cleared for building. So you don't clear until you have a vision and then say, "Okay, I'm ready to go, I have cleared the ground." *Translations* may seem to be clearer, it has some of the older poems. I took "Dread Season," "Prodigal," and some others and edited them, cut some things from somewhere else and added them on quite freely to create a clearer movement. So there is a clarity of vision there. I was particularly pleased with the title poem, "Translations," which deals with my experience in Boston, where I tried to write clearly in physical terms, plain-statement terms, and yet with the lyricism of what I actually saw around me in Boston. I think in my later poetry, I have moved to that. It's something that a number of us here have been trying to do in recent years. But I think it is different because of a lot of editing I did of older poems. I am now, after time has passed, freed up from the original sentiment and attachment to things that seemed good then. After several years, you can more easily let go and dispense with lines which may be very nice, but they don't achieve much; and you edit and cut more closely. I think I did this with this book. If you look at the titles, all the titles are one-word titles, and that was very deliberate, and probably that reflects what I am trying to say about the whole thing: a kind of editing and cutting to try and get at the essence of things; to try to achieve a clearer vision.

KD: I have observed in your verse a willingness to experiment with form. Very often the cadence is founded on folk traditions and music, but increasingly the rhythm and repetitive (clustered) structures of Hebrew versification (so prevalent in the Psalms) reveal themselves in your work. How much effort do you put into uncovering and honing the formal structures of your verse? Who are your models?

RL: In terms of form in my verse, I think I take a lot of time on that. I think about it very carefully in terms of how I want to say what I want to say, in what form I want to say it. I spend a lot of time on the verse, on the forming of the verse. Now something I will say, in recent times (and this influenced what I was doing in *Translations* and in the "Translations" poem and the later poems) I became more and more aware of American verse and what the Americans were doing. I became aware of what they call the breath, the length of the line decided by the breath. Now when I wrote a poem like "Translations," I deliberately did that. I chose my stanza structures very definitively. I wanted fourteen-line stanzas. I wanted certain line endings which I sat down and schemed very carefully. I wanted half-rhymes. I thought through what I wanted at the time. But I decided that once I started to write, though, even though I had decided on line endings and half-rhymes and whatever, I was going to allow the length of the line to be the length of my speaking breath. So when I actually read the poem aloud, it would be as near as possible to my own voice, my own speaking voice. And so in terms of cadence and the rhythm of lines, I have been working more, using the modern American kind of thing as the model. In terms of the business of Hebrew versification, now I am aware of some of this, but I haven't consciously done this. But I think what has happened is that for years I have been reading the bible regularly; the Psalms, the New Testament, the Old Testament. And I think subconsciously, this whole parallelism in bible verse and so on is in my head. If you hear people in churches reciting a very familiar verse of scripture, there is a certain cadence which you can pick up. The King James version, of course, is very beautiful for that. But there is a certain biblical cadence and biblical rhythm that emerges. I have listened to Jamaicans in rural Jamaica talk. A man gets up to pray and you listen and you hear a pure Jamaican rural voice in the most beautiful language, most beautiful cadences, and it's obviously based on that deep beauty of the King James Bible.

KD: Walcott has spoken about your control, the absence of the grandiose. It suggests a terseness and a commitment to very focused editing. What is your writing process like? Are you a scrupulous and finicky editor when it comes to line breaks, word choice? Do you write religiously each day or are you driven by the sparked image — the muse, if you will?

RL: When I write poetry (I will put it that way since I don't write poetry every day) I do try to go for what Walcott calls sort of scrupulous editing to get away from what he meant by the "grandiose." I try, as he says, "not to over-extend the range of the truth of [my] emotions." And I keep using the term editing and self-editing. I think

I want to stay away from the self-indulgence. You have to be so careful about this when you want to write good poetry. I mean, if one is recording a true "heartical" experience, that will come out even if one is describing a glass on a table, a mango, or a thing. And when one does talk about one's self, one has to be so careful about how one does it. Generally speaking, one wants to get to the heart of the statement. And I think that as one matures one comes to an understanding of the equality of the human race. There is always the temptation among artists to believe artists, people who create, are better than the carpenter or the baker or the plumber or the man who fixes yuh fridge. Well, you know, that ain't so. Maybe you do have to go through that period for a while just to find your identity as a creative person. But once that is established, you don't need that again, you move on from that and say well I am a unique individual being and my gift happens to be putting words together and this man's gift happens to be making chairs, that man's gift is making music—fine. And then, I now try to share my experience in as simple and plain and clear a way as possible with whoever is going to look at it. So, there is a terseness, there is a trimming down, there is a self-editing, a focused editing, yes.

KD: Your poem "Hologram" speaks of poems as children. In it there is a hope that the poem would be found "honest." Is this the quality that justifies the poem, that makes it complete and ready? How and when do you determine that a poem can be "let go"?

RL: Yes, I think that quality justifies a poem or a piece of writing. I think at this stage one is struggling to explain, but honesty obviously is kind of relative, in a sense. But I think in writing prose or poetry, and especially poems where one is operating within such a limited space as it were, I think one wants to be honest, one wants to be true to what one has really experienced, what one really feels, what one really sees and perceives. And so the quality that I would strive for in my poetry is honesty. Now as to when you determine the poem can be "let go," I don't know. You work on it as much as you can and then you just know you need to let it go. Now in *Translations*, I looked at some of the poems again and said, "Well, maybe your clothes need patching up here and there. You need some new shoes or something." I still felt it was okay to do some things with them. And I felt quite justified when I did so. So, it may be I don't know when one lets go a poem. Maybe one lets go most of one's poems, but maybe some will come back for a kind of reworking or re-dressing, or tightening up if one feels the poem is good enough. And so the poem itself grows with you. Maybe that's it. That some poems can grow with us, some poems you have to leave behind.

KD: In the world of Caribbean poetry, there is a community of artists, but it is disparate community, and often we don't even get a chance to hear each other speak. Do you feel isolated as a poet or do you find yourself feeding off the energies of other poets in the region? Who would these poets be?

RL: I think this business of isolation as a poet, I think it is something I have come to a kind of resolve about. I think it is inevitable because when you go back to the existentialists and so on, you see that ultimately we are all alone. And even from my own religious viewpoint — the Christian, spiritual — ultimately I do think man is alone. My Christian spiritual view says man is alone before his creator. Only my creator knows me in a way that nobody else can know me. And so there is a real kind of isolation. And even in that religious experience, the cries that Jesus cried, "My God, my God, why hast thou forsaken me!" one feels so much walking through darkness. "The Lord is my shepherd; I shall not want" because one is walking through darkness. So I think that experience of isolation is something that one must come to terms with as a mature human being, as a mature person; that one is essentially always alone. Not necessarily lonely. The old cliché of being alone in the middle of a crowd. I mean you have people who truly love you, your children and so on. Yet ultimately (go back to the "Hologram" poem) you know that your children themselves will have to learn to be alone. Maybe that is something we need to teach our children too. That I am here with you, I am there with you and so on. I will try to help you out, but don't be afraid to be alone. There are some people who can't bear to be alone. They have to have something on, some music on, or people always talking away. I personally like to be alone. And it is a thing I have learnt and all my spiritual experiences have only deepened that. So the business of aloneness and isolation is something inevitable, in a kind of way. But even though we live in an artistic community, I think I am at a stage where I believe if there was a vibrant artistic community around, if you are doing really good and serious work, one will always feel one's self outside, one will always feel a bit alienated. I mean, yes, there are people who understand what yuh doing, but as far as I can see, and I think that is probably true in New York and London or wherever, the people who are working hard at the craft always feel a bit alone, outside. And even when you've done the work and people receive it there will always be still time before they fully understand.

But there is another side to the question where being human, ourselves, we want appreciation, we want appreciative communities, we want rewards for our work, we want our books to win prizes, we want people to publish us. And that is quite valid. Nothing wrong with that. But I think even as one struggles for those quite valid things which are good and necessary, one must also be prepared for the isolation. So on one hand I would say, yes, I feel isolated as a poet, but I accept it as part of the condition. But also, in St. Lucia there is a small community of poets, people who I know, with whom I work and so on. We read each other's work and appreciate each other's work.

Grace Nichols

BORN 1950

GRACE NICHOLS WAS born in Guyana, where she went to school and later embarked on a career as a journalist. It was during those early years that she began to write seriously, experimenting with prose and some poetry; some of her work was published while she lived in Guyana. With her partner, John Agard, Nichols moved to the United Kingdom in 1977, where she began to pursue writing with greater intensity and drive. Remaining one of an industrious group of black British artists who are able to make a living primarily as writers, she is regarded today as one of Britain's leading women poets.

Her reputation was built primarily around her poetry. Her first collection of poems, *I Is a Long Memoried Woman*, was published to significant acclaim in 1983, winning the Commonwealth Poetry Prize that year. The work was especially novel because it brought to bear a vividly realized female sensibility on the colonial and racial dynamics of Caribbean society. In this collection, Nichols established her inimitable style: the terseness of language, the sparseness of adjectival indulgence, and the constant quest for the simply rendered and resonating image that suggests both dream and stubborn reality.

She has published children's stories and a novel, *Whole of a Morning Sky* (Virago, 1986). Her other books of poetry include *The Fat Black Woman's Poems* (Virago, 1984), *Lazy Thoughts of a Lazy Woman and Other Poems* (Virago, 1989) and *Sunris* (Virago, 1996), which won the Guyana Prize.

KWAME DAWES: Grace, what prompted you to start writing?

GRACE NICHOLS: I read an awful lot as a child because my father was a head teacher. And our home was always full of books, so maybe the seed was sown somewhere around there. When I was about twenty-one, I began working as a reporter with the *Chronicle* newspaper back in Guyana. I used to love writing feature articles instead of just news stories. I used to go around the marketplace and interview women about bush medicines or just write about people who I thought were interesting. So I guess you could say I began writing around then. Gradually I got more and more into expressing myself in other ways. I'd write the occasional short story and one of my short stories, "Manna Come Home," was read on radio in Guyana. And while working with the Government Information Services, we used to bring out a magazine, a house organ called *In Focal,* and I contributed what must have been my first poem, about a waterfall, Kaieteur Falls.

KD: What were the processes involved in moving into poetry? How do you see the two genres working in your own mind? How do you make the decision whether to write fiction or whether to write poetry?

GN: Well, it's not a big conscious decision, because, as I said, in Guyana, I began writing fiction and I had already started my novel, *Whole of a Morning Sky,* so that when I came to England I had the first few chapters of it and I had written short stories in Guyana. I had also written a few poems—not many, I could count them on my hand; about three or four poems. But after coming to England, maybe because of the whole emotional separation thing from the Caribbean, I just found myself getting more and more involved in poetry, and actually, I'm now much better known for my poetry than my fiction. After my first book of poems, *I Is a Long Memoried Woman,* won the Commonwealth Poetry Prize, I got lots of work in schools, universities, and libraries and so on. And I began doing readings a lot more and writing much more poetry.

KD: As a poet living in "exile" (and I use the term guardedly), there must be an increasing tension between the competing landscapes of your imagination. I've noted in some of your poetry a fascination with the complexities of living in a new landscape. How do you resolve this tension as a black woman living in Britain, or is it resolvable? You said your move may have even influenced the instinct to write poetry, but how do you deal with that tension?

GN: I mean the tension is very much there; I don't think it could be reconciled. You try to reconcile it. But the tension is always there and maybe it's a good thing. And it's not only the tension of physical difference between Guyana (or the Caribbean) and England, it's also in terms of language, culture—Creole versus Standard English, for example. I find it exciting, actually, using that tension especially in terms of language, between Creole and Standard English. I like slipping back and forth from one to the other. There are so many registers and mixtures which I like using and exploring. But at a day-to-day level, I suppose the tension is felt in very concrete ways. The grayness in England is one of my constant moans. The amount of light in the sky does affect me. So a lot of my poems, I suppose, come out of that kind of feeling of being in a different culture. You know, I might be walking down the street (I live in Lewes, near Brighton) and suddenly both landscapes collide—the English and the Caribbean; the gray becomes blue, the trees grow hibiscuses or whatever—in your mind's eye, just for some moments, there is a sense of unreality. A lot of my work still comes out of the Caribbean, in terms of what really excites me at a deep level, but more recently, I have been writing about England. And I've sort of been even getting into the English landscape, more especially in my latest collection *Sunris*. The pagan past of England excites me. I have written a long poem about an ancient hillside figure called the Long Man of Wilmington not far from where I live in Sussex. The collection also has other poems about life in England in general. So, I mean, if yuh living in a new society, away from your homeland, sooner or later, your canvas will have to change to accommodate what's happening around you. And this has happened in my work. But coming back to the tension, having had a British education—we did writers like Shakespeare, Chaucer, Keats—there is a big connection there, and this is always in contrast to that other powerful link with Africa and other cultures of the Caribbean.

KD: One of the most striking features of your poetry is a clear focus on the Afrocentric reality of blacks living within what I call the Diaspora. In a real sense your poems celebrate the connections with Africa through a self-conscious process of naming Africa in the context of this Diasporal world. How central is that to your imaginative process? Is there a certain didactic quality to your recall of Africa in your work?

GN: Were you referring to all my work or specifically to *I Is a Long Memoried Woman*?

KD: Yes, from *I Is a Long Memoried Woman* . . . and . . .

GN: Because that particular book very much comes out of an African source. The whole book was inspired by a dream I had one night of this young African girl swimming to the Caribbean from Africa. She had a garland of flowers around her. So when I woke up, I interpreted this to mean that she was trying to actually cleanse the ocean of the pain and suffering she knew her ancestors had gone through. So, the whole book sprang from the first few lines: "Even in dreams I will submerge myself swimming as one possessed back and forth across this course, strewing it with sweet smelling flowers . . ., one for everyone who made the journey." So the whole book came out of that. It began at that kind of dreamlike, psychic level. It didn't begin with any didactic intentions at all. But as the book progressed, obviously, I had to go back and do a bit of research into things, to refresh my own mind on the history—different customs, the past, different tribes who came out of Africa. I feel very multicultural as a writer, though Africa has always been the strongest spiritual strand for me. And whenever I think of the ancestor, the ancestor is to me an African ancestor in that sense; an African woman. She may be the muse for me, I think. And from her, I get that kind of strength, because she is the woman who has been, in history, negated and voiceless, but has persisted and flowered regardless.

KD: I find what you are saying interesting. It always comes to that discussion about the connection with Africa that we make as writers in the Caribbean, which has been talked about in Brathwaite's work, and now increasingly in Walcott's work. But there is a sense in which there are these two worlds, these two influences, Europe and Africa, that have an impact on the work that we do. But in the more recent writers like yourself and Lorna Goodison, Olive Senior, and so on, there is not a battle established—a battle of cultures, so to speak—but it seems more a kind of acceptance of these strands as they affect the work, and you can pull from anywhere. This is my sense of your work, but is it true about how you relate to disparate cultural strands, or do you see them as sources of internal tension?

GN: I see them as both, if I understand you correctly. At times, you know, the different cultural strands as a poet and as a writer, I do find exciting and enriching—whether it's Amerindian, African, Asian,

European—it is enriching to have at your disposal all these different cultures; the whole language thing, Creole, Standard English—it is enriching to me. But at another level, there is, at times, a tension especially with the European strand because of colonial history, because of the fact that all of our cultural "things" were denigrated and looked down upon while the European "things" were the ones celebrated in every way, even in terms of physical beauty. So there is always going to be that tension because some of these things still exist even today.

KD: Now I want to talk about your writing process. I suspect that with many poets there is a curious correlation between the physical space in which you write and the kind of work that you generate. Is this true about you? Does physical space, literally where you sit down to write the poetry, have an impact on your work? Do you need isolation, quiet? You have a home, you have responsibilities. Do you juggle both, or do you need distraction to create?

GN: Oh no. I need a quiet space in which to work. I know for some writers, they can write with people around. I can write on trains, but I need, when I am at home, a quiet space which nobody else must come into or invade to be able to be at my best and create—you know, to have that sense of freedom.

KD: Do you write in bursts, a lot in one spurt, or are you a careful, meticulous writer, going slowly, line by line? Or does it vary? Some writers approach things by just pouring out the material in waves and then they return to clean up and find the poem. For other writers, it is as if each line becomes a labor. Does it work both ways?

GN: When I was working on my novel, to actually finish it (and for every writer it's different) I did have to push myself and say, I must finish it this year, because it could just go on and on endlessly. Physically, you have to get to the typewriter every day and do some work on it. But with my poetry, it's a bit different. As long as I am excited about something, it will flow. It will come fairly quickly, like *The Fat Black Woman's Poems*. I had fun writing it and the poems came quite quickly. While *I Is a Long Memoried Woman* took about two years to write. So it varies. Sometimes I get poems and they come just as they are, and I leave them exactly. I don't change anything. In other poems I have to do a lot of work on them, a lot of shaping, and chipping, and chopping, and going back, and changing until I get it exactly right, or at least until I am happy with it. So it varies.

KD: How do you see yourself in terms of your role as an artist? The griot figure is an appealing one because she represents that distinctive traditional quality of being at once artist, historian, custodian of the community's stories, politician, warrior. And many of us have seen that to be an attractive role. Do you share this understanding of the role of the artist in society? Do you think there is something distinctly Caribbean, African, or "Third World" about it? Is that an appealing concept for you?

GN: Yes, the griot figure is appealing. In the sense that you are not just a writer and that's it; you're performing, you're connecting to the larger community. But whether I'm all of those things you outlined, I don't know. Balancing motherhood, writing, and performing takes up most of my energy. But in terms of my work, I hope it does all of those different things because poetry is such a radical type of synthesizing force and so much is happening when you write a piece or a poem. So many things come into play, not just your feelings and the thoughts that you are communicating. The erotic comes in, the political, the religious, and everything kind of merges. But it is appealing, the griot concept, in the sense that you feel your work is reaching out to people in a much wider way and connecting to them in an immediate way, hopefully.

KD: Within the past ten years a plethora of studies has emerged in an area that is termed postcolonial studies. A number of Caribbean writers and so-called "Third World" scholars and artists have felt the need to speak out against the premise of postcolonialism, arguing that it is a dated and backward-looking philosophy that perpetuates the concept of the "Third World" writers as being defined primarily by colonialism. Others have argued that to deny the colonial past that has grown and shaped our literature is naive. Have you given much thought to this debate—the idea of postcoloniality?

GN: No, I haven't really given much thought to it, but I do find labels are limiting by their very nature. If you examine terms, like postcolonialism which does sound dated, you just don't want to be defined by that. There was an article in the *Guardian* some time ago and they were speaking about "the New Transcultural writers." They were writers living now in London who had a past from which they have been uprooted and they were addressing an audience as uprooted as themselves and not any one particular kind of audience. I suppose that, in a way, is a bit more appealing than "postcolonial," because not just black writers have been uprooted; you have so many writers from Eastern Europe living in London, living in America, but yet still, you are addressing a much wider audience through the English language which you are using. I mean, even though you might be using English a bit differently, using it in a Caribbean way or whatever, at the same time you are addressing a much wider kind of audience that might be as uprooted as yourself. So I suppose that is more appealing because it makes you a part of a much wider kind of movement.

KD: It makes sense because the principle is that you carry to another culture something of your older culture, and there is that shared sense. Transcultural does sound more appealing . . .

GN: Well, it's more appealing than "postcolonial." Some writers writing now haven't really experienced life under colonialism. They might be born here, black British, they came here when they were very young. So the term doesn't really apply to them.

KD: How do you relate to the generational dynamics of Caribbean literature? I speak here of the fact that we can now see, and hopefully identify, at least three generations of Caribbean poets, writers. It is possible to write about influences. I think this reality has had little study, but writers appear to be very aware of it. Have you tried to understand yourself in terms of this generational reality?

GN: I don't know if I have tried to understand myself through this, but I do feel part of it in the sense that you do feel a sense of a kind of tradition and continuation. Like the older Caribbean writers who were writing in the '30s, people like C. L. R. James and V. S. Reid, Edgar Mittelholzer, and so on, the older writers. And then you have after that period people like V. S. Naipaul, Sam Selvon, Derek Walcott, and Edward Brathwaite who made their presence felt. I suppose, now we are like a third generation, maybe part of a movement, a generation after theirs. So it gives you that sense of continuity and a feeling of a tradition. But, I mean, on the whole, the whole tradition of Caribbean writing is still fairly new, still fairly young. When compared (though you shouldn't) with English literature, that dates back several centuries, they can look back to a much, much longer tradition than we can in the Caribbean. But I do feel part of that.

KD: And as somebody who was influenced by those writers . . .

GN: Yes. I feel that I have been influenced by them. But I can't really pinpoint any of them in any big way, but just the fact that I did read books by Walcott and Brathwaite and the fiction writers, subconsciously and consciously they do give you a certain inspiration. Even their themes, how they write about them, inspire you. To pinpoint clearly and say I have been influenced directly by Martin Carter or by Derek Walcott would be difficult for me to say because I have read so widely not just Caribbean writers, but black American writers, English writers, writers on the whole. People have compared *I Is a Long Memoried Woman* to Edward [Kamau] Brathwaite.

KD: That is an inevitable comparison. The other thing that struck me was the dialogue with other emerging women writers—a dialogue that speaks more to the notion of giving voice to the feminine experience, which seems to create a parallel reality to the predominantly male writing that preceded you . . .

GN: That is true, because Brathwaite did explore that [African/Caribbean themes in *The Arrivants*], but as I said, I wasn't really reading much Brathwaite. I would have looked at *The Arrivants,* not in any big conscious way of really fully appreciating his work, which I came to do later. Even Walcott, I came to Walcott very late. I began reading Walcott like in my thirties, which is pretty late, and really appreciating him and what he's doing. And like his book *Another Life,* I could see myself doing a similar thing for Guyana, a kind of autobiography written in poetry. It appeals to me. So the parallel thing that you are talking about is true, where you appreciate what they've done, they haven't really given voice to the kind of female experience in a big way, not in a way that I feel is true to me. And so Oxford University Press, who saw the manuscript of *I Is a Long Memoried Woman* when I had finished it, said that Brathwaite had done that journey already; so even though they liked the poems a lot, they didn't publish it. So it was published by Karnac House, which is a small Caribbean publishing house based in London.

KD: There is no doubt that Caribbean poetry has been shaped and guided by the writing of a strong generation of women writers today. Names like Lorna Goodison, Olive Senior, Velma Pollard, Christine Craig, and Jane King come to mind. What has happened? How do you account for the emergence of those writers?

GN: Well, I mean, writing don't happen in a vacuum. As I said, Caribbean literature itself is still fairly young. When I look back, we didn't study any of our writers in school when I was going to school as a young child. Brathwaite and Walcott probably were then making their presence felt on the whole literary scene, so we haven't had a long tradition. And to create you need that whole climate around you in which you can feel empowered and kind of a sense of freedom which women haven't had in the Caribbean. I mean, take my mother's generation, for example—she was a talented woman in her own right; she played the piano and so on, but she had seven children and was completely financially, economically dependent on her husband. A lot of women were like that. They weren't really going into the professions, and certainly, writing would not have been seen as a career in which to make a living. But some of these women might quietly have poems tucked away, women of an older generation, and never would do anything about it. But to name yourself as a writer and come out and really perform your poetry on stage, and bring out records, and try to get published, would have been something that would have been alien to their generation, because, as I said, writing especially for a woman (for a man it's always been easier to name yourself as an artist), it's seen as a bit presumptuous; you're naming yourself, you know, "I am an artist, I am a writer, I am a poet" or whatever—defining yourself in those terms. Being able to make a living from it would not have been an easy thing to do for a lot of women. So you needed a feminist movement, you needed lots of things to happen for this emergence of women because women have been writing in the past, but might have kept it quiet and certainly would not have been making a living from it as lots of women writers I know in England are doing today. That's what we do. Writers, both black and white, writers from Asia and elsewhere, we make our living that way. So I think those factors contributed towards a whole feeling of freedom, psychically and creatively and in every way. But why it only happened in the last fifteen, twenty years is interesting. So that's why I am saying it's also related to the broader developments in the broader society. And the feminist movement was a big contribution. I mean feminism is seen as a dirty word these days. Especially our younger women see it as old hat. They see it as something passé, but it has had an impact, whether we like it or not. Even though younger women like my big daughter would not acknowledge a debt to feminism, she takes the freedom of doing this and that in her stride. She has that confidence, she is doing everything, doing kick-boxing, dressing up in the latest fashion, and she has a natural confidence, I suppose, which we had to work for.

KD: But she wouldn't characterize herself as a feminist?

GN: Oh, no! Not at all! She sees feminists as boring people who won't dress up. So, as I said, it's related to what has happened in the wider society. Like she grew up with a woman prime minister, Margaret Thatcher, her whole life. So women could do anything. It was not something she even had to think about. She could do anything she wants to do. Any area. Because that whole climate of freedom, of people feeling they had a right to express themselves in every area, that has led more and more women to come out.

KD: You've written a number of children's books. Do you see yourself as a children's writer or does the term mean anything useful? I know a number of writers have written children's books: Andrew Salkey, Jan Carew, Merle Collins, Lillian Allen, Afua Cooper, and many others. I recently saw a marvelous book of poetry for children by John Agard. What is the instinct to generate these kinds of work? Did you have any Caribbean works to read when you were a child?

GN: No, no. When I was growing up, apart from Louise Bennett's Anancy stories (and using the Creole), we didn't really have any books coming out of our own kind of culture or environment. But I read an amazing amount when I was a child. So when you write and you have children, it comes quite naturally to want to write for them, because, in any case, part of you feels that there should be books around for black children where they could see themselves reflected, their own lives and experiences. Not necessarily didactic books, just imaginative books, books that children would like. So I began writing for children also. When I came to England, I had already had a young daughter. She was four at the time so I began writing for her.

KD: What kind of challenges face you when you start writing for children? Does the kind of increased pressure that we have in society about what is good for children, does that have an impact on the topics you pick, the ideas you contend with in the writing?

GN: Well, obviously, you would be aware of that. That would impinge on your consciousness. You know, like issues of stereotypes, I mean the mum stuck at home while the father goes out to work. It is too neat and it's no longer true because our society has changed so much. When I write for children, I suppose I write in a way for the child in me. I write the things that the child in me would love to hear about. Quite a few of my poems for children can be quite funny poems; exploring sounds and rhythms, because children love sounds, the actual sound of the word can send them into stitches. Like John and his calypso alphabet; whenever my young daughter reaches the part "e," for "eh-eh," she laughs and keeps saying "eh-eh," and we explain what it means — the sound of surprise. Writing for children may seem deceptively simple, but it isn't. There are people who have looked at picture books and said "Oh, it looks so easy," but then ask them to write it and they see that it is difficult.

KD: What place does music have in your work? There is rhythm which is constant in the verse, but there is a clear sense in which many writers working today can't avoid reacting, whether consciously or unconsciously, to the popular music that beats out of our sound systems everywhere. What impact has reggae or calypso had on your work and what other musical styles are you drawn to?

GN: I think music must have had a big part because I grew up with a lot of music like most people in the Caribbean. There was a woman who lived next door to us after we moved to Georgetown. She'd be blaring out her music, much to my father's annoyance, because he was a head teacher who suffered from constant headaches. And all hours of the day she'd be blaring out the latest Sparrow calypso, so you'd be hearing "Dove and Pigeon" and all these kinds of things. So you grew up with all these rhythms, especially calypso, in your head, which I loved as a child. She could play her music whole day as far as I was concerned. It just livened up things whenever she put on her music. And then on the radio you would be hearing music. At weddings and so on, you would be getting some of the *Queh-Queh* ceremonies — I don't know if you had that in Jamaica, but when I was a child in Guyana in a country village before we moved to Georgetown, there were always weddings in the village, and the night before, at the ceremony (this was very African) you had *Queh-Queh* night where they hid the bride and the women would be singing lots of bawdy songs and then they would eventually go and find the bride. So all these old songs like "Hear Auntie Bess, hear Auntie Bess, hear Auntie Bess ah halla" we grew up with. Some were plain folk songs, but most of them had the sexual, you know calypso, suggestiveness. I loved that. I absolutely loved it. I took in all these songs. I have just finished working on a long poem about a woman going through carnival (*Sunris*) and being transformed by it. And that, I know, is directly linked to steel pan and calypso—that influence. So music has been a big part of my work. Even in simple poems, that musical awareness, and awareness of sound and the way words sound is very much in my head when I am writing.

KD: This is both in the musicality, the rhythm and so on and the content, the lyrical statement...

GN: Yes, because in that particular long poem called *Sunris*, the calypso rhythm is very strong in it. That can't be helped because that is what I associate with Carnival and with the steel band. So that's very strong, and I am trying to keep up that kind of rhythm all the way through.

KD: Many of our women poets appear to have taken a rather ambivalent position towards Western feminism. I find it ambivalent because while there is an open unwillingness to be labeled a feminist writer, these writers, clearly because of their radical position on issues of gender, are challenging the status quo. Where do you stand in all of this? Would you define yourself as a feminist writer? How do you read the various positions taken by other women writers about feminism? It's as if I am asking you to put a label on yourself, but it's not that, I am more interested in your ideas about the discussion itself.

GN: No, I mean, I just wouldn't call myself a feminist writer. Nor would I simply say that I am a black writer. I mean, these things just don't occur to you. Or that I am a woman writer, a Guyanese writer, or a postcolonial writer. They are all labels and at times they have a relevant context, depending on the situation you're in. Someone might organize a festival and you willingly take part under that name which might be a label at one level, but it's specific and it's defining what is going to happen and what you're looking at. And even though I am saying I don't call myself a feminist writer in that sense, feminism and the idea of the feminist is very much a part of my philosophy and what I have always believed in, in any case. The feminist movement was important, you can't get away from that, in terms of the impact it has had around the world. In the past you might have had a big conference and you would find that all the writers were men. Now they are forced to take note, which is as it should be. We are now living in a complex culture, so you can't have the male Eurocentric voice defining what is literature all the time, what deserves to be preserved as literature, what belongs to the great canon of literature, with no one else having a say in terms of defining what we think is literature also and what we think is important. Now you have a much wider and varied kind of debate and communication going on.

Lillian Allen

BORN 1951

LILLIAN ALLEN WAS born in Spanish Town, Jamaica, where she spent most of her formative years—the years that would help to shape her sensibility and self-identity. As a teenager, she left for New York, where she spent several years attending school. During that time she became immersed in American culture, particularly black American culture, at a time of significant activity in that community. She attended New York University, where she majored in English and developed her skills as a writer of children's literature. After returning briefly to Jamaica, Allen soon settled in Canada, where she has lived since.

In 1979, after meeting Jamaican dub poet Oku Onuora in Cuba at the CARIFESTA Conference, she returned to Canada and teamed with a number of Toronto poets and artists, notably the poet Clifton Joseph, and began to work in the dub poetry mode. She has toured throughout the world as a performer of her work and is a committed activist for cultural and political diversity in Canadian society. She teaches literature and writing in Toronto colleges and is a regular consultant to national arts and political organizations.

Lillian Allen has produced three albums for adults and one for children, and two books for children and young people. Her poetry collections include *Nothing But a Hero Dub* (Women's Press, 1987), *Some Imagining Women* (Women's Press, 1990), *Why Me?* (Well Versed, 1991) and *Women Do This Every Day: Selected Poems* (Women's Press, 1993).

KWAME DAWES: When did you start writing? Did it begin with poetry or prose?

LILLIAN ALLEN: I always have problems with beginnings because I don't believe in beginnings, I don't believe in ends. It's just a circle. People who remember me from my past remember that I was always writing. When I go back home, people I know from thirty-odd years back say, "Yuh still writing?" I grew up in the church, in a large family, a community. I was very active in school. I was always involved in elocution and activities like that; church activities and getting together with other kids to do plays and so on. I must have distinguished myself as a writer back then. That's before I was ten or so. I didn't realize it until I went back and people, you know, started talking about it. But I remember sort of around age twelve, being amazed at writing, thinking about writing and I wasn't quite sure where writing came from. I remember going through the geometry book where you had to learn three hundred theorems or something like that, and when I was done, I figured, even if I thought somebody wrote books, after geometry, I wasn't quite sure. I thought it may have come from some tree, or factory, right. So it was much later, actually, that it really clued in to me that there is something called an author, a writer, and I remember when I realized that I figured, yes, that's what I want to do, I can do that and I'd love to do that. And I started to think of writing, not as a profession, because I had no conception of the profession—I knew no writers, I probably just found out that somebody wrote a book by accident. But it just gave me that "in." I could say, "Yeah, I wanna write books, I wanna create with words the journey that I've taken with books." And just every opportunity I have gotten since then, I write. People doing things in school plays, I would write. If there was a band or singers around, I would say, let me write a song. And I also realized pretty early that the other side to writing was learning about writing. So as soon as I got a chance to, I did literature and I made a real big effort to read a lot. Also, as soon as I got a chance, I started attending writing workshops. This is when I left Jamaica.

KD: You left Jamaica when?

LA: '69, aged seventeen.

KD: And you came straight to Canada?

LA: Yeah, I came to Canada. But somebody like Miss Lou was already indelible in my mind as an artist. I mean, I didn't even associate her that much with writing, but as an artist and a persona; when I looked in society at what the possibilities were—she looked like she was having more fun than anybody else.

KD: Can you talk about your own movement towards dub poetry? In fact, before you do, can you define the term and speak to whether you regard what you do as falling squarely under the rubric of "dub poetry"?

LA: You know, it's like you talk about a reggae musician, right, people say, "'im don' haffe learn nuh chords, no beat, 'im jus' haffe learn reggae"—that is so silly. This is how we categorize things. Dub poets are activists and writers coming out of that postcolonialist movement, influenced by the Black Power anti-imperialist movement and the politics of daily engagement, who brought that energy and those principles to their work. Art was part of activism. We were doing it differently. All over the Caribbean, all over the black world. The thing that made dub poetry unique is that one person pressed the term into the consciousness of the Jamaican people. If Oku had got up and left it, it would have just been anything else.

I met Oku in 1978 in Cuba. I went to Cuba to read poetry, Oku went to Cuba to read poetry, and Linton Kwesi Johnson went to Cuba to read poetry. I met Oku, and we talked and I was so impressed with him. I missed his main performance because I was of the "First World," Canada, and he was of the "Third World," Jamaica. I couldn't get to see his performance because I was performing at the same time. And he did a performance for me—a full performance at the broken-down wall at the José Martí School. It was one of the most magical moments of my life. Almost a full hour. The man did a show as if he was doing it to a stadium of people, and I mean, I was so transfixed and transformed and so touched by that man's spirit, that I figured I wanna be part of what he's doing. And living in a place like Canada and coming up in a colonized place like Jamaica where all there was to aspire for was whitening up and lightening up—here was a black man, who was blazing the trail in a form—making it more contemporary (he can't replace Louise Bennett, that's a place and time). He's not quite reggae, 'cause that is a different level of the culture, the music, but here is somebody who is doing something that's closest to what I am doing and what I want to do. And he was naming the form. I was so proud, man, 360 degree black!

I came back to Canada and gathered up everybody and I said, "We are doing this stuff, and we know what it's gonna be? It's gonna be dub poetry. We have a brother, right, who is connected in spirit to us and he's doing it. We need to be part of it. We are not individuals, we are a part of this movement, right, and we need to have a signifier and symbol that we are connected to." And that was sort of Oku's expression and wish. And I think that's what basically fueled the movement. This Canadian center fueled the movement and gave it articulation and analysis and actually moved it towards a literary place because of the background; myself and Clifton [Joseph] who had English degrees and were part of the literary community in Canada.

So the form is a crystallization. And having named it, then you can actually develop it. And as I said if it wasn't named, it would have been diffused. But once you named it, you actually had to develop some characteristics around it. And I am still proud of it. I don't care who likes it or who don't like it; I think it speaks to a lot of people, it speaks to 360 degrees Africa in terms of the sheer sensuality of it, the sheer beauty, the sheer rhythm of it. Forget the words and the politics (I mean that's great too, for there is always a message to dub poetry) but that African way of bringing soul to something—I mean, that's our gift, man, that's definitely our gift.

KD: I would like you to talk a bit about your compositional practice. In dub poetry you are working with two basic "instruments," the voice and the musical instrument. Do you script the "lyrics" first and then find the rhythm to work with the piece or is the process less structured than that? Do you do your own musical composition or do you work with a particular musician or group of musicians?

LA: About a hundred questions in there. Again, the process of beginnings. If you look far enough, there is no beginning. It's just an organic kind of thing. But again, from how we tend to look at this or for the kind of answers you might want, I need to find a structure. And at one time I had it down pat. But when I really meditate on it, when I go back into the layers that I have to go through to come to a finished work, the layers gone, man, and them gone and them gone and them gone. Them just become organic. So it's not a beginning thing, it's a thing that feeds on whatever spiral is happening, and feeds itself.

I guess the easiest thing to say for somebody to get a grasp on it is that some stuff you sit down and you write it, some stuff you get a vibe or a rhythm. I think basically for me, my passion for expression, and my emotional capacity is basically what defines my life so my movement, the way I shape things, is a materialization of that. So words and utterances are a vocalization, a materialization of the emotional and the expressive space. So at some point that takes some form — that is communicable. The words or the rhythms. When the whole process . . . or the part . . . it's really hard to put a finger on because it is a personal sort of process. It is like a compost dump. You have everything in, and it stays in and it goes through a whole transformation and it comes out again. And I keep going in and coming in and whatever. So you just have to artificially stop and assign a beginning, middle, end. I don't think there is a real natural break at all. If your art is a process of expressing a process then that process just goes on. So it's harder now.

It was easier then, when I only had certain skills. I developed my musical skills after. I developed my writing skills first, so it was easier then to say you do the writing and then the dah dah dah. Now the musical skills and the greater consciousness of my own process is harder. I mean, I have worked with musicians and basically they work on the pulse and the beat and the chords that come, the musicality, more or less. Now, I have come also in my own development, I have learnt to make the music as another craft. I basically do most of the music myself. I teach people how to do it. It involves chord, melody, and beat and you've got your music. You don't have to write down music or play an instrument. I mean if you sing "Yesterday / All my troubles seemed so far away" and somebody come and strum a guitar, it don't mean them write the song (although they are likely to claim that). 'Cause music existed before instruments and guitars and all that. So all this big thing about structure and all that, just play the music, man. It's not a black cultural thing to worry about who can write down the chords.

KD: Your work has very strong feminist/womanist overtones — a strong articulation of the experience of women, black women and minority women, in fairly patriarchal societies. Not many Caribbean women writers like the label "feminist," even as they consciously work to ameliorate the condition of women. Do you have such qualms about the label; and do you see a working tension between your advocacy as a woman and your advocacy as a black person?

LA: I see myself as black and a woman every single moment in my life. It's like there are some black men who would like you to be black and there are some feminist women, white women, who would like you to be woman. I am woman and black. I can only be who I am at every single moment. How you negotiate those I think has to do with what I call the shared and the sharable, right. I don't see it as a dichotomy or as a conflict. I mean there are things that we can share as black people from the same culture that we share, and there are things that are sharable as human beings, and all human beings can share. I'd look at my work to see what are the values in that and who are these values shared with, and what are the sharable values. I just think that gives more room and more focus and more depth to each issue that one deals with.

In terms of feminism stuff, I'd rather be called feminist than not, any day. In fact, I feel quite proud to be feminist in the late twentieth century because I see feminism in a long line of struggle for human liberation. If I reject feminism then I would be doing the same thing that some white folks did in rejecting the Black Power movement. Because black people came together and talked about their liberation. They are to be supported by all people who love humanity, and going back to the abolitionist movement and the antislavery movement that gave white women the experience and the practicality of fighting for their freedom and the suffragette movement and the whole feminist movement that sort of developed out of that, I can't not support any movement for liberation for any group of people. So I am actually quite proud to be part of the feminist movement despite its contradictions. I was in the Black Power movement and it had a lot of contradictions, also. And I am prepared to struggle along. That's my position. What is the alternative? My poetic definition is: "Instead of being the doormat, get up and be the door"—Feminism 101.

KD: Can you speak about Jamaica and its place in your sensibilities, in your poetic instincts?

LA: It's interesting because my actual formative years, my coming together as an independent person happened in New York. I lived in New York for four years. And it's interesting because having lived in New York, I had lived in a different community—although I had relatives, I just basically abandoned myself into the culture I was surrounded by, black culture and white New York, and at one point I did not know how to speak Jamaican. I was in a West Indian store and I stood up for about half an hour listening and I couldn't figure out what they were saying. It scared the shit out of me. That was a wake-up call. I was pretty surprised and I just kind of slipped by as a New York person anywhere I went. I went to Europe and they said "Oh, you're from New York," I went to Jamaica and they said "Oh, you're from New York" and so on. It made me realize that somehow I was drifting out there and made me take the time to start figuring out who I am. That was the turning point. I remember that specifically.

That was the point at which I made a specific effort to reconnect with Jamaica, with my grammar, with my roots. And of course, once you do that, then somehow your life becomes infinitely better. You feel differently, you see things differently, you're more grounded. So Jamaica, then, not only became a home, in terms of where my family was and where I needed to go back to, but it also became a psychic nurturing place where, when I was down or in between or I couldn't quite hang onto something . . . wasn't sure what was going on, I put on "Natty Dread" or phone (my phone bill coulda tek me on an airplane and back!). It's just the idea of being connected, right, and having that connection and knowing that there is rightness about it, a feeling about it. I can't explain it in words—a feeling that was important to me and still is, although I live in Canada now. I don't know what the future will hold, but Jamaica is like . . . well, Africa is like my grandmother, Jamaica is like my mother, and Canada is like my spouse. That is the only way I can explain it. It can't be a conflict. It's just that I have all this richness and they all have something special and they are all a part of me and I have begun to figure how they fit in my life. I am certain that they are all there.

KD: A related question has to do with the "problematic" of audience. In many ways, your poetic ethos is more akin to the griot and other African models of artists whose roles are defined by their service to the community—in other words, you appear to eschew the concept of the poet as an isolated, introspective soul locked away in a room making verse for him/herself. The African model, the griot/folk poet, is defined by the assumption of a community. The griot is appointed by the community. There are implications to this ownership: shared values, shared histories, shared sense of identity, etc. Can you say that such a community exists for you here in Canada? Are African Canadian poets searching for a village or is there a village? More critically, are their voices, is your voice, first given to that village?

LA: That's a pretty complex question, but I think a very good one, only in terms of the way the question keeps coming up. I mean people don't say that about the Nobel Prize and the Pulitzer Prize, right. Yet, for most writers, or writers who work in the so-called mainstream, that's their village, that's the environment that dictates their values—that's the highest ideal in life. When people talk about the community for black writers or writers who work most closely in the culture, there is that little undertone as if it is a burden. But if you get the Pulitzer Prize or the Nobel Prize, it's not a burden. An' yet, when the community come out and laugh an' clap an' praise yuh, right, an' somebody say "write a poem for me," that's supposed to be a burden, and you are supposed to be censured by that.

I think that culture comes from community and art comes from culture. I think those of us who are involved in cultural practice experience it as a process to recreate and transform ourselves and the values that are part of us. Our work is accountable to those values of liberation and beauty and that place that we would/should have been had it not been for racism and so on. Now as an artist, I am working on my life. I am not working on my art or a book, I am working on my life. And all that stuff is a product of working on my life. So what happens with me is that I am connected to family, small community (which is alternate family) neighborhoods, community, creative value, pan-Africanism, humanism, world humanism, moral life, etc. My values get tested in my work and in my relationships with people, get expanded in my communication. My passion in my relationships brings meaning to what I am doing, and I take those and they go in my writing. So it's all circular. It is part and parcel of it. I couldn't be doing what I'm doing if I wasn't out there working on my life, working on myself. I couldn't have the vision, right? So for me it's about that process and about life. And life is the process.

In terms of that responsibility, I like to see it in a very positive way—Oh yeah, I have responsibilities! I wanna have responsibilities, I want to have mirrors and connection and "looking glass." I feel the work is appreciated. I know with absolute certainty that I've done great work. I don't have to wait until I die. It gives my life and work great meaning. My work helps to preserve and challenge the values of my community and pushes forward new ideas, and I think that's important, that's how I want to live my life. Everything that I am a part of provides that framework and acts as a testing ground for me. So the shared ownership, shared values, shared history, that's pretty important. I think we all come to it from a different position, but the one thing about an artist is that the artist is like a midwife and the birth mother is the culture, so the artist is gonna birth the baby. And if the baby is stillborn, the artist is going to have to deal with that first, and feel its pain. Then the community has to deal with that next. But the community is not birthing the baby. The artist's role is to labor and give birth. The community incubates the baby, provides the genetic makeup, whatever, but the artist has to do the laboring and bring the baby out. So I don't see the danger of the community censoring or censuring the artist. An artist's role is to raise the questions, to blaze the trail. If as an artist all you do is feed back the median value of the community to the community, you would have achieved the heights of mediocrity. There would be no passion, no vision. That whole process of creating art, singing and dancing, is a spiritual process; that is the medium of communication with the universal spirit, with the soul, with the ancestors. That's what we need to do, that is the higher calling. Show me a higher calling. Show me a higher calling. I don't see any higher calling.

KD: I have been throwing around this thesis that the period of the emergence of reggae, the late '60s, early '70s, in that period the music represented the kind of "literary" voice of Jamaica. In other words, if you took a generational view of the development of writing and creativity in Jamaica, you would talk about the '50s and '40s with the Maises and the Hearnes and in the '60s the Morrises, etc. There is a solid gap in the '70s with no distinctively new voice, and in the '80s, the women emerge in great force. I've always said that the real voice, the clearest voices, in the '70s were Spear, Lee "Scratch" Perry, Marley — these were the voices that gave everybody else a way to speak. We still haven't even fathomed it fully as yet. I wonder if you have any ideas on that. I am talking about the ethos of reggae music, that combination of the song and dance and the statement quality — its politics, if you will. How have you observed that to have transformed what we call "writing" in Jamaica, the Caribbean, and elsewhere?

LA: The thing with writing for me is it doesn't have to be what you have on the page. You talk about ethos of it and so on. Reggae created a whole new space. I think it does what you say. There are at least twenty artists who were articulating the conditions of Jamaica, dealing with the situation. When I talk about reggae I say that is Jamaican popular culture—that reggae scene and the early dance hall. I think Olive Senior talks about the influence of reggae and dub poetry, and of course everybody comes to all this late. Reggae brought a new dimension. When I look at the early reggae, it had pure artistic value. It was accountable to the artistic value of the artist and the artist's community. And I heard some early Trench Town stuff, even the early Bob [Marley], they were singing for their lives. They were singing themselves out of a wastepaper basket. Them nah sing fe nuh stadium, no nutting. Dem was singing because dem had to do dat. They had to put those values out there. They had to assert themselves, they had to exert their existence. They were fighting for their existence. And to me, that was one of the major influences in terms of the whole Caribbean culture and it brought it into being in a popular way.

And you know there are no themes that you can find that have been written about that are not in the music. I link back with Miss Lou and my position is that if it wasn't for Miss Lou, we wouldn't have reggae music till about 2050. Miss Lou was a major catalyst. Miss Lou basically came and changed the course and that she, both in her presence and her work, was like the source that people drew on, the backbone, the stone, the rockstone. And you know, I understand the Workers Movement and [Ralph] Campbell and all of them and so on, but somehow I don't think ordinary Jamaicans felt that them coulda go rest on anyone else for them never give the spiritual, the 360 degree that Miss Lou offered. She got an award in the States not long ago for being one of the most significant personalities of the twentieth century. But I certainly mark her and Bob as two of the most significant personalities of the twentieth century. Period. No apology.

I have a short story about two girls coming into awakening and the birth of reggae music. They went to a summer camp in Orange Street. They were from various political families and they met and hooked up with some of the guys in the ghetto and their awakening to womanhood and a sense of possibilities and the birth of reggae music happened at the same time. I think that's pretty significant for the world. I think that basically how the world renews itself is through black music, how the universe as we know it renews itself is through black music, the vibes and the rhythms and the vision. And reggae was just another renewal (if not redemption) for the world. It is a thing of the spirit, you know.

KD: Can you talk a bit about your influences? Do you think you have been shaped by any specific writer or writers? The fact that you are writing in a form that is still defining itself means that you are pioneering, yet there are models that may have helped shape your own sensibility?

LA: It is a "pioneer" form. The way I usually describe it is that a crystallization happens. It is like a crystallization of an oral form within the context of the African tradition. So there is a whole heap a' influences coming down that some a' we don't even know. I think that Africa is both a continent and a people and you talk about the holograph—you know how that work—if you take a piece, the whole thing is in it. This is the African people; there is a lot of Africa in us and she expresses herself through us. So for that not to happen you really have to do some stuff to yourself. But I think that that's the way of things. That's who we are. So, once you reach for an instrument, then that expression of Africa is gonna find itself in you. So that is the context. Louise Bennett certainly. I don't think I would exist as a dub poet if Louise Bennett didn't exist or Oku for that matter. I would be writing, I would always be doing stuff, I am sure, but not in the same way.

I think the reggae artists influenced me greatly. I mean, they put a body (an embodiment), a continent, a consciousness behind the words and the rhythms. There was a fearlessness about them—something that's different from calypso where there is a demand on the system—that really attracted me, that really, you know moved me. So certainly, reggae artists—Bob for sure. I can't imagine anybody not being influenced by the commitment, the artistry, the coming together of the rhythm and the message. Basically, he was the guy who made the message the primal thing, the form of the song. If you listen to Bob's stuff, some of it is not song, you know—it's poetry and music. That was the thing. And once that happened, it was—Booom! The power of it was greater than the parts.

I did English literature, I studied black American writers, I studied American and Euro classics. The truth is, everything in my life influenced me, everything I've read, whether negative or positive, it has become a part. Those that give me the strength and make me imagine something for myself are most of the black writers. There are people I love like bpNichol. I would go to bed with a bpNichol. I mean a good afternoon for me is just me and bp and some music, under my covers. Then working with Clifton [Joseph], working with dub poets was pretty important to me. It was pretty important because, particularly with Clifton and a few other people, we had a forum to talk, to research and discuss among ourselves, which a lot of people don't have — that process of talking, of going back and forth. We loved and respected each other so much that we could disagree and fight and go find our sources and quotes and then come to the realization collectively that no quote could save us. So that meant a whole development for both of us.

The other thing that happened was that people like Clifton and I were engaged in actual community work, so we had a basis, a dialectic, we saw the sheer practicality, the sheer passion for change in the community. Just straightening out the bends, just correcting any problems and filling in any gaps. And we went around the country. I am so happy for that experience because we were there on the frontline, we were doing our stuff, right. At some places three hundred people would show up to listen to poetry! We were fearless, we were bold, and both of us together, we would say anything. We would be doing gigs where a Minister of Government this or that was at and everybody would be hush-hush and we would get wild, like the devil would take us over. It was just as if we felt we had a chance to say what black and dispossessed people hadn't had a chance to say in those forums and we had the ability: art. So that was something else. And you could feel that sense of your own power rising, just "getting away," you can't hold yourself back because there is so much . . . It was just the greatest thing. I remember once we were invited to perform at the black community center in Halifax in a pretty conservative setting. They have the kids under manners and the kids were bubbling over, on the balcony panting, dying to do something — and Clifton did his "Looking for a Job" piece at the end of his performance. You know, this piece ends with "I will take the day, I will take the night." He was so wild. The kids were riotous, they jumped from the balcony and cheered. Needless to say the evening went quite differently after that. Chains and fears are sometimes the same things. The thing I like most about Margaret Atwood the writer is that she's fearless. Fearlessness . . . that is revolutionary.

KD: Do you think there was a defining moment for you, a moment when you felt you had found what is (perhaps vaguely and misleadingly) called your "voice"? Can you talk about your process of arriving at a sense of style and sensibility?

LA: I had a sense of voice before meeting Oku. But that meeting helped it. I think probably, from the Black Power movement in the States, some of the poetry scene then, I think that is where I solidified a voice. I remember a time when I didn't have a voice, when I could write and do well on essays that sounded nice and good, but it wasn't really the substance of self, the stuff, but then, I remember distinctly when the dub poems happened—I mean the classical sense of the dub poem, since some of the poems are poems that were not conceived as dub poems but were transformed by the dub poetry process—but I remember when I made my first conscious attempt at a dub poem. That was an amazing experience. I didn't sleep for four days. I just knew that my life would be different. It was just like an opening, a river meets the sea. It was just one of those things, totally amazing. A whole new universe opened up for me. It was just something that fit, there was a rightness about it. Before there was sort of an intellectual insincerity that you were not conscious of, you know, but you sort of bore it, and the more insincere it felt the more you worked harder at it, and then when I did "Riddim on Hard Times," my first consciously crafted dub poem, everything just fit, the sensual, the intellectual, the rhythm, the music, everything. So there were several defining moments throughout the process. And even now it's still kind of changing, for it's definitely moving to the spiritual, which has to do with being guided by spiritual values that define and refine the political values instead of being guided by the political values and deciding what side people are on and that kind of thing. So it's been a turnaround, which is another defining kind of thing—which transforms you and everything you do, not to mention the art.

Kendel Hippolyte
BORN 1952

KENDEL HIPPOLYTE WAS born in St. Lucia, where he attended school and became involved in the performing arts. In the mid-1970s, he attended the University of the West Indies in Jamaica, where he became deeply immersed in the cultural life of that society. His plays were staged at the University's Creative Arts Center, and he began to write and publish his poetry during that time. His poetry represents a fascinating waltz between a clearly engaged political advocacy and a deep lyricism; it is carefully crafted, with rigorous attention to language and the structure of the line. Hippolyte's vision is an updated, starker version of the world of St. Lucian drawn by Derek Walcott. But as the work collected in Hippolyte's substantial volume *Birthright* (Peepal Tree, 1997) demonstrates, Walcott and Hippolyte share a devotion to the discipline of form and to the almost priestly belief in the business of writing.

Hippolyte is the resident playwright, cofounder, and artistic director of the innovative Lighthouse Theater Company in St. Lucia. His credentials as a poet of remarkable skill and imagination are firmly established: he is anthologized in virtually every important anthology of Caribbean literature, and is a frequent object of critical attention in survey studies of West Indian poetry. His volumes of poetry, each one published modestly in St. Lucia, have been variously hailed by critics as the voicings of a very important talent.

He has published four collections of poetry: *Island in the Sun-Side Two* (UWI Extra Mural Dept., 1980), *Bearings* ([St. Lucia], 1986), *The Labyrinth* (The Source, 1993), and *Birthright*. He has been described by *The Heinemann Book of Caribbean Poetry* as "perhaps *the* outstanding

Caribbean poet of his generation." His work has also been anthologized in The *Penguin Book of Caribbean Verse, Voiceprint,* and *Caribbean Poetry Now.*

KWAME DAWES: When did you start writing poetry? What prompted that activity?

KENDEL HIPPOLYTE: Oh God! The first clear memory I have of actually trying to shape a poem goes back to Standard Six. I would have been around ten years old, I suspect. There was a brief period for some of us when we were in Standard Six for a few weeks—you know, after you finish the scholarship exams and you sit around until the results come out and either you stay in Standard Six or you go on to secondary school. And I remember writing some poem there about dawn, and I don't remember all of it, but there was some recurring line about "all the birds and beasts awake for it is dawn." The teacher of the class at the time, I can't remember how she got ahold of it, but she liked it and she read it to the class and the class seemed to like it. That is my earliest memory of actually trying to shape something—perhaps because there was an actual public response to it that fixed it in my mind. I used to read a lot when I was growing up. I used to like the sound of words. I liked the way the words always made my imagination create pictures and so on—I mean, it's normal kinds of things, I suppose, that any child goes through. I used to be alone a lot, very much by choice, and I guess when you on your own a lot, you dream a lot, and you create little things for yourself with words. I guess that's how it started.

KD: The new generation of Caribbean poets share two critical characteristics: (1) a strong awareness of a real tradition in Caribbean writing forged by the pioneering work of some of the older writers, and (2) an appreciation of the importance of reggae music and popular culture to creative expression. I think your work epitomizes this thesis. Do you see reggae as a critical feature of your writing? Can you talk about reggae and poetry?

KH: I've never thought of reggae specifically as a critical feature in the writing—not in terms of determining the form. I suspect it may be more to do with the fact of when reggae was happening and the kinds of ideas it was carrying. Reggae for me is very much associated with the '70s, with a time of a lot of self-questioning, nationally, individually. And not just self-questioning, because also I think it was very much a time when people were open to ideas about what I will just loosely call the spiritual world, you know, the inner world. And there was a sense that both things were important—that is, making things right in the world of the here and now, the social world, kind of building a New Jerusalem impulse; and also the other important thing was attending to what was going on inside of you and becoming right, becoming what the rastaman referred to as the higher man, or the Iya-man. So yes, I think reggae was important in terms of keeping the significance of those two strands of living very alive and real and accepted and normal for a lot of us. As far as direct experiments of reggae rhythm in the poetry go, for myself, I think they've been few and far between and very, very fragmentary. I can think of one piece in *Island in the Sun*, "Worker Chant," which actually I don't even think of as a reggae rhythm so much as a nyabingi rhythm, a Rasta rhythm. So I don't know. I have always felt for myself, rightly or wrongly, that what music has influenced me in the shaping of the poetry has really more to do with jazz. And I don't necessarily mean that jazz rhythms get directly into the poetry, but more that the way that the jazz musician's lines in the solo, particularly in the solo, the way that the lines are going to come out—they really aren't dependent on anything more than just an ear for how it feels. And it's guided really by just that, just a trust, and the instinct of the ear that the shape of the line, the length of the line, the hit of the line, if you have the right technique, will be right. I kind of trust that that kind of thing could happen in the lines of poetry as well. So, to go back to your question, I don't really think of reggae itself as a shaping, technical influence. Maybe it's there in a way that I don't know, but that's not really how I think of it.

KD: I note at least two central influences in your work: the lyricism of Walcott and the political/folk clarity of Brathwaite. Those are easy, but I also sense a fascination with the *idea* of the poem that we see in Anthony McNeill and Dennis Scott, as well as a spiritual engagement reminiscent of Lorna Goodison and Robert Lee. These are my observations, but can you talk about some of the writers whose work has helped shape your vision?

KH: I think when I started to take writing more seriously—and when I say "to take writing seriously," I always go back to the question of craft, because we all know it's not the ideas you have or the feelings that you have that make the poem the poem, it's when you start to pay attention to the shaping of it. I think when I began to take writing seriously, to get an idea of the size of work and the importance of work that is involved in crafting a poem, I probably was more conscious of Brathwaite as a technician than I was of Walcott. I really feel that it's more now, in fact, that I really have come to appreciate the range of technique that Walcott has mastered and is so comfortable with. But I know that at the time (and I am talking about the middle to late '70s), I am certain I was more interested in the kind of stuff Brathwaite was doing. Because I mean, for one thing, he had connected with the music, the various folk musics of the Caribbean. And there was his sense of history—I found it more accessible, more in accordance with what I was probing and interested in at the time. But even so, I don't know. I really find it difficult to say that Brathwaite was for me a definite poetic influence. I can remember in the '70s when a lot of people were writing "Brathwaite" poems; there were a lot of people who were writing poems that were trying to do stuff like what "Negus" was doing, or that were deliberately going in for calypso rhythms and so on. I didn't do that. But I think that for me Brathwaite's influence was more a kind of a validating of the oral aspect of poetry. Because it worked. What he did worked. And it was so very much dependent on the oral tradition, the various oral techniques, if you like, that had been carried through in songs, storytelling and so on. To see it working in poetry of high-high seriousness and of a vision that was very integrated, that seemed to have a very well worked out historical viewpoint of the movement of a whole set of people, and beyond that too, a kind of a cosmology—because I think that very, very early, you could sense that Brathwaite had a kind of cosmology that he was trying to work towards—to see that level of seriousness and vision happening and happening in what might have been at one time simply labeled as dialect poetry—it was a kind of—not even so much a permission—it was as if, if you had had any lingering doubts that such a thing was possible, it just removed them. It was okay to just go ahead and go wherever you wanted to with the language that you were hearing around you. So I think Brathwaite was an influence in that sense. For a whole lot of people and certainly for me. But in terms of consciously trying to work with his particular kinds of techniques, his particular kind of drum sounds (again I may be wrong), I don't think so. Walcott for me is very much, I think, a later influence and the most important thing still remains the understanding of the need for precision of the image. And the idea too. Of, apart from metaphor as an image within the poem, the idea of the whole of language as metaphor. It's an idea that you come across over and over and over once you are into poetry at all—but somehow his work, more than any other, solidified more for me how the whole of language is a metaphor for the world that we are seeing through the senses. There is a way in which Walcott's poetry absolutely consolidated that for me.

The influence of other poets, I don't know. I can think of persons whose poetry I admire for one reason or another. There is an American poet called Wendell Berry whose poetry I really admire tremendously for its clarity, for the way in which he uses language that really has a music in it and yet that really has an ordinary, everyday quality to it which never ever gets prosaic. I believe in that kind of poetry. In that respect, in Martin Carter's poetry, too, I also find what is, again, not really permission, but validation. You see that, yes, it can work, it does work, because, look, there is somebody who is doing it with the highest of intentions, with profundity, not shrinking from confronting things in themselves—all these huge things that have to happen in poetry when you get more and more serious about it—and yet, it's happening within a language that is accessible enough to a whole range of people. There is a black American poet called Robert Hayden, who is dead now, but in his poetry, what I found to be very, very crucial was the way he was able to ground himself in his own history as an African American, but he is also a Baha'i, so that his vision of persons, of the movement of human history, goes beyond the more narrow African American, black nationalist type of perspective. And yet he is very, very grounded in his own history. It is as though if you dig down deep enough through poetry, even if you are starting just with technique, if you dig deep enough even into technique, eventually you will arrive at an ethic that is just built into it. And if you dig down deep into that ethic you will find yourself traveling the same kind of path that religious people, and not conventionally religious people, that mystics and seekers after that kind of wisdom, have also trod. I think MacNeill really believes that. He really trusts the poetry and the process of creating poetry to take him there without any aid or any support from a religious system, an ideological system. Poetry is its own way, its own path. Someone like Robert [Lee], one of the things he made me more conscious of is just grounding yourself here where you are. I always think of Robert in a lot of ways as a transitional figure between somebody like Walcott and other persons like myself, although there is not much of a big age difference between us. But I think Robert has a very strong sense of the generations, of the movement of generations, or what each generation in St. Lucia was facing, is facing, will face. So history in that very, very localized and personal sense was something that I saw very early in his poetry, and in talking to him too, that made it more important for me.

KD: What is the writing process like for you? Are you driven primarily by metaphor, idea, or narrative? I know the question could be answered with "all of the above," but could you speak of what impact each motivation has on the shape and content of your verse?

KH: My gut reaction is to say: the idea first off. Another gut reaction is to say: narrative?—no! Although it may be in there, but certainly, I don't think the narrative motivates; I mean, not even in plays—I have to work very hard in plays to try to get stories, to get plots. It's always ideas that I start off with, even in something like a play. Very often the troublesome part, I find, of working on a play is finding, making a story that can be turned into a plot that can allow you to explore the ideas. So I can't say narrative is what takes me off. It seems to me, offhand, that it's always ideas. Okay, so I mean, of course, images naturally are just going to end up clamping themselves onto, or bursting out of the particular idea that you are following through. Like I know that for months now (well, I suppose it's more than months, but it seems like it has gotten more intense over the last few months) I've been haunted by the really age-old idea of the natural world around us, just the mineral world, the vegetable world, you know, the world of nature, as a kind of a book, a kind of parable, as a language all in itself—I mean, it's an idea that's always been there, but I find myself getting more and more intrigued by it. So I mean, in doing so, naturally some images just seem to be more cogent. Anytime I see grass growing in sidewalks, I almost want to just laugh because there's something so amazingly unstoppable and enormous about that, it's just an image that's so potent. It came up in the "Jah-Son" poem, for example. But more and more, I feel myself when I am writing a poem—more from the conception of it than really when I'm going into the shaping of it and everything—I feel myself more on the track of an idea. Poetry for me is very much connected with trying to understand things, to understand. But of course the idea has a certain kind of tone and feeling attached to it, and I have to stay true to that tone and feeling.

KD: What has the publishing scene been like for you? Quite clearly, you have successfully established yourself as a distinct and vital Caribbean voice without publication by any of the few "big name" publishers that handle Caribbean poetry. Do you think that this is a product of having remained in the Caribbean, or is it more complicated than that? How has it affected your work, your writing?

KH: The publishing thing is a pain in the tail, and I think when I first started doing it—I suppose it was 1980 when I had done the first book, *Island in the Sun-Side Two*—I really just kind of felt it's time to, like, throw certain vibes into the air or to get some dialogue going with the society. And I have always thought of that as a stage that a person who is writing will come to and will then make a decision about. I think it's possible to be a poet, to be a writer for yourself (as stupid as that sounds) and the writing just remains with you, and might be purely a means of clarifying your own inner life. I think that is just as valid as publishing; in some ways it's more valid. But there is also another role, another dimension that a person can decide to take on. The book was published in 1980, and the mindset it was coming out of was very much of the 1970s, of the writer as griot, the writer as the one that's going to engage the society and share insights with the society and get feedback. And also, I have had a very definite sense (which is there still) that in a lot of ways I was lucky to be born in St. Lucia, where even though hardly anybody really reads Walcott's poetry, there was still in a sort of a ghostly way, a sense of a literary tradition. So I felt that part of the reason I gravitated towards writing and found myself doing it was because the society I had grown up in had, in its own small way, said it was okay to do. I felt that there was a way in which I had to keep a tradition going. You know, if I hadn't grown up reading books of poems then I probably wouldn't be writing poetry. So in a way, I had to throw my books back out there again, and some other person, perhaps ten years younger than myself, would come across them and read them and would find that that's okay to do and would do it, so that the whole thing would be kept going.

But, honestly, as the years have gone on, I have just felt that self-publishing is, frankly, not worth the effort and time because of the toll it takes on your own feeling and your own sense of yourself and the sense of value of what you are doing. Because if you walk up and down the streets for how many months to collect a couple thousand dollars, even though at one level you know that what you doing, you believe it's important and necessary, you know, but you do start to wonder: well, okay, you think it's necessary, but, if people felt it was that necessary, would it be that difficult for you to accumulate the money for you to do it? After I did the last book, *Labyrinth*, at home I told myself that I would never self-publish again, and I don't think I ever will. So I am glad Peepal Tree Books is interested in this thing, because, for myself, I wouldn't self-publish again. And I mean, one can understand how a large publishing firm, a reputable publishing firm, would not take on the work of a writer who is entirely unknown or very, very little known. Certainly, one understands the economics of that. And because of that I really don't see any short-term alternative for some of the younger writers I see in St. Lucia but to self-publish. Once the work is good enough, I would encourage them to self-publish because they strengthen each other and they have to create an audience. But publishing is a pain, man. I have also been quite lucky, because work of mine has gone out without me making any serious efforts whatsoever. I mean, people have come across the self-publications here and there and have written to ask whether they could use this and that, and once it has appeared in one anthology, somebody else writes to ask to use the same one somewhere else, and then you can tell them you have another one.

KD: Images of the sea are inevitable features of your work. The sea is a curious entity, for it is a carrier of sorts. Later you ask the question, "Can you name a single wave you ever saw?" This implicit transience of the sea has been used by some Caribbean poets (David Dabydeen) to suggest a historylessness—a land/seascape that promises constant mutability and the possibility of new creativity from a "blank slate." Does that work for you as a kind of metaphorical encapsulation of the Caribbean context within which you write, or are you consciously working against such notions (notions of rootlessness and void) in your verse?

KH: I'm not consciously working against notions of rootlessness and void, partly because I think, from my perspective, that the whole historical question—historical roots, antecedents and so on—has been narrowed and politicized in a way which I don't think a lot of people actually experience on a day to-day basis. I mean, when I look around Castries, I don't really think that what people are walking around experiencing on a day-to-day basis is a sense of historical rootlessness. In other words, those people that I see around me every day, whether it's in school or the fellers who liming, you know, outside the house where I live; you know, the people I see around me in town and so on, I don't think that if over the next couple of years they were infused with a whole lot of information about their past, about the lives of the ancestors from before, or how the various peoples from the Caribbean came here and so on, that that would necessarily give them a different bedrock kind of feeling about themselves. I don't really think that that's what it's about. Even when Walcott talks about, say, the Caribbean as the place and possibility of new beginnings and so on—I mean that's closer to how I see it and yet to me, even that is like coming out of a consciousness of history and how history has influenced us, that I personally find too weighty. It may be stupid, but I really do not finally give all that much weight to history. I mean there is a way in which to me all history is parable, you know. All history is stories that illustrate principles about people; it's not really about this side winning and that side losing—this side the victor and that side the victim. That's not really, really, finally, what I think a useful sense of history is all about. So I mean, my concern with the history of the Caribbean, with the histories of the peoples who came to the Caribbean, arises in order for me to try to deepen my understanding of human motive, and for me to try to understand the impulses in my own self that make us behave in ways that give rise to the typical histories of the world. Things always come down to the individual. People experience their lives individually—even when you see yourself as part of a historical mass, part of a particular set of persons and so on. You still live your life individually, you know, *you* walking on your two legs and breathing the air through your nose, and it's *you* in the relationship with a particular person, and *you* dying on your deathbed. History can help you to understand your inner self, if you interpret it rightly. On the other hand, it can give you a whole lot of baggage to carry around if you don't watch it.

KD: When one speaks of form, the traditional associations are with Western poetic forms as models for good verse. Your verse is seemingly "free" in the tradition of much of the recent poetry from the Caribbean, but occasionally you indulge in a few set pieces: the "Villanelle for Blake" in *Bearings* comes to mind. Are you very self-conscious about form in your work, and how do you evolve a distinctive Caribbean form in your work?

KH: I am trying to puzzle out the sense in which you mean "self-conscious about form." I'm not self-conscious about it in the sense of being embarrassed by it. I give you the old cliché: "There is no such thing as free verse." Free verse is a form, if it's well done. If it is not well done, it's not even free verse — I don't know what the hell it is. I don't think of poems like, say, "Villanelle for Blake" as "set pieces." I think I have a kind of a completely unproven and maybe unprovable idea that these traditional forms, or any form, for that matter, while they are shapes, external shapes that we can see, they're also shapes of the mind itself. It's something that strikes me quite often when I read a really good sonnet. That a sonnet finally represents a particular kind of way in which the mind works. That's really what it *is*. I mean, we call it a poetic form, and externally, it is that in terms of literary theory and so on, but I think that at the level at which we most deeply live, what it is really is a kind of a minuscule example of an archetype, of a certain kind of a movement that the mind goes through when it's trying to work out things. And I think all poetic forms, to one degree or another, really represent particular twists and turns that the mind makes and must make when it's involved in exploring itself. I don't think consciously again of trying to create a Caribbean form. It comes back to the thing of audience. The people I am talking to are Caribbean people, and if I'm listening internally or just waiting internally for the poem to ring true, then I just have to have the faith that when it rings true, then that ringing true is going to ring true because of how it's gonna resonate in the psyches of Caribbean people. So I don't worry about that sort of programmatic or ideological aspect of it. The English language, like any language, has a history, and that history includes the various poetic shapes that have evolved within it, and if I inherit the language, which I have, then I inherit all those things as well, and they're mine as part of my legacy and I use it how I want, when I want. Hopefully, as I understand myself more deeply, I'll find ways of making these forms, and any other forms that I end up working with, ring in my mind and people's minds in ways that feel true, and maybe that might end up bending the shapes of them in certain ways. But I don't see a dichotomy between writing villanelles and writing what's referred to as free verse. It's all grist for the mill.

KD: To what extent do you feel that your physical connection with the landscape and with the voices of the Caribbean is critical to your work? Do you ever feel inclined to move away for a while or does the prospect fill you with a fear of losing a sense of voice or a rootedness in experience?

KH: At one time, I would have [felt fear]. Right now, no. I wouldn't mind, in a couple years from now, getting out for a couple of years. The landscape of the Caribbean is becoming more and more important to me, and yet not so much in the sense of the fact that it's Caribbean but as land, as nature. I mean, I find where my head is going now, what I find my thoughts turning to more and more is toward trying to understand how (and I don't mean a scientific how, I mean a psychological how) we came from this thing that we call the earth; what really is our connection with it. I find myself thinking more and more about the kind of categorizations that ancient philosophy uses, of earth and fire and water and air, and an understanding of the chain of being that we live in; from the mineral world to the world of plants, to the animals, to the world of humanity. And therefore, to me, there is a way in which I need to be looking at landscape around and really trying to see it and remember, in a kind of a way, the kind of enormous processes (for want of a better word) that have to go on, I mean millisecond by millisecond, to keep all this happening — the fact that trees grow, and wind blows. Just the complexity of scientific understanding that would have to happen to explain those things is mind-boggling and yet it's just happening. I keep thinking that there are ways in which what we call nature is one huge metaphor, and contains a set of metaphors within that metaphor. I find myself reading people like Wordsworth all over again or reading the Austrian poet, Rilke, all over again. And seeing more deeply how they were able to see parables in nature and how nature was presenting a set of parables about our existence. Not homilies, and not morals and so on, but I mean in a more twentieth-century existential way. So, yes, the Caribbean landscape is what I grew up with, it's what I understand and instinctively respond to most. So all the landscape that I always used to see around me, and love, is having for me, more and more, a meaning that is more personal and more philosophical. What I know I would like to see happen (but you can't force these things) is a kind of an understanding that would allow the landscape to illuminate the history that the Caribbean has gone through. I realize that sounds very, very, vague, but things have to be explained in the temporal realm of history as well as in the atemporal realm of the human psyche. And I think there is a way in which landscape in the Caribbean is a reflection of both of these worlds, and I would like to move towards an understanding of that and see if it can happen in the poetry. But I don't think if I moved away from the Caribbean for a few years that I would lose that connection. Because sometimes it feels more real to you when you think about it, when you remember it, than when you are actually looking at it.

Jane King
BORN 1952

BORN IN ST. LUCIA, Jane King moved with her family during her early childhood to Trinidad, Tobago, Barbados, and Scotland. After completing her high school education at St. Joseph's Convent in St. Lucia, she was determined to attend a university as far away from St. Lucia as possible, and opted to go to the University of Edinburgh in Scotland. She returned to St. Lucia to teach at the Sir Arthur Lewis Community College in Castries. She was one of the founding members of the Lighthouse Theater Company along with her husband, Kendel Hippolyte.

Thematically, her poetry offers intriguing insight into issues of race, identity, and gender, and the delicately wrought playfulness to her tone in many of her poems suggests an inclination toward irony and self-reflexivity. The themes of poems in her two volumes, *Into the Centre* ([St. Lucia], 1990) and *Fellow Traveller* (Sandberry Press, 1994), include a sophisticated examination of male-female relationships, the place of women in society, and the complex issues of death and the afterlife. Jane King began *Fellow Traveller* while holding a Witter Bynner fellowship at the Yaddo artist colony in New York in 1992; she completed it while she was holder of the James Michener Fellowship at the Caribbean Writers Summer Institute at the University of Miami in 1993.

She is working on new poetry for another volume of poems, and continues to live and teach in St. Lucia.

KWAME DAWES: The first thing that struck me about your work is your clear commitment to the rhyming line. There is something that this quality of your verse says about poetic influence and your attitude to form and structure in verse. Can you talk a bit about these things in relation to your poetry?

JANE KING: I know that before I started showing anybody my poetry I never really bothered about form at all. Most of the stuff that I hid under the bed or threw away, in fact, was free verse. So, I mean, I am very much aware that form was something that came later. That said, I do have a very strong commitment to form of one kind or another. Partly because I am only beginning to analyze in my free verse what it is that I am doing as opposed to just saying things. The difference between poetry and prose is what I'm talking about, really: whether the ideas are more important than the form or whether the form is more important than the ideas. I am saying this very badly. The poet I pick, then, would be someone like Gerard Manley Hopkins. When I did my A-levels and studied him, I was very, very struck by how much the man needed form. His sonnets are so good, and in "Deutschland," a long poem, the verse format is very tightly crafted. It seems to me that when Hopkins didn't give himself a tight form, he ended up making a terrible mess which nobody really wanted to read. And so when I wanted other people to start reading my poems, I was very conscious of not wanting to do that. It doesn't mean that I always wanted to stick to standard forms, but I do find that I often make little forms for myself and stick to them from verse to verse. I think "Neighbors" is the first poem in which I actually did that. It was done for a workshop for Walcott when he had suggested that free verse has to be like jazz and there had to be an underlying form that you can take off from. So I decided that why not invent a little form. And I did it a lot with poems like "Negative Space" and "Postulant" and stuff like that. My favorite poets, the people I like to read most, are in fact people who use form and structure, and I suppose that's relevant to the answer. In terms of modern poetry, I really, really like Elizabeth Jennings and Tom Gunn. I'm not kidding when I say I would like to be able to write like Yeats had come again. I do love Hopkins as well. The poets that I like absolutely the best are the poets who do deal in structures.

KD: In "Of Men and Mermaids" the persona says, "I must heal myself. / I must swim in sunset waters." This poem then ends, "this poem would / implode into godness. // Love is the way," suggesting that poetry, "the healer's Art," is what you are philosophizing about in the piece. I would like you to talk about what the poetic instinct has to do with healing. Is your inclination to write poetry part of a process of self-actualizing your own healing; and in the process, the healing of others?

JK: Yes, poetry is healing. Yes, at a very simple level, as a child, when I became fascinated with poetry, I first started (and it seems probably everybody does) really getting drawn to poems where you think, "Oh yes, that's what I was thinking about; really, that's exactly what I think only I couldn't have said it that well." And it was a sense of being not alone, if you like, because it was usually in areas that were a problem for me, and I could say, "Well, somebody else has felt like that. I am not crazy." Or maybe, "I'm crazy but there are other crazy people out there," which is kind of nice. Poetry as my own healing? Well, that is a particular poem about healing; healing isn't quite what I would think of it as, although it obviously follows from it. I think of it as . . . let me see: my favorite metaphor being the artesian well, but I have never managed to articulate it; but I have a very strong sense of it. I come across it in places like Virginia Woolf's *The Waves* and in various other pieces of literature, and I suppose Jungian collective unconsciouses and that kind of thing. I have a very strong feeling that if you go down deep enough into the human being, you find that we are all the same, that we are all from the same source. If I was going to get really heavy today, I would even call it God or something like that. But if we dig down deep enough we will discover that we are all from the same source and that source can manifest itself through art and at particular times through various art forms. I believe that's the value of art. I mean, obviously there is frivolous stuff, and I have written frivolous stuff, but at root, what it really is is a manifestation of the source of all of us, and if that is done truly then I think that yes, it can be a source of healing, even if it is just the type of recognition that I was talking about: that other people have felt the same way. I like the well metaphor because it always leads back to form and shape. Wells gush. The artesian well that springs up does come up in a particular shape, as fountains can be crafted to come up in particular shapes. So the poem becomes something that has to have a shape, if it is to hold the spark of the origin, which is what real poetry is to be about.

KD: In some of your poems, you position yourself as an observer, a kind of voyeur of the folk, looking and writing down. But this role does not sit easily with the poet, it seems. It is as if you are always aware of the mammoth responsibility that you have as an observer of society. Is this a fair assessment? I am really asking you to talk about the challenges inherent in the statement: "And I'm a spy, when I look down at them, when / I try to chronicle their daily life in pen."

JK: Did I say "look down" in the poem? It's interesting because it sounds very politically incorrect, when in actual fact it is simply the way the view from the window is structured. But that said, there is an element of pure chance and the geography of the house involved, but there is also a sense of myself as an outsider. That's true. I have always felt that. It's always been very difficult. Growing up "pale" in the Caribbean has always made me feel outside of things. People have made me feel that way. I mean, my mother is English, which means that I wasn't growing up straight Caribbean pale; there is the extra dimension of outsideness. But I suspect that most writers, probably most artists, do feel themselves outside in some kind of way. And they probably wouldn't be writing if they didn't. So I don't think it's necessarily a terribly bad thing to be of the people but not completely of them — of the people but slightly obliquely, so that one can look and perhaps see things that one doesn't see immediately when one looks at one's familiar life.

I am sure that Jane King as human being would be far happier if she could just blend in with the mob and nobody could ever notice her. Like with Walcott, I want to say "I am your poet. YOURS!" I think it's probably necessary for poets to feel different. I don't think I have ever met a poet who didn't feel different in some sort of way, whatever the reason for the difference may be, and I suppose different poets have different reasons for feeling different. Maybe it's like pearls and oysters and you don't get the pearl unless the oyster has something making it itch. Whatever the itch is, it's uncomfortable for the oyster, but if it doesn't have it, it won't produce the pearl.

KD: The mermaid appears to be an important figure in your verse. It manifests itself in direct reference, but more tellingly in the casting of the poet as singer and of the song as a source of spell-binding or spell-making — conjuring if you will. There is something assertive and radical about the ownership of the woman poet as "siren" and "witch" in your verse. So that, unlike in [Lorna] Goodison's verse in which the mermaid figure is a negative one — a kind of sterile, sexless creature—your mermaid appears empowered and sweetly dangerous. Do you agree with this? Is there evidence here of how you handle the portrayal of the female in your verse?

JK: When you look at my more recent work you'll find lots more "negative" females in the sense of more sort of torn open woman and secreting women—perhaps less pleasant views of women. Yes, mermaids aren't negative to me; mermaids are very sexy, poetry is sexy. Singing is important. And yes, the mermaid is a kind of a siren singer. In the first of the mermaid poems, which is the one you already quoted about "imploding into godness," I was obviously thinking of the Little Mermaid who gave up her mermaidness so that she could try and capture the prince. I mean she got legs and every step it was as if she was walking on glass and so on. And so clearly she was whole when she was a mermaid, before she fell in love and got distracted by love and men and all those problems. So the mermaid was very whole and virginal, sexy but virginal. And similarly, I think in the "Dream Poem," where mermaids are all Lilith's daughters, there is a sense in which the mermaid trades her tail for legs; she splits herself wide open and she then can people the world, but she has lost her wholeness. That's why she was Lilith's daughter, because when she was a mermaid she was refusing to lie with any man. So that, yes, she's a figure of spellbinding innocence and all the rest of it, but she knows she has to give that up and she has to become split and then find some other way of working towards some other form of integration. There is a problem with men and women in the Caribbean, and my poetry, insofar as it has that sort of focus, does have, from time to time, political concerns about the problems between men and women. I think it's the big rift in the Caribbean at the moment. It would be nice to think that that was healable. If that's what you mean. And I think women are less troubled before they start looking for men. I mean, a lot of the problems between women are problems because of men. But there's also a metaphor of death and rebirth in the mermaid splitting. The "Mandala Dream Song #3" has it in the dismembered god—I was thinking of Dionysus. I think that's the mermaid figure. As for spells, and witches, and enchantments, yes, yes, yes. Part of the fact that I think that poetry comes from that very deep place means that I think it's very possible that poems are spells and enchantments. In my very worst moments, I have even written curse poems, but I have torn them up and thrown them away because actually I am afraid of them. I have to be in a very bad way to do that.

KD: In a number of your poems you suggest that writing poetry involves *hearing* poems or ideas for poems in dreams and visions. The effect is a metaphysical and mystical rationalization or de-rationalization of the creative process. And yet there is an intense craft at work in your verse. Do you find that these two seemingly conflicting elements are a source of tension in your writing process?

JK: Only when I'm not dreaming. Dreams are very important to me, and dream images do find their way into my poems. I have a stack of dream poems that I have not published. I suspect one of these days I'm gonna do a dream poem book by itself so that people aren't too startled by the weirdness of it. There are quite a lot of the dream poems at the end of *Into the Centre*, I guess. The haiku that opens the poem about the slave ships: "Thousands of birds / are flying / through an orchard"—that is a haiku that I dreamed whole with a picture that went with it, but I couldn't manage to work the picture into anything, but it will get there one of these days. I don't know how "de-rational" it is; if one can dream a haiku, then one's subconscious is behaving reasonably rationally—because I dreamed it with the lineation and everything correct. I think dreams are telling us a lot more than we know. I start with phrases out of dreams perhaps, sometimes, and then work towards finding a crafted poem. I think when one is really working, in a period when one can be writing a lot over a period of time, then everything starts to come together, and the dreams start feeding the waking life and the dreams get a coherence and rationality which obviously I don't think is irrational at all.

KD: What is your writing process like? Do you compose in your head before putting pen to paper? Are you committed to writing on a daily basis for a certain length of time or are you driven by what we call "inspiration"?

JK: All of the above. Yes, there are poems that I think have been pure inspiration, and yes, there are poems that have been absolutely whole in my head before I put them onto paper. "Fellow Traveller" is one of those that was completely whole in my head before I put a single word of it on paper and I hardly changed it at all after that. It doesn't always happen. Sometimes I just write down phrases, sometimes I write really bad poems which I then go back and say, "Well that's a horrible poem, but it's got really nice phrases, it's got nice something or the other; let me see if I can rewrite it," or "This is a poem that is a wrong form, let me see if it would work as a sonnet, let me see if it would work as something else." There've been a couple of times in my life where I have been lucky enough to get a chunky period, you know a month maybe, where I can do what I like and what I do then, I have a method. The poet, Claudia Rankine, who says all she needs to write is to be able to sleep as long as she wants and not have to talk to anyone in the morning. I think that's a brilliant quotation. I keep using it. Yes, so I sleep as long as I want, I refuse to talk to anyone in the morning, and I just write. Now, when that happens what I do is some days I get good poems straightaway, some days I just get complete and utter garbage; and I may get complete and utter garbage for two days, and then sooner or later the poem starts to shape itself. Now, it's probably important to say that I am not sitting down to say I'm going to write a poem about X. I was at Yaddo [writers' colony] at one stage and there was a poet who said, "This morning I am going to write a pastoral sonnet and tomorrow I'll write a . . ." and so on. I don't. I just sit there and let what comes come, and quite often it is conditioned by things that are lying around the room. I mean, like when I did "Negative Space" and I had that verse about "did you stuff your womb with paper / to make it hold its shape?" it was because there was a big pile of paper there that I had just taken out of a handbag that I'd just bought, and I mean the image came out of the room. And similarly, a lot of the "neighbor" poems arrive because we are in an upstairs house on the top of a hill. If somebody is outside making a noise, that noise is likely to find its way into my poem, and obviously it then becomes a metaphor for something else that is going on inside of my head. But it all comes from what is going on around me at the time.

KD: When do you determine that a poem is finished? Mervyn Morris likes to speak of "finding the poem" in the midst of a lot of words. Is this how you edit?

JK: Yeah, sometimes I will sift through ten pages of garbage and say okay, this is a lovely phrase, this is a nice little couplet, this is whatever, and I will pull that out and work on it. I love the way Mervyn says "All right, let's take off the first three verses, take out all this bottom bit and, there, these four lines, that's the poem." I determine it's finished when I figure I can't do nothing else with it. And then sometimes I find that's not true. I have gone and put it out somewhere and I think, "Yuck! If I'd just crossed out that word!" But at the time, I think I am never gonna do anything else with this; it ain't perfect, but it's the best I can do with this particular piece so I just have to let it go as it is.

How do I edit? Not as carefully as I should. I don't know, I just fiddle around until I think I have got it right. I mean, if I'm in workshops, I listen to other people, and mainly, I listen to know whether they are getting what I intend. That's what bothers me and that's what I like about workshops. If somebody is going to grossly misinterpret something, then I will go back and edit it until I think it says more precisely what I really, really want to say.

KD: Landscape is important in your verse, but it is often a landscape that is not static: it becomes personified, it moves, reflects the people on it. You resist landscape that is there simply for decorative purposes. Can you talk a bit about how the St. Lucian landscape has affected your writing? How much do you rely on being in a given space when you are writing?

JK: Well, I'll answer the last bit first. No, I don't rely on being in a given space, but as I said before, the space that I am in is going to affect what goes into the poem. I mean, what I really need for writing is time, not particular spaces. But the space will condition the poem. I mean, most of my most recent poems have been written in fact in Miami or at Yaddo, I suppose. There's a chunk of them in *In the Centre* that were written when I did a sort of little writers' colony thing in our own backyard the year I wrote "Kingston Ramble." St. Lucian landscape is tremendously important to me because it is my home landscape. I don't seem to feel terribly impelled to describe it in any great detail, but it's there, it's very much there for me. "Moments" is the poem I think of, but then again, perhaps nobody recognizes that "Moments" is about St. Lucian landscape and the importance of it. I've got bits and pieces of poems that have more landscape that just aren't finished yet. The things that I see around me tend to have to sort of fit themselves into the metaphors that I'm playing with and it's not that I'm not doing landscape, it will happen one of these days if it needs to. I don't have the Walcott thing about giving things their names and so on. I feel quite well-named as it is.

KD: In "How Not to Write a Poem," you point out one of the pitfalls of verse that is fixated on form (rhyme, meter, etc.). Can you tell me your philosophy about the poem as sound-fixated/driven? Is it sound first or are the "thoughts and feelings" more important?

JK: Well, when I wrote "How Not to Write a Poem," it was just a wicked little piece of slander for Kendel [Hippolyte] and Robert [Lee] who are forever telling me that form was what was important and content is really (I felt they were saying) negligible compared to form. So I just thought I would be a little bit rude to them. But, no, obviously one needs both. I mean, you don't want to be a technically perfect poet who has got absolutely nothing to say. You want to sense that there is something to say. But I really feel what I am trying to do when I am working at my best is I am really trying to dredge as deep down into myself and to find the right shape. I think I wrote it in some poem somewhere or the other, about the waiting urn/vase of one only possible shape. That the two have to come together as one thing—the form and the content have to be one thing. You cannot separate the two. And of course I love sound and that's why I am always talking about singing and mermaids and being Yeats and Crazy Jane, and I want the poems to sing, I want music in them.

KD: When did you begin to write poetry and why?

JK: I can remember writing verses to put on my Granny's Christmas cards when I was five or six. I mean practically as soon as I could write, I was doing something, whether you could call it poetry or not; most of it was pretty garbage. But little verses. I love rhyming. Rhymes come very easily and naturally to me. After that, one goes through that revolting adolescent period of needing to do it because one is all tangled and mangled and meshed and conflicted and miserable and one feels that if one vomits enough of it out on a page it will somehow magically straighten out one's head. Adolescent poetry as therapy. And then you just keep on trucking. I think the deeper reasons, I've already spoken about. The spiritual needs of one's self and other people and the need for exploration and so on.

KD: What impact did your time in the U.K. have on your writing and your will to write?

JK: It made me keep it very much to myself because I felt, in any case, so much was already being done, there was no need for some little Caribbean person to come along and do very much else. I mean, as I say, I was in Scotland, and Scotland, Edinburgh. Edinburgh is a very interesting city. I had no idea how to access markets or anything or whether any markets would be interested in me. I mean I never felt there would be so I just kept it all to myself and did a lot of reading and going to a lot of theater and going to a lot of film. It was a very, very important educational time for me. I mean it broadened me tremendously. And I wouldn't have missed the kind of education you get from art galleries (Edinburgh has wonderful art galleries, marvelous theater). That was all very important, but it didn't really make me publish. I do remember feeling very, very strongly when I came home again in 1981; I do remember then, within a couple of months, having a sense of, "My God, this island needs theater, it needs books, it needs . . . And if we don't do it, it isn't gonna get done." You know, a sense of, all right, jump in there with both feet and start helping out with theatrical productions. It has to be done because there is a spiritual death going on. It is very, very, very frightening to me that, okay, people go to church on Sunday and think that's it. The spirit doesn't need anything else, and they are dying out there. And so it was, in fact, coming back from the U.K. out of that great wealth of cultural exploration and the fascinating experiments that were going on. Theater companies like 784, for instance, in Scotland. Not yet ready to publish as a poet, but I was an artistic person who had to take some responsibility to put something into the island.

KD: What are your future projects in verse? Do you have directions that you want the poetry to take?

JK: I wanna do more and more. I'm in the process of giving up an upper administrative job which has been eating up all my time and making me think and behave like a little corporate American executive and I want space and time. I wanna get back into teaching and so on. I want to read more poetry. I want to use my summers to write more poetry. What comes comes. I will just keep doing more of the self-exploration in whatever context I find myself and letting context work through me and make shapes for me. I have a kind of a confidence at this stage that simply using that kind of process will make something happen. And that every time you do it, it gets more and more important, I feel.

Opal Palmer Adisa

BORN 1954

OPAL PALMER ADISA was born and grew up in Jamaica. After high school she traveled to the United States, where she undertook college studies in New York. She returned to Jamaica in the mid-1970s, where she was employed with the government as an education officer for the Educational Broadcasting Service in Jamaica. While there, she worked with Jamaican poet Mervyn Morris on several writing initiatives, including an outreach effort for creative expression with prison inmates in Kingston. In 1979 she moved to California.

She works variously and simultaneously as a storyteller, an artistic director, a community organizer and activist, a creative collaborator and facilitator for many writers and performers, and as a published author. She has published short stories, poetry collections, and one novel to date.

Her *Tamarind and Mango Women* (Sister Vision, 1992) won the PEN Oakland–Josephine Miles Award. Her other publications include *Pina, The Many-Eyed Fruit* (Julian Richardson, 1985), *Bake-Face and Other Guava Stories* (Kelsey Street Press, 1986), and *Traveling Women* (Jukebox Press, 1989), which she coauthored with Devorah Major. Her stories and essays were included in *Daughters of Africa* (Pantheon, 1992) and *Caribbean Women Writers* (Calaloux, 1990). She lives and writes in Oakland, California.

KWAME DAWES: In an early poem, "Will the Real Island Please Stand Up," you offer a litany of woes about a paradise blasted by poverty and exploitation in your description of Jamaica. Yet the poem ends with a certain ambivalence—"still I can't leave connected through birth pains." But you did leave. What were the circumstances and feelings surrounding your departure from Jamaica? There's a sense in which the poem is still true, isn't there?

OPAL PALMER ADISA: I can never leave Jamaica, certainly not spiritually. And that's what the poem expresses—the inability to leave spiritually even though because of the socioeconomic conditions one has to leave. I wrote the poem shortly after I left in '79, I think, and came to California. And when I left Jamaica in '79, I left rather unhappy. I had gone back to Jamaica in '76 after five years of college in New York, very optimistic, wanting to make changes. I discovered the gap that existed between myself and Jamaica, the Jamaica that I grew up in when I left and this new one. When I left I was just sixteen and I returned when I was just a little over twenty. And while I was aware of the class, color boundaries, and the way in which, certainly at that time, people didn't cross over, I didn't expect to confront it. Basically, what I felt on returning in '76 and leaving in '79 was that there was no place for me. That I felt very much Jamaican, and yet I was being accused of bringing my Americanism there. I wasn't aware that I was Americanized, and I don't think I was. But also at that time the island was going through tremendous change. Violence had started in the early '70s, and by '79 was in full swing. And I began to witness some social ills that belie independence—certainly, what I thought about as independence. So the poem, in a sense, was dealing with certain issues. It was asking where is this independence. The title even says that: "Will the Real Island Please Stand Up." I was saying, I want to see this other part of Jamaica. This other part of Jamaica standing tall, you know, with its head, its head high. This Jamaica that is not denying a segment of its population who are for the most part black and working class and poor. I wanted that part of Jamaica to stand up. And I wanted those of us who are more privileged, either because of education or because we were raised middle-class, to help Jamaica stand up. So that's what that poem was. Yes, I left, but in one way I never left and can never leave Jamaica. There's another poem of mine that talks about the fact that, you know, Jamaica's in my blood. Because of the banana, the salt fish, and the people. I was raised there, culturally, socially, in every way. I am Jamaican. And so my departure was fraught with disappointment, anger, and frustration at the classism that prevailed.

Vexation characterized my feelings that those of us who were middle-class and who were educated seemed to be doing very little to bring about true transformation, that somehow we had believed the lie, as I saw it, that somehow having a flag and a national anthem meant that we were independent. And it seemed to me in so many ways that we were near colonialism. We were not even celebrating the cultural nuances of Jamaica. And yes, the poem is still true. I'm still waiting, and still optimistic, because that happens to be my disposition. I'm still optimistic that the real Jamaica will stand up and until it does, you see, none of us have any right to celebrate. Until the poorest people in the most rural areas of Jamaica (like in St. James where my mother comes from, where many people still don't have running water or electricity) until those people can celebrate Jamaica and not eke out a living, eke out an existence, have to walk fifteen to twenty miles without a bus to get to the hospital, or for a dentist; until there are schools for all the children, and kids won't be eliminated by the ten-plus or the eleven-plus [examination] because there are no spaces. The social conditions are worse. It's all of those litanies which unfortunately continue, nonstop, and which still force a good section of the population to leave, to not be able to find a place, to not be able to build, to not be able to make this real island stand up.

I go home often. I try to go home every two years. My youngest child who's four said, when I got her from preschool, "Mommy, my friends didn't know that my brother and I are Jamaican." So I laughed, because she really believes she's a Jamaican, though she was born here in California. And I do speak to my children in the Jamaican language, I don't refer to it as Patois and I don't particularly like the academic term "Creole"; I rather like the notion of a Nation Language. So I speak the Jamaican Nation Language to my kids and my kids know it. They can speak it to me in their own way. And there are times when we're relaxing and having a wonderful time, and they speak it because that's a part of who they are. They love ackee and saltfish and dumpling and all of that stuff because that's what I cook. And they love going to Jamaica, they love the freedom of Jamaica. There's a certain amount of ambivalence that I'm having now, because I feel that my kids need to be in Jamaica, or at least they need to be in what I perceive to be a black environment that's not so hostile to who they are. And yet, in many ways, I don't feel I can go to Jamaica, because I go to Jamaica and my mother doesn't even want me to sit on the verandah. And even on the verandah, I feel imprisoned because there are burglar bars. And so in some ways I don't feel imprisoned here. You know, on the one hand, there's that sense of freedom, and openness, and on the other hand, there's a tremendous sense of imprisonment, enclosure, because middle-class people and poor people who have a little are trying to protect themselves from the tremendous rampant and nondirected violence that is prevalent in the society. And, of course, the cost of living is so exorbitant that I couldn't even think about going there to live. And so there's a part of me that mourns the fact that I can't give my children the Jamaica that I had, you know.

KD: I am drawn to your love poems both for their unabashed sensuality and for their doggedness about dismantling traditional dichotomies that are placed between notions of love and romance and notions of politics. In many ways, your love poems achieve what Marley achieves in his "love songs," "No Woman No Cry" and "Is This Love?" You are breaking stereotypes constantly. Is this something you are consciously striving to do?

OPA: Yes. I do wonder why more poems by Caribbean women writers specifically (although I think there's a parallel even with the men) do not celebrate love and sexuality in the way in which I think it is celebrated in North America. Certainly growing up in Jamaica, and going to Jamaica, people were always having sex. People were always sensual and sexual. But it's the kind of thing that happens all the time but doesn't get talked about. It's like the way we dance and grind. I happen to love sex, you know, on many different levels. And it's one of the things that I want to celebrate in my work because it's an important part of who I am as a woman. I would like to think that I am a very sexual and sensual woman. And I want to shatter the notion that a woman can't talk about deriving tremendous pleasure from having sex or sexual encounters that are not somehow coated in love and marriage and these other traditional ways in which women are allowed to express love.

Yes, what I want to do in my writing—and I think this is happening more in my novel, in my prose—is in fact to break tradition. I don't want to write to toe the line. I'm constantly asking myself questions and I'm trying (but I haven't found it yet) to find the language and the route through which to expose myself, for want of a better word. Oh, God, does that sound narcissistic? When I say expose myself, not expose myself personally, but expose the womanness of myself and the Caribbean woman that I've always known, both in the Caribbean and here. I think sexuality and sensuality are still areas that we shy away from, that we still seem to think should be relegated to the private, domestic sphere. And I'm saying, "To hell with that." In addition to being private and domestic, it is also very public. Because I know when I walk on the street, and I feel men's eyes eating into me, or I'm feeling particularly sexy because I hear some music or I'm just feeling good about my body, and I just bounce a little bit more. Particularly if I see somebody I want to tease. You know, in the Caribbean, we're very flirtatious. We're always teasing and touching each other. Men and women, women and women, men and men. So there is that kind of sensuality that prevails in that environment and yet I'm hard-pressed to find that in the literature. And I'm saying, why? In the Caribbean we talk with our hands. Some people in North America find that disturbing with me, because it doesn't matter who you are, man or woman, and I'm sitting down beside you and I'm talking to you, I'm going to be touching you. You know, I'll be touching you on your arm, leg, wherever my hand falls. That's sexual, that's sensual. Yes, and I want to shatter the notion of sex and sensuality as being restricted to the erotic or being restricted to a private act. I think in the Caribbean it's very public, and it's displayed in numerous ways all throughout the society. And part of what I do in my writing is to point to these instances, these numerous instances where sensuality and sexuality meet in a kind of explosive flamboyance.

KD: In your poetry you clearly position yourself as part of a feminist, womanist sensibility that is deeply rooted in an African American sensibility. This is not mere polemics; indeed, it emerges in your literary allusions, your "samplings," if you will, of other African American women like Ntosake Shange, Toni Morrison, and a host of other witnesses in poems that evoke the power of African American women. But your poetic influences are more expansive and not entirely defined by gender. There are echoes of Brathwaite everywhere, as well. Can you talk about influences a bit?

OPA: Let me just go back to the beginning here and say, yes, I consider myself a feminist or a womanist. I think I prefer (I think it is Walker who uses that term) "womanist." Or in Jamaica we say "womanish," you know, when a girl child approaches adolescence. And certainly much of my attitude toward feminism or womanism comes from Jamaica, comes specifically from my mother, who was a forerunner, and it comes from, and was embedded in, the word *talawah*. I was always referred to as little but *talawah*. And that word refers to a woman who irrespective of her size is fierce, is independent. Or there is the term "big woman." When a woman in Jamaica says she's a big woman, it's not about size. It's about her clearly defined economic and emotional independence from men. It is saying, "I can take care of myself, I will not be beholden to anyone. I am a big woman. I am independent." So my feminism and my womanism is rooted in Jamaica. It's rooted in observing those market women. It comes across in the poem "Market Woman." It is the Granny Nannies, the market women who have influenced me.

Kamau Brathwaite is a dear friend. And certainly, when I went back home to Jamaica in '76, he and Mervyn Morris took me into their folds, and I consider them both very dear, dear friends. Whenever I go home, I would never go home and not see Mervyn. We have our customary little lunch or whatever—just talk shop. I haven't been influenced so much by Mervyn's poetry because I always perceived him more as a scholar than a poet. Definitely by Brathwaite, you know. Definitely by Brathwaite. Other influences. When I came back to the USA in '79 and decided to pursue a graduate degree in creative writing, it was Neruda's fabulous sense of language, tremendous sensuality and sexuality and eroticism that informed much of my poems. Well, I was trying to imitate him, let's put it that way. I was trying to look at his absolutely chiseled use of language. I love his work. So he was a big influence. And then much later I discovered Margaret Walker's poems, and I think she's also a very fabulous poet. I particularly like her narrative work, because I think a lot of my stuff is narrative. And Lucille Clifton, who I can't touch. You know, I am long-winded, and Lucille Clifton gets to the heart and meat and soul of stuff with brevity. She has mastered that. And I haven't mastered that at all. And I dare say I probably won't. I think I've been influenced a lot more so by fiction or prose than by poetry. I read a lot, I think in general I read more fiction than I do poetry. So I was influenced a lot by fiction writers, such as Vic Reid, whose work I like, Samuel Selvon, Roger Mais (I really like Roger Mais). So I don't think there's a singular tradition that has informed me, but I think in terms of poetics, the writers who inform my poems are, in fact, Brathwaite, Neruda, Margaret Walker, Lucille Clifton, Sonia Sanchez, Langston Hughes. I studied Claude McKay and read him for my master's oral, but I can't say his poetics influenced me primarily because he wrote the sonnet, and that didn't appeal to me as a form.

KD: How have you coped with the pressure to silence the sexuality of language and poetic expression, as in poems such as "Feeding," pressure placed on you by your own upbringing, by society, by the tradition of poetic expression you may have grown up with?

OPA: Because I'm a rebel. I don't give a damn. And that might sound somewhat flip, but in many ways it's true. I hated being told as a child to be a lady. My mother drilled it into me, and I didn't want to be a lady because all the ladies I saw seemed to have absolutely boring lives. And I often wonder, those women who didn't have men, my God maybe that was the reason they were so miserable—you know I had some teachers who were spinsters and mean—was because they needed a good piece, kind of stuff. In fact, a couple friends of mine, Jamaican friends, two male friends, said I speak about sex like a man. I don't know if that's complimentary or not. But I just hated the restriction imposed on women, you know. I absolutely detested it, I absolutely hate and hated having to wait for men to make the move because I was quite capable and able to make the first move and why the hell should I have to wait for any man? I'm rebelling against my upbringing that I thought was Victorian, that I thought did women a disservice and repressed us in a very fundamental way by directing how much pleasure we would have, because that's really what sensuality and sexuality is all about. It's about pleasure. And if you say to a woman, good women or ladies don't do this, then what you are in fact doing is denying woman pleasure. And I will not be denied pleasure. Straight up the line, I will absolutely not be denied pleasure. Because it's just too wonderful. You know, I think life is very short. And I do believe in pleasure

Well, certainly, my mother does not like this poem, "Feeding." Actually, I think that she likes it, but it frightens her, because she was never able to express that publicly. You know, I remember when I got my period, how she took me in her room with the curtains drawn and told me absolutely nothing. Oh, I'm a woman now and if I let boys play with me I'll get pregnant. Whoop-dee-do! You know, who the hell told me that sex was pleasurable? They said keep your legs closed. But they didn't say, "and be a virgin," which was what my mother said to me. And nobody explained to me that okay, maybe I should be a virgin, but a boy I like, if he touches me a certain way, I'm going to feel damn good. And maybe I shouldn't respond to it, even though it feels good. So you can imagine the, not so much confusion, but the pull it was. On the one hand, being told that you should be a virgin till you get married (and certainly for a very long time I prescribed to that). I just assumed that that's what a woman should be; and on the other hand, meeting boys, liking them, and having them touch me and feeling this absolute fire burning in my body and thinking that maybe I'm not such a good person after all because I'm not supposed to feel this way. And finally I resolved it, like, this was the secret: they wanted you to be a virgin because they didn't want you to have fun. They didn't want you to explore your body and the kinds of absolute pleasure that you could derive from your body. So, yeah, I'm a rebel. And I don't care if people say that I'm preoccupied with sex. A couple of people have said that. I say, "Yes, I am preoccupied with sex. Sex is damn good." I don't mind being preoccupied with it.

KD: Your encounter with Africa in your poetry is complex. There is celebration but there is also hurt. At what point do you think you came into a sense of Africa in your development as a writer? Did you go through various changes before arriving at this seemingly Pan-Africanist anxiety ideology that permeates your writing?

OPA: I don't think so, no. I came to Africa through Egypt and I came to it when I was about eight or somewhere between eight and ten. My mother's younger brother who was an artist in Jamaica (he's now dead), Lloyd Walcott, had decided he wanted to be an artist. And while he was getting it together, he was living with my mother and us. We lived just outside of Spanish Town. We had a big lawn in the front, and he would set up his easel and set up an easel for me, and I would attempt to paint, imitating him. And he would talk to me about Egypt. And I knew Egypt was in Africa. So we would dream and talk about going to Egypt. And at that time, I think for me Africa was Egypt and Ethiopia. Because there were Rastafarians who were in tune with Ethiopia and then there was my uncle who was talking about Egypt. I don't remember seeing any art books or any images of Africa. I remember the first time I made the connection with Africa was . . . God, when was it? Whenever the World's Fair was in New

York. My mother took my sister and I to the World's Fair in New York for vacation. And I remember when we were at the World's Fair, we saw a number of people who were Africans in African dress. And these Africans had their hair parted and twisted and it stuck out. I remember thinking how absolutely beautiful that was. So I think there was a part of my family and the circle that I was in, where Africa was always home. It wasn't England. I never perceived of England as the mother country, although I said it. England was never real to me, ironically, but Africa was.

And of course, when I left Jamaica and went to New York, in college I became involved in a group, I think we called ourselves Students against Imperialism. And one of the things we looked at was colonialism of Africa and the Caribbean. And it was there that I also realized my nationalistic posture as a Jamaican. The Caribbean became real to me. I realized that there was not that much difference between us, and we shouldn't be talking about Jamaicans and Trinidadians and Barbadians, being so nationalistic, we should be more regionalistic. And then I discovered Africa. And Africa now became a real place, a real map, with real countries. My older brother had turned me on to Nkrumah and I was turned on to Fanon, and to C. L. R. James's work. You know, I studied the Harlem Renaissance and the Negritude movement. That was Pan-Africanism. That's where I was. That's where I located myself. But for a long time, I didn't want to blame Africa for me being out. Africa was blameless. And so it took on another kind of nationalism. Africa then became romanticized. You know, we were descendants from queens and kings, that kind of stuff. And I think that's an important process for black people in the Diaspora who were oppressed. They need to understand that they are kings and queens, but most of us didn't descend from kings and queens, you know. We were on the bottom of the totem pole; that's why we got sold. And I wanted Africa to acknowledge that blame and that hurt and that pain and that something very wrong was happening in that society for it to have sold so many of us and forgot about us like it did. And that's what hurt. That's the pain of that connection that hurts. You know, and I think the movie *Sankofa* attempts to address that pain—that they sold us and forgot about us. And in fact, when I went to Nigeria in '86 (I went to East and West Africa in '86 for six weeks), I was speaking to an old man in Nigeria in one of these villages where slaves were sold. He said to me, as we were standing by the seashore, "I didn't know people who look like me were in Jamaica." And it was like he turned a knife in me. Jesus Christ, people, you sold me, and then you forgot about me! You turned your goddamn backs on me. You know? That pain is real. I don't know what can heal that pain—a monument? I think that's why black people in the Diaspora are in such turmoil. It's because we have no monuments to commemorate slavery. We have no shores on which we have stacked the boats. There's no place we have etched the names. We haven't mourned. So the poems that deal with those themes are a mourning. Mourning for what I lost. The fact that Nigerians in particular, once they discovered I wasn't them, because I didn't speak the language, would use the same goddamn word which I've just forgotten that means "white" for me, and that hurts. You know what I'm saying? That hurts and I want them to acknowledge it. While it is true that many of them didn't participate in selling me, and while it is true even those who actively advocated selling me didn't understand the system that they were selling me into, I still want them to say "I'm sorry," to say, "forgive me," to say, "I did wrong," to say, "I was greedy, and in my greed, I forgot about you. And you are my sister and my brother and my cousin and my child. And I embrace you even though we no longer speak the same language." So the complexity of the poem is the complex relationship I feel with Africa. That there will always be a part of Africa that is lost to me. We all want the white man to take responsibility, to own the fact that they enslaved us and they still enslave us, you know? Well, I want Africans to do the same thing. I want Africans to do the same thing.

KD: And is this view of Africa related to your treatment of Rasta in "Ethiopia and the Mango Tree"?

OPA: "Ethiopia and the Mango Trees" is in many ways a naive poem. It was written when I was back home in the '70s, when I just went back home. To me, a Rastafarian is still male. Although I know many women have since joined the sect independent of men, and are in fact Rastafarian. But my image of a Rastafarian is still the image that is located in my childhood, you know. And I remember those Rastafarians, clean, proud, quiet. There was always a kind of peace, a kind of quietness that seemed to pervade a Rastafarian's presence. And that they were very clear about who they were, particularly in relationship to Babylon, the rest of us Jamaicans. And they were industrious. And they were not about profit. They were like the earth. That rich Jamaican soil that grew whatever you'd plant in it. They were about spirituality which was not secularized like Christianity and Anglicanism—you know the kind of church you go to on Sundays where everybody might act crazy the rest of the time and sin and lie and sleep with somebody's husband then go to church and pray and have the audacity to say who was going to be in heaven and who was going to be in hell. Rastafarians didn't play that game. What they were involved with was living. Their philosophy, their spirituality was interwoven into the daily fabric of their lives. There was no sense of haste. There was no sense of confusion. There was no sense of being burdened by the average thing that the Westerners were burdened by. They were at peace. They were "I and I." They were infused with the spirit of Jah. And that allowed for a certain kind of tranquility. And even more so, they knew and welcomed and longed for their ancestral home, Ethiopia. So my experience with Rastafarians are of a group of men, primarily, who had tremendous self-restraint, pride in self, peace . . .

KD: Your poetry is replete with feminine images: birthing, menstruating, mothering. It is almost as if you are shaping and founding a poetic on images that work against phallocentric or patriarchal languages. Is this a conscious project of yours and how has it evolved in your writing?

OPA: Yes, definitely so. Barbara Christian (who I don't think many people realize is Caribbean, although I don't think many of us know how we want to talk about the Virgin Islands, specifically St. Croix, which although being very much Americanized is also very much Caribbean), is a Caribbean feminist critic, and we did a conference, a feminist conference, at Berkeley together and during that paper the entire audience paused because rather than a "seminal work," she said it was a "vaginal work." I thought, yes, yes. And vaginal is much more fluid and grounded and deep, I think, than seminal. Again, it goes back to an earlier question about using those images that clearly define me as female and evoking them and trying to refashion them in the work. I'm very conscious of that. Also, I'm still very much writing myself, in that I am a mother, and I am a feminist, and I've given birth three times, and I have lengthy periods which I hate, you know? And in many ways, so much of who I am is relegated to a private, domestic sphere. And I'm saying, "Uh-uh. No. We're not going to have that. We're not going to say that this is not political, that this is not important. This *is* political. This is as political as it gets. There's nothing more political than giving birth. Hello?" I think that the Trinidadian [Marlene] Nourbese Philip, in her very brilliant poem "The Logic of Language," talks about "mama tongue" and "papa tongue" and she's talking about us as a colonized people; Caribbeans as a colonized people and that English is a father, foreign tongue, and she's trying to find her "mama tongue," her "mommy tongue." But then just a couple months ago when I was in Miami, I met this fine and fabulous young Bahamian poet, Michael Pintard. I was just swept away by his performance. He has a poem in which he takes another step beyond Nourbese Philip. He says English was the language he was given because of experience, and he's going to use it as a weapon. It's a fabulous poem. And he did, the way he performed it was just incredible. So I think Caribbean writers both male and female are beginning to use language to define who they are and how they see themselves. So in terms of me attempting to insert feminist idioms, lexicons, if I might, in the language, then yes, I'm very conscious of that. I'm definitely trying to highlight, illuminate, the feeling of the words.

KD: In your poems "First Sound" and "Let Them Laugh" you celebrate music, women singers in one and jazz in another. In both pieces there is a life-giving quality that you attribute to music. Something inextricably linked to the creative process. Your references are largely American, African American specifically, although elsewhere you evoke calypso, and some South African stylings and a somewhat subtle nod to Marley's "No Woman No Cry." Can you expand upon the place of music in your work and your life?

OPA: There is no music that speaks to me more than reggae and calypso. Nowadays I'm bordering more on calypso. And certainly some of the dance-hall/hip-hop culture appeals to me. But I also grew up in Jamaica at a time when ska was born, and reggae. Yet a lot of the music that we listened to on the radio was foreign music and a lot of it was African American music. So African American music is very dear to me, and I still listen to it more than I listen to any other music. I've been much more conscious of this in the last couple of years, because I want my children to be very familiar with Caribbean music, and now they recognize it, and they like it. I play reggae music, and calypso music, but also music from Haiti and other places for them. So that music is important to me, but it is not a part of my daily life any more. And in many ways I feel out of touch with that music, yet when it's played and I go somewhere and I dance, it just cruises through my body and it sends me . . . Music is important to me. It stabilizes me and it helps to center me. I listen to music a lot. I need it. It is like the food that I need to nourish me so I can write.

To a certain extent I feel sad, and I feel somewhat cheated, because I really would like to write dub poetry, and post-dub poetry. There's a young friend of mine, a Jamaican who is talking about post-reggae, or post-dance hall culture or whatever; that's his thing. And there's a part of me that would like to be a part of that rhythm, and I feel I've been away for a very long time. And although not consciously, because I've become somewhat immersed in the African American culture, I have been shut off from that part of my life. So I don't feel as familiar with it. And there's a part of me that wants to do it, that wants to write more in the rhythm of reggae or dance-hall culture. And I don't think I'm proficient to do that. But the music is important to me. I feel that reggae language has abandoned me. Notice I didn't say I have abandoned it, but that it has abandoned me. And at this critical juncture, I would like to try to reclaim it, to retrieve it, to find out where we left each other. It's like two friends walking, and then suddenly one friend takes another route and the other one keeps going, and it's after a while that she realizes that this friend went another route and another way, and she was so absorbed in her own thoughts or what was immediately in front of her that she didn't realize it. And there's this great longing, and regret, you know, so . . . I still love reggae music. But I don't feel as close to that language as I would like to.

David Dabydeen

BORN 1955

DAVID DABYDEEN WAS born in Guyana and grew up in both rural and urban parts of the country. In 1969 his family moved to the United Kingdom, where he attended secondary school and went on to secure a place at Cambridge University. His studies would also lead to stints at Oxford University, London University, and Yale University in the United States. Dabydeen is a senior lecturer at the University of Warwick where, he heads the Caribbean Studies Department. Dabydeen also served for several years as Guyanese ambassador to the United Kingdom.

As one of the leading writers among the new wave of immigrant writers in Britain, David Dabydeen has devoted a significant amount of his time and creative output to exploring the complexities of race in British society. His work, shaped and influenced greatly by stalwart West Indian writers like V. S. Naipaul, Kamau Brathwaite, Wilson Harris, Samuel Selvon, and Derek Walcott, offers fresh approaches to the themes of exile and cultural schizophrenia that are distinguished by their capacity to examine with candor and intellectual vigor the construction of race and difference in British literature and art. His critical texts *The Black Presence in English Literature* (1985), *Hogarth's Blacks: Images of Blacks in Eighteenth-Century English Art* (1985), *Hogarth, Walpole, and Commercial Britain* (1987), and *Black Writers in Britain, 1760–1890* (1991) are important examinations of the position of black people and blackness in Britain over the last three centuries; they have contributed to his reputation as a scholar of prodigious giftedness and insight. Dabydeen has published four novels, *The Intended* (1991), *Disappearance* (1993), *The Counting House* (1996), and *A Harlot's Progress* (Jonathan Cape, 1999).

His poetry collections include *Slave Song* (Dangaroo Press, 1984), *Coolie Odyssey* (Dangaroo Press, 1988), and *Turner: New and Selected Poems* (Jonathan Cape, 1994).

KWAME DAWES: T. S. Eliot's poetry is founded upon a certain dispensational philosophy that posits that in order for Europe (core of Western Civilization) to understand its current schizophrenic self, it must return to its primordial origin, its history: "Time present and time past contained in time future" and all that. Two interesting things are operating here: the first is the metaphor of society as mad and the need to heal that madness, and the second is the place of history in that process of healing. I detect a certain application of that dispensational reasoning in your tendency to return to the slave and indentured labor past of Caribbean people—it is almost as if there is a need to understand that past before the present can be grasped. Is this part of your rationale for returning to the past?

DAVID DABYDEEN: I think it's a kind of excavation of self. The layers of the self have been buried in a forgetfulness—which is why I like the "Turner" painting, because it's the black figure who is submerged in the sea, head first, not feet first. My "Turner" poem ends on a great note of pessimism. When Brathwaite talks about recovering a sense of the West African Anancy by sight of a cobweb, or when anthropologists go peering behind every sage bush in the Caribbean for evidence of African retentions, I don't find it altogether convincing. The other selves, the ancestral selves, are so buried that they cannot be easily recovered. So, that frees you up to then say, "I have no past." Now, that's not a glorious freedom, because it's still immersed in a kind of a sorrow over what has been lost. But then you just have to realize that that is the situation. So I kind of misquote Eliot by saying that, yes, time past is time present and future for the European maybe. In England, where I live, the myth of national identity has been one of an unbroken lineage from Magna Carta days to today in terms of the rule of law, say, or the sense that history has been continuous and peaceful with no major fractures (in contrast, say, to the French Revolution). So England's national identity is based on a sense of gradual progress towards fair play and justice. Now, our condition as Caribbeans is a broken one. And the brokenness is all the more intensely felt when we live in a place like England. "Turner" was a great howl of pessimism about the inability to recover anything meaningful from the past. But it's a kind of howl that is also a release into the future.

KD: Isn't there, at the same time, this effort—that is, you go through "Turner" still? I mean, part of the process is going *through* "Turner," which takes you to that place.

DD: Yes. Because I tend to write inside out. If you want to write about love, you write about hate. So the denial of hope at the very end of "Turner" is contradicted by everything that went on before. A degree of recovery can take place through what Wilson Harris calls "magical processes of intuition." You can intuit the past. So it's not just a matter of scholarly recovery of data, or reading books about philosophy, or whatever. Moments of intuition can actually provoke in you a sense of the past in relation to the present; you know, a little strain of a sitar might awaken something in you, some kind of sorrow or memory. "Turner" deals with that, but then it negates it at the end. After all, it's a poem rather than a piece of social or political or philosophical discourse.

KD: Slavery plays a pivotal role in "Turner" and in many of the poems in *Slave Song*. The most striking characteristic of this treatment of slavery is not the propensity to list its horrors as it would appear in an abolitionist pamphlet, but to try and salvage the stories of everyday living that one would imagine belonged to the slave experience. The impact of this approach seems to me to be such that it readily allows us to connect the past with the present in a disturbing way. Can you talk a bit about your encounter with the slave past of the Caribbean and how that encounter has affected your own writing?

DD: I encountered the slave past in two ways. One was just by growing up in a kind of plantation environment, where, whilst the African Guyanese no longer cut cane, they are there—in terms of being buried in the cane fields—there are black ghosts, black jumbies. So it's there because it's the cane experience, it's the parent experience. But then also through study. I mean, my academic work has been on the eighteenth century, which was the period of enslavement of Africans. So you recover the stories in the way that *Beloved* was triggered off by a story that Toni Morrison read about the killing of little children. I've got to say that why I don't dwell on the suffering is that that would be obvious; it seems to me that the triumph of *Beloved* is in the way it does what Eliot does, which is to fuse the intellect and the senses with great potency. Eliot described poetry as "the direct sensuous apprehension of thought." In other words, Morrison wasn't being politically correct, she wasn't starting off with a kind of deliberation or with a set of beliefs—these are given, the intentions are given—but it's her ability to create stories around the philosophy that make *Beloved* a work of art, rather than a political tract or a piece of documentation. Morrison is more interested in how she can recreate sensuously the kinds of stories that allow suffering and grief to come through. I like the distinction Seamus Heaney makes between the expression of grief, which is art, and the expression of grievance, which is social/political protest.

KD: One of the obvious dualities that operates in your work entails the combined heritages of the African past and the Indian past. There is a kind of dialectic triad that has emerged in your three collections which reflects this synthesis. Your first collection, *Slave Song*, explored the African past, while *Coolie Odyssey*, the second, focuses in some detail on the Indian presence in the Caribbean; "Turner" establishes a synthesis of the two, for while, ostensibly, "Turner" is about the tossing of an African slave over the sides of a slaver, the mythic framework of the piece includes the rather central figure of Manu, Hindu god of the deluge. The presence of these two heritages is unassuming in "Turner," as if you are trying to articulate a new mythology of identity that marries both elements. Is this a product of your own "creolization" as a Guyanese Indian? In this instance, Walcott's "divided to the vein" takes on a peculiarly distinct twist.

DD: In the Caribbean we use that term creolization so easily when, in fact, we don't "creolize." For example, there is a massive body of Hindu texts that came over in the nineteenth-century boats—I speak of the *Ramayana*, the *Mahabarata* and such—which are epic in theme and bulk, and they've been there for a hundred and fifty years, and yet very few of our Caribbean intellectuals have even looked at these texts. So, how can we say we are creolized? What I am saying about the Indians you can say about the Amerindians and the Chinese. The first book on Chinese history and culture came out last year, a book by Wally Lok Lai. The unfortunate thing about all these matters is that it's up to the different ethnic groups to write their own history and culture. To me, that's outrageous, because that reveals a kind of a self-apartheid. Walter Rodney, in *How Europe Underdeveloped Africa*, called upon Indian scholars to investigate African history—he was seeking a realignment of our perspectives in terms of historiography, at a time of decolonization when the two great continents, Africa and India, were becoming free, and he's saying, "Well, let's look at one another now, rather than the gaze always being European or transatlantic." I don't think we've done that in the Caribbean, and I speak objectively in view of the massive ignorance that we entertain about our Amerindian, and our Indian, and our Chinese and Portuguese heritages. Obviously, we have to correct that, otherwise how can we boast about being a tapestry of peoples and cultures? That can just be rhetoric, and basically, what it would mean is that we are still offspring of Britain. We don't talk about Indianness or Amerindianness because we don't make the effort to understand those languages and concepts, whereas we go and read James Joyce, which is more difficult than any Vedic scripture. So we are, it seems to me, still laboring in mimicry in the Caribbean, which is all right if we acknowledge that we are Naipaul's "mimic men"; if people just acknowledge it and move on, fair enough. But we don't; we create this kind of rhetoric of independence when we're really dependent on British, and increasingly American, sources.

Now, in terms of transfusions of cultures, *Slave Song* considered something of the African experience, or rather experiences (because you don't want to be monolithic about it). But the African experiences are fictions because I'm writing intuitively (I'm living in the twentieth century in a position of privilege; nobody ever beat me, I never cut cane, I don't know the weight of a cutlass). *Slave Song* was an Indian book as well because the agricultural environment is Indian. If you talk about planting and reaping you're talking about an Indo-Caribbean activity, in Guyana anyway. So you can't write about planting or anything agricultural, even with an African theme, without the Indianness inevitably and unconsciously fusing into that African body of experience. So these fusions are not necessarily conscious acts, they just are.

With "Turner," I didn't know what I was doing with Manu. Manu was a total accident. It was just a name I'd plucked out from memory. And it was not until the book was reviewed in *The New Statesman* by an English scholar who edited the *Penguin Book of Caribbean Verse* [Paula Burnett] and identified Manu as the Noah of Indian myth, that I went to my encyclopedia, my *Encyclopedia Britannica* (!) and checked it out and thought, "What a curious accident!" It reminded me of what Wilson Harris says, that when you write something, it's only in revising it that you get clues to a much deeper meaning or a deeper structure. Now the deeper sense of Indianness did not reside with Manu but in descriptions of planting and reaping. Manu was just a kind of trigger, which in some peculiar way forced me to express an Indianness.

KD: There is at work in the "Turner" poem both a narrative quality akin to the art of storytelling (I think here of the retrieved memories of the drowning/drowned slave Turner, which appear to be set in some mythic landscape) and a complex series of philosophical explorations which echo the poetics of someone like T. S. Eliot. At the heart of this philosophizing is an unconcealed indictment of slavery and the society that allowed slavery to continue. Was it the narrative instinct—the instinct to "recall the sources of [Turner, the slave's] life" through a reconstruction of his past (through storytelling) that became the engine for the poem, or were you perhaps drawn more to the irony contained in this act of human abuse as caught by Turner the painter? Is it possible to make such a dichotomy, anyway?

DD: Let me say first of all that the preface which you quote from, and all prefaces I've written to everything, including *Slave Song, Coolie Odyssey*, everything, have, in fact, no necessary correlation to what goes on in the writing. They are, if you like, what makes sense of what you've done. Because I really believe, as Walcott does, and definitely as R. K. Narayan does, that (and this isn't getting into mysticism or romanticism) the writer can't really explain what has been written. In the actual process of writing you are feeling your way confusedly towards some kind of pattern of meaning. You are trying to order experience in a certain way. Nevertheless, you have to write prefaces, and I love Aubrey Williams's preface to the catalogue of one of his exhibitions—the Maya Exhibition at the Commonwealth Institute in the '70s—when he said, "Look, I'm being forced to write a preface, don't believe a word of it or believe everything. Take or leave it. I hate having to do it. Look at the painting!"

In terms of your question. I would come back to two things, and maybe this is answering it indirectly. First of all, most of the names of animals and birds and fish in the poem are fabricated. I just plucked them out of my mind one late night whilst writing. The desire was twofold: one was to erase recognition of a *particular* landscape, whether India or Africa, and secondly, to suggest the possibility of remaking a landscape by renaming it, which is of course going against the colonial experience. The second thing is that I deliberately set the poem in the sea. Most of it takes place in the actuality of the sea, and the sea is actual, not just as the location of the drowned man, but in the rhythms of the poem. The drowned man's landscape is ghostly and part of that ghostliness is the fabricated names of the fauna and the flora. This is another aspect of creolization: I don't want to be "authentic" about the African experience, nor do I want to be "authentic" about the Indian experience, because I'm neither, but I'm both in a kind of ghostly way. England has a very concrete sense of its past which is very visible in terms of fortresses and castles and displays of ancient weaponry and statues of men wielding weaponry and monuments to national heroes who were also mass murderers—you know, the "hero" of the Morant Bay rebellion, the "hero" of the Indian mutiny; if you killed more than four or five thousand people you got a statue erected in your honor. So if you live in England where the English have a very powerful concrete (or stone/marble) sense of their histories, and you as a Caribbean person come to a sense that your history is nebulous and shifting, it means that you have a tremendous capacity for a new kind of freedom, which is what Manu was talking about in the poem. He's saying, you can dream, you can surmise, you can invent. The nebulousness of one's background gives one a kind of epistemological freedom, an existential freedom. To me that's what creolization should be, coming to an awareness that we are free, not because it was the British intention to make us free, but in a peculiar way we became free, we were freed of certain traditions, knowledges, and so on, and while we have sorrow about the loss of those, nevertheless, we are always on the threshold of originality.

KD: I am fascinated by this act of inventing names for the fruits and birds of the mythic land that you describe in "Turner." I am reminded of Brathwaite's fascination with naming in *The Arrivants,* but in his poem, the names are retrieved through a journey back, through a journey to an existing origin which is found, in that instance, in the ancient civilizations of West and North Africa. When things are named again, they are reclaimed. This reclaiming occurs in your poem, but the names are made up. It is as if the amnesia is insurmountable and the Africa that is constructed is mythic and defined in terms of the current space of exile. The statement that this makes about Caribbean society and its relationship to Africa or India is fascinating. In some ways, it patterns or confirms the ideology of Rastafarianism, for instance. To what extent do you think the process of constructing one's past, even if that past has no resemblance to the "real" past (whatever that is), is important to survival in the Caribbean?

DD: I'm really pleased that you picked up the Rastafarianness of the poem's mood. Before "Turner," I published a novel where I had a Rastafarian character who is a peculiar character, a peculiarly intellectual kind of figure—basically he floats, and the rest of the characters are rooted. It's set in London. I'm not talking about the Rastafarian as a Rastafarian, but about the notion of the Rastafarian. Rastafarianism was important as a "concept" to me because of course there is the overlap with Hinduism, the smoking of ganja (supplied on the plantations to the Indians by the British) or all kinds of other ritual and mystical correspondences. At this stage in my life I wouldn't mind exploring the possibilities of freedom—freedom being the desire to invent totally, and to live in a body of myth of one's own invention. There are, I suppose, echoes of Blake, and definitely D. H. Lawrence—because I grew up on D. H. Lawrence—who was trying to create a private myth by which he could exist in a place like England. The idea of art, or the writing of an individual artist, being ultimately a social death and withdrawal into a self-mythologizing is fascinating. What it doesn't mean is an abandonment of social and political responsibility. In other words, I am not going to shave my head, grow hairs on my chest, and sit under the nearest peepal tree and fast unto death; not just in the Indian way, but, you know, all those Catholic martyrs living up nut trees and that, I am not going to do that, because at the end of the day you have to live and eat and live in a community and your imagination is nurtured by that community. So you'll still write political tracts or you'll still be a Paki at a bus stop in England, ten thugs around, and you're still shit-scared because you don't have enough money for a taxi fare—you don't get away from those things. But I think in art anyway, I want to explore the possibilities of a total freedom from the social being.

KD: "Turner" is a departure for you in several respects. On the one hand, it is written predominantly, if not entirely, in standard English. As well, there is a far more sustained attempt to contain the poem in a complex of images that play on the sea, sailing, ship-lore, drowning, etc., through the use of echoes, metaphors, and densely fused images:

> First a woman sobs
> Above the creak of timbers and the cleaving
> Of the sea, sobs from the depths of true
> Hurt and grief, as you will never hear
> But from woman giving birth, belly
> Blown and flapping loose and torn like sails,
> Rough sailors' hands jerking and tugging
> At ropes of veins, to no avail. Blood vessels
> Burst asunder, all below-deck are drowned.

Do you see "Turner" as a watermark for you, the kind of opus that represents a technical and intellectual "arrival" in your poetry? I suppose I am struck by the confidence that seems inherent in the perceived voice.

DD: "Turner" is the only thing that I have written so far which I feel comfortable with. I suppose I spent twenty years just trying to find an Africanness or find an Indianness or find a Creoleness; a kind of constant grind to find something, and now you settle for a world of your own making, and you settle for metaphor—the sheer beauty and autonomy of the metaphor. We live in a world where we are burdened by meaning. In this politically correct world, we are trying to find meaning all the time, and to express that meaning in rational terms. Given the race relations situation in America and the Caribbean or Britain, writers are expected to be very correct, to bear all kinds of responsibilities towards the notion of being "truthful" and "moral" and to provide a kind of explanatory system by which people can live. What pisses me off about critics or about community activists (I used to be one of each, in earlier years) is that they expect a consistency from you and they expect a kind of linear development or they expect sense from you all the time, and you have to be "one of the boys," and you have to be saying the right things on television, and defending the race. It's a very sincere expectation but I think it goes against the nature of the very processes of writing, where what you are much more interested in at times is transgression, and abandonment, and the confusion of metaphor, and opaqueness, and multiple fused yet contradictory perspectives, and reveling in contradictions, muddle, wrong-headedness, hydra-headedness.

KD: Your poetry is filled with "classical" echoes, poetic echoes from various cultures, as if you see your palette as being quite unlimited and unrestricting. Is this how you feel? Your work engages in a certain flattery of other writers in some instances. Walcott's maritime metaphoring in *Omeros* has some echoes in "Turner," Brathwaite's rhythm and line breaks are clearly a presence in "Love Song," and Eliot makes his appearance in "Turner" along with Shakespeare and Homer; and in other instances, you appear to be taking on these writers, the most obvious being Ruskin's narrative on Turner the painter and your reworking of Shakespeare's Caliban mythos in "Miranda," "Caliban," "Water with Berries," "Rebel Love," and "New World Words." This layering of echoes and references along with internal debates and feuds lends to some of your work what appears to be an intensity which can be interpreted as elitist or alienating in some contexts. Are you very conscious of all of this as you construct/create?

DD: I'm conscious when I write prose of Selvon, Harris, Naipaul, Lamming, and others; I'm conscious. In fact, in the last novel I did, I used a character from Wilson Harris' *The Secret Ladder,* Fenwick. And I asked Harris. I said, "Bwoy, you mind if I . . . ?" He said, "No, man." And I said, "Well, would I go overboard if I take a quote from *The Secret Ladder* and use it as an epigraph?" He said, "No man. Go!" And then I used a character called Jack from Naipaul's *Enigma of Arrival.* And Selvon is everywhere in terms of a certain peasantry and boyhood, growing up in an Indian environment; Lamming is there —when I talk about Miranda and Caliban I'm thinking of Lamming's *Water with Berries* and *Pleasures of Exile*. I suppose, when I look back at it, what I'm trying to do is to say that whereas our writers had to rewrite the "master scripts" of Europe, my interest now, from another generation, is to rewrite or respond to our ancestral writers (who, incidentally, are all male—Brathwaite, Selvon, Harris, etc.— since the literature of the '40s to the '60s was overwhelmingly by males. No one knew of Rajkumari Singh or Louise Bennett until very recently). So my particular interest now is fuck the "master scripts," let me write instead to Harris and to Naipaul, write back, quarrel with, borrow from, love, praise, worship them. So, if there is a certain kind of eclecticism, it is not a knee-jerk response to Western texts. The other thing is that all these writers are living, and they've helped me. Wilson Harris said, "Give up criticism, go and write poetry." Aubrey Williams provided paintings for my front covers. Sam Selvon—he and I would go and drink and smoke and behave bad. They are a very living presence, these older figures. Sometimes I feel, though, that I am an allusion to an allusion to an allusion. I'm like one of Eliot's footnotes. I'm just a footnote to an Eliot poem which is in turn a footnote to other writings by other people. That's part of the idea of disappearing—there is no fixity, there is no structure; in my head are just echoes of everything. What I am in myself, in essence, I don't know. I'm living in Britain, I'm not living in the Caribbean. If I were living in the Caribbean, I'd probably turn out, hopefully, like Lovelace, who is rooted in landscape and communities. Eliot is modernism, Eliot is fragmentation, Eliot is the disembodied consciousness. Eliot is the great escape artist, Eliot is Anancy in the way that he escapes from Victorian verse, from meaning or from epistemologies, and in a peculiar sense Eliot is the parent of Caribbean poetry. Isn't that peculiar? A racist, conservative, Anglo-loving fucker like him, right! But these are some of the beautiful ironies of literature.

KD: All this brings us to the question of audience and your understanding of who your audience is as you write. Is it important to you to have a clear sense of your audience? Being a resident of Britain yet working with a clear Caribbean focus, what kinds of challenges do you face with regards to the question, "Who are you writing for?" Jean Breeze, for instance, has said that she writes to a black audience —anyone else who happens to hear is overhearing. She welcomes the eavesdropping but she does not plan to do the work of explaining what she means for them. It is an interesting perspective . . .

DD: The business of writing is so blasted difficult and takes so long and takes so much out of your life and gives you so much, that believe me, you haven't got time for "audience." You just want to write the fucker on the paper. After it's finished, the question of "audience" comes in. The audience I seek are people like Wilson Harris. I'm scared of George Lamming, and I'm scared of Wilson Harris. Now that Aubrey Williams is dead, I'm no longer scared of him except in a kind of jumbie way. These are the people to whom you have a responsibility, and I feel that very consciously. I was so torn when I heard rumors that Brathwaite didn't like *Slave Song*. If fifty thousand others didn't like it and fifty thousand others liked it, it was Brathwaite that I was scared of. When I would see Selvon, I used to say, "Yuh know Sam, man, I'm trying to hustle a bit of fiction here to give you a bit of competition; wha' yuh think of it?" And he would say, "Don't worry, you know . . ." Those are the people I clear my work with. Whether the English understand it or not, whether they are white or black, I don't worry about those things too much, because one realizes that art is so private at times that nobody will understand it, anyway. Secondly, every time you utter you're open to misinterpretations; some creative, and some willfully malicious. I haven't got a romantic view of black audiences or West Indian audiences. I move with "the boys," they would eat food with me, they would like the idea of a book —"the boy writing book" and so on— and they will always look after you because you are a writer, but they are not gonna read the stuff, and if they read it some of them might be offended.

The first novel I did was set in a village in Guyana; I used some of the names of the characters who were still there. I felt I could do that with members of my family, but I stupidly took the novel back and the next day, somebody had flicked through it, and I was really in trouble. They said, "We didn't like this at all . . ." I was worried as to whether they were attacking the themes or the way life was represented. They were, but they were more offended by the fact that I used the word "fuck." One man said to me, "Man, yuh get permission to write 'fuck' in a book?" So I said, "You know, in Englan' you don' need to." He said, "Still, man, why yuh use 'fuck,' why yuh don' say something else; it look so nasty." So that was a really interesting (mis)reading, but it didn't necessarily teach me anything. And of course, once you buy the rum, all the differences are forgotten. The way out of hostile criticism in a Caribbean village is to buy rum for everybody. I am being flippant, but you know what I mean. What I mean is that they don't really necessarily care for the books. They've got their own lives to live. "So all right, so the boy bring home a book, so what?" It gives you status, but at the same time it doesn't seem to be anything special when you are a villager looking after cow and sheep.

There is comedy as well as a pathos in the presence of a "book" in a peasant village. I came across the comedy a couple of years ago when one of the villagers, hearing of my arrival, wandered into the yard where I was drinking with relatives. He was an uninvited guest, so to secure his share of rum he came up directly to me and said, "Man I hear you is a writer and ting. What you think 'bout Dickens, eh? What you think about Dickens?" And he spent the next four hours asking the same question, and drinking, until he collapsed in utter inebriation. In other words, Dickens, whom he'd heard about somewhere and somehow, was suddenly of moment; what was obscure and irrelevant in his life suddenly became a very necessary passport to unlimited rum. That pathos I came across in a conversation with my mother, who, as a peasant-child in the village, had the job of sweeping her uncle's house. Although a total alcoholic and utterly self-destructive, he was rare in having books in his house. This was extraordinary—books in a village-house in 1940s Guyana. My mother said that one day, some pages fell from a book which was by an open window. The book's binding was rotten with age and the tropical weather and the wind blew some pages from it. She picked one up and it was headed "Iliad." She told me recently, "I hold it up and I read I-L-L-I-A-D and I wonder, what name so?" Fifty years later she still didn't know what it was all about, but the triumph of our Caribbean achievement is that her children—Brathwaite, Walcott, Kincaid—can not only read, but rewrite Homer.

KD: In poetry, personal memory can be both a rich source of inspiration and material as well as a treacherous taskmaster that desires to consume all that you create with sentimentality and nostalgia. I am struck by the absence of these qualities in your poems that appear to retrieve old memories. But there are times when the eschewing of sentimentality creates a hardened realism and irony that seems cold and detached. How do you contend with these pressures as you try to construct a sense of your personal past in your poetry?

DD: I like Brathwaite's view of poetry, which echoes Eliot's view of poetry—which is that poetry is rhythm. And I think rhythm creates music that is deeply sensuous. So if your theme is utterly bleak or hard or lacking in sentiment, if it's done with a kind of rhythmic beauty and with metaphoric color, that helps to assuage the kind of tight-arsed, conservative retreat from life which sometimes you get in Naipaul. I mean, I quite like Naipaul's absence of sentiment, but if I have a quarrel with Naipaul, it is that I don't like the way that that absence of sentiment is not conveyed or expressed with richness of metaphor or generosity of character-creating. *King Lear* is fucking bleak, man, nothing is more bleak, but look how beautiful it is. So while one eschews sentiment because it creates bad art, I think one has got to express bleakness with a generosity of creativity, with music and sensuousness, otherwise it's just a dry, tedious self-denial.

KD: Your poem "For Rohan Babulal Kanhai" is one of the most moving cricket poems from the Caribbean that I have read. I suppose it stands on par with Brathwaite's "Rites." In your poem the centrality of cricket as a way of understanding the Caribbean identity is most vividly and touchingly articulated. Perhaps the most telling image is that of Kanhai in some foreign place alone in the middle accumulating centuries. Can you talk a bit about cricket as a kind of mythmaking entity, a central idiom in Caribbean society that in many ways defines the society and helps to shape that society?

DD: I got to answer that by acknowledging a couple of things that I've read that helped to provoke that poem. One was a quite beautiful essay on Rohan Kanhai by a Guyanese scholar called Clem Seecharan, who grew up as an Indian in the Indian parts of Guyana and hero-worshipped Kanhai as most Indians did. And then, I read an exhilarating poem by a Trinidadian writer called Faustin Charles which connected up the force of cricket with conquistadoral energies. That's how the Kanhai poem came about. It's about the West Indian experience in two ways. One is Kanhai batting lonely in some far county called Warwickshire, which is the West Indian pioneering moment. We are all pioneers, you can find us in all corners of the earth, in darkest Russia or darkest England, there is some West Indian somewhere, doing his thing. And he's creolizing the thing. And Kanhai created a sweep shot. C. L. R. James said of Kanhai, he was one of the few people to create a new stroke in cricket—the sweep shot. And what CLR was saying was that the boy took on all the rules and regulations of cricket, which is an English game, and he created a shot. In the same way we created the steel band or we created a creole. But then, the sadness of the poem is that that creativity, because of the barbarism in our own native society at times, that creativity, instead of being seen and received as the grand feat of creolization and celebrated as that, becomes the weaponry of one race against the other. I wanted to reflect the conditions of Guyana where we broke into ethnic enclaves. Whilst we had the rhetoric of creolization, we were in fact ethnocized. So there's a paradox of Kanhai being a creole figure in England but not a creole figure in Guyana. So it comes back to that question that we started off with: Are we gonna be properly creolized or not? The other thing, of course, is that cricket is a form of energy that is the same form of energy as cane cutting, and Carnival. So that you can't separate the activities. It's a metaphor of the transformation of the middle passage. The root of it is an inventiveness—not just survival; you can survive with a bit of food—but it's the inventing that matters, the inventiveness, in this instance, of the Guyanese people.

What pisses me off most when I meet Indo-Caribbeans or Afro-Caribbeans—and I don't want to be innocent here—but they have rabid racial views. In Miami, an Indo-Caribbean accosted me and said, "Well you know all these black people don't understand our Hindu aesthetics and Jees, we gotta hold on to our . . ." Yeah, fair enough, I accept all that stuff, but I'm not gonna express or politicize it in that way. Or else I meet some black guy who says to me "How come you put Manu in there? Are you blotting out my African teachers?" And I say, "No, man, it's just there as a kind of a way of exploring possibilities of being together." So you always get that kind of shit. But the best thing about the Kanhai poem is that just as I have always been afraid of Lamming and Naipaul, I've been afraid of Kanhai, because I grew up with Kanhai as the great Indian hero in a racially polarized Guyana. And when I was in Guyana in 1993, I saw Kanhai in a boat, crossing the Berbice River. And I fumbled in my suitcase, I really fumbled about in my suitcase because I had taken some books home for people, and books to leave in the libraries, and I went up to Kanhai very shyly with *Coolie Odyssey* and the Kanhai poem. I went up to him and I said, "Excuse me, my name is David Dabydeen and I teach at the University of Warwick." And he said, "Yeah?" No recognition, just "Yeah?" That kind of hoggish, plantation response. He said, "Yeah?" So I said, "I'm a writer and I wrote a poem for you." He said, "Yeah?" And then I opened up the book to the Kanhai page and he looked at it, and this is God's truth, he looked at it and he said, "Yuh spell me name wrong." Not, "By the way, thank you, but the name is spelt wrongly." He said, just straight out, in a kind of plantation staccato, "Yuh spell me name wrong." So I said, "How you mean?" And he said, "Well, middle name, it get two *l*, it get two *l* dere, boy." So I said, "Well, aww, I didn't know that. In the next edition, I'll get it corrected." Well he doesn't know what a "next edition" is, he doesn't know about editions and all that kind of stuff; and that was it. He just closed the book and I just walked away sheepishly, thinking, "You coolie bastard!" That total uncouth coolie . . . I mean, when I say uncouth, it's also the beauty of the Guyanese; that lack of reverence, that rumshop kind of wit and readiness in putting you down, which you've got to admire. And I suppose if you look at it, what I could interpret him as saying is, "How come you spelt my name wrong? Everybody spells my name wrong. That's why I'm a plantation coolie. They, the whites, spelt our names wrong or changed our names. You can't spell my name wrong like that!" What he did not understand, which I couldn't explain to him, was that I got it from Wisden, the bible of cricket, the white man's text. So, in a curious sense, to discover his middle name (Babulall) I had to go through Wisden which didn't recover his name. All these kinds of ironies. The reception of a poem like that becomes a metaphor of our Caribbean transformation.

KD: The Guyanese landscape is legendary for its influence on the work of Guyanese writers—that sense of expanse, an understanding of the river as source of sustenance and as enemy. Your poetry reflects this grounding in the landscape, particularly the dialect poems of *Slave Song* and *Coolie Odyssey*. The Canje River is a constant presence that has the capacity of assuming mythic proportions. Can you talk a little bit about the importance of this landscape to your writing? Has being away from Guyana all these years and living in another kind of landscape had an impact on your own sense of place as it emerges in your poetry?

DD: I think so. Probably in a variety of ways, but the most obvious way for me is living in England, where the landscape is very tame, you know, the only wildness in England are the human lager louts, but the landscape is very tame and gentle; almost a classically lyrical landscape. It is interesting that whenever Naipaul describes the landscape in *Enigma of Arrival*, which is set in the English countryside, he always alludes to Wordsworth and Constable. In other words, living in England, the landscape for me is a literary landscape. And that's partly because we are colonials and we read the literature so the places have a kind of mythic literary quality. England has been written about, so that everywhere is very alive with literary evocation. The Guyana landscape is terrible and unwritten. It has a terror, the terror of the unwritten. And I don't mean that in a negative sense. The unwritten is terrible because it is unknown. And it also has terrors in real ways. I mean, I can't swim because my mother would prevent me from going to the pond because in the pond lived all kinds of dangerous creatures. And there were alligators, and we grew up with snakes in the countryside and even in the towns. Snakes and alligators, and we were always being stung by malabunters and there was always something there to make you scream, scorpions and centipedes—everybody got bitten by mosquitoes and so on. So living in England really emphasizes my sense of the "frontier" dangerousness of the Guyanese landscape.

The other thing, of course, is that I can't live in the English rural landscape. I don't feel committed to England. I mean, I can survive in the English urban setting because a city is a city is a city, but in England a rose is not a rose is not a rose. It's not my rose. I don't know the names of birds and trees and flowers and I don't feel as if I'm interested because I don't feel as if I could really get in there. Migration is too young a process for us to actually evolve into the landscape and creolize it. So England's landscape then becomes iconic. It is never a real tree, it is always an icon of something else, and that's probably the way landscape comes into whatever I'm writing. This is why I like the idea of the sea, you see. The last novel was about the sea. It was set in the sea off the Hastings coast. The sea frees one up from landscape. It's the sea, and the idea of being born in the sea and being an Adam in the sea . . . and dreaming one's own landscape . . . starting all over again. Imagine it!

KD: Your poems that deal with sexuality and sexual relations appear to be marked by deeply complex interracial tensions which lead, very often, to a certain impotence or dysfunctional sexuality. This idea of racial disquiet as imaged through the metaphor of interracial sexuality is at once provocative and deeply pessimistic—in many ways it reminds me of the peculiar sexual dynamics in Naipaul's *Mimic Men*. My question may sound like one about your sexual experience, but it isn't, the problem is simply that you deal with racial dynamics through the situation of sexual relations. I am interested in your thoughts on the racial dynamics that operate for an artist "of color" in Britain. Is the racial landscape as festered with aborted fetuses and impotence as your poems seem to suggest?

DD: It's what's most obvious about what I write; the interconnection of racial, historical, and sexual themes. It's partly autobiographical and partly not autobiographical. I mean, I feel as if I'm an abortion, at times. I feel like the stillborn child in "Turner," definitely. Or even worse than that, I feel like an abortion, messy and bloody and unborn, and that's partly because of a racism, where other people are trying to reduce you to nothing all the time and erase everything that you brought with you, or else they remind you of what you could have brought with you had they not taken it away. But it's also a kind of general human feeling, we all feel deeply pessimistic at times; the greatest emotion is really the sense of the tragic rather than the sense of the comic, which is why *King Lear* is better than any of Shakespeare's comedies. The tragic sense is what galvanizes all of us. We switch the television on and we see people dying in Rwanda — tragedy is much more and always with us. So that's partly it. The other thing is that I suppose I wanted to explore the idea that the "Empire" was a pornographic project, it wasn't just an economic or a sociological or a political project, it was also a project of pornography. And Wilson Harris in providing a blurb for *Coolie Odyssey* talks about the ways the poems reveal the disturbing pornography of Empire. I suppose that's all I wanted to say, that ultimately, the plantation experience had severe and traumatic psychic impacts that had to do with the loss of, or the traumatic changes in, epistemologies and philosophies, but overwhelmingly had to do with what is the very ground of our being, which is our body. Now, that's how I've seen it, but believe me, other people don't see it like that — and thank God, right? Then again, it's always been easier for me to write the morbid and the tragic than it is for me to write something else. I don't know why. That's all there is. I wouldn't want what I write to be a manifesto of colonial feelings. Yes, it has a dimension of truth, but there are other truths which should compete with it. There are deeply autobiographical moments as well. I grew up without a mother, so that the absent mother is probably what moves me very deeply and creates writing. "Turner" is really about the absent mother, too. So there are those moments of autobiography. So when one speaks of an abortion, one is also speaking of the absent mother; the absence is the mother, not the life in the child. Then there are autobiographical moments that are also related to the disgust that I felt, when I was young in Guyana, at men beating up women. Some of my most painful memories of Guyana are of men beating up women; not just in my own family, but neighbors, and women crying late at night. I was trying to highlight things that moved me for a variety of reasons—certain social experiences, certain family experiences, certain deeply personal experiences that create a mood of, at times, disgust and, at times, bleakness. But I certainly wouldn't want it to be used as a manifesto of black/white relations or male/female relations.

BORN 1957

AFUA COOPER WAS born in the parish of Westmoreland in Jamaica. She moved to Kingston when she was fairly young and spent some of her formative years in that city during the late 1960s and early 1970s. She attended high school in Kingston where she was involved in the arts, and started writing at a fairly early age. In 1980 Cooper moved to Canada, where she studied history and began her career as a writer.

Cooper's work is constantly trying to reconcile two seemingly disparate spheres of experience: political action and activism, and personal self-actualization — the personal inner narrative, as she has called it. Bringing those two into some kind of meaningful and productive dialogue is a project that reflects her own development as an artist and as a feminist activist who has described her life in Canada as one spent "fighting a racist and patriarchal structure."

Cooper published her first collection of poems, *Breakin Chains* (Weelahs), in 1983. Several years later she published her first children's book, *The Red Caterpillar on College Street* (Sister Vision, 1989). Sister Vision then published *Memories Have Tongue* (1992), which collected poems written between 1985 and 1991. This collection was the first runner-up for the 1992 Casa de las Américas Prize. She is the editor of a recent anthology, *Utterances and Incantations: Women, Poetry and Dub* (Sister Vision, 1999).

Cooper lives in Toronto with her family.

KWAME DAWES: In an interview with Makeda Silvera you seemed to suggest that she may have doubted the veracity of your belief in ghosts and so on. But this connection with the supernatural is important to you and to your work.

AFUA COOPER: I never had any disbelief about ghosts. Growing up in rural Jamaica, in Westmoreland, we didn't get light—electric light—until the Rural Electrification Program under Michael Manley in 1972. So everything was dark all the time. Six o'clock was pitch black. So you lived with ghosts. And you also lived in yards where people buried their dead—right there. You never buried the dead in cemeteries. So there were ghosts all over the place and so we grew up hearing them. So I know this experience that I had (the one I described in my interview with Makeda) was real. Because I saw the person, the actual spirit. So I grew up with that, and so there was no doubt in my mind about that. Also, there was the sense that we humans were always living at the border between human reality and another reality. For example, at night, you wouldn't open your door and throw water; you could throw it out but you had to say something: "Excuse me!" or "Coming!" before you throw out the thing. Or you wouldn't move into a house until you burned it out with incense, frankincense or sage, or you sprinkled lavender water. I mean, to this day I do it. I just did it. I just moved into a house on November first and mi never sleep at night until mi burn out the house. It's not that I'm superstitious or that I figure that if I sleep without burning out the house something will come and kill me, no, because I figure if I sleep nothing will happen. It's just growing up and having that instilled in you at an early age and figuring that it's real and that as human beings, I think we need to be cognizant of these things. We are living in such a mundane secular world where you just jump in your car and move here and there, blah, blah, blah; but part of that whole thing for me is having rituals in my life. So I just don't jump out of my bed and brush my teeth and drink my tea and go off to where I am going. I say my prayers. I don't go church or anything like that, but I say my prayers, you know, because that grounds me for the day. An' night time me jus' don' jump inna de bed an fall asleep; I have to do a little meditation. Because, again, it's like preparing before sleep, preparing for that journey because you might not even wake up, which is okay. So it is not myth in the sense of not true, but it's myth in the sense of a social and cultural and psychological creation. And ancestors are very real to me, and when I go to Jamaica and I go to the country which is Westmoreland for me, I have to go and visit my grandparents' graves and my father's grave. And I took my children when we went the last time to do these things. I mean they might not grow up doing that. But I do it because it just kinda feel funny if you go the place and you don' visit the grave. And one of the things that we do is if the grave have a lot of weeds on it you clear it. I don't drink rum, I don't drink alcohol, but they say when you visit a grave you mus' t'row rum even though the person might not be a rum drinker. So I do that right, because you don't know. I experienced this thing when I was small, and then my grandmother's sister, when she died I was in town, but when she died, I knew because she came and told. And in the evening, I called my mother and I said, you know Aunt Princess dead, and then the next day the phone call came to say she dead. So I am not gonna slight those things and say they are not real because these are things that happened to me. And, of course, if I am being true to my poetic voice or living in that voice or living in that body, then I have to write about those things. Not that I *have* to. Not that I am going to sit down and say let me write a poem about graves or ancestors. But when you go into your meditation, and as you write down your reflections, these things come out because these things are in your body and are in your life.

Now with regards to the Taino and Maroons and stuff: Jamaica is a violent place, man. If you think about the history. Not just Jamaica, but North America. There is a history of violence done to the land and to the people and so much blood was shed in that place, and I don't believe that things just go away just like that. I believe that you need to have rituals to placate the dead and to placate the spirits and say to them, "Go on now, you can rest." For I am sure you have heard things like "You see dis man dead or dis woman dead an' 'im jus' a walk up an' down the street an' a torment de people an you have fe do a lickle ting fe get dem out." I remember I was reading this thing: I can't remember who it was but it was a psychiatrist or psychologist or some kind of therapist, and she said that a lot of the patients coming to her were having these dreams of Native Americans. Some of these people had never seen a Native American in their life, and when she inquired into the dreams, these come from a long, long time, some of the things they were dreaming. And she said, but why not, you know, because the land speaks and these people were living on the land. And now these new people who have come and lived there, these things would just seep into their unconscious. And I think it is the same thing with Jamaica and the Caribbean. The original population were wiped out and we act as if nothing never happened. And I think that is one of the reasons why you have this terrible violence going on now. Because no sort of prayer or collective therapy has been done to say, okay, this is where we have come from and this is where we are now; this is what has happened to us, and okay, with all this violence, how can we move on? What can we do? There is no sense of acknowledgment of that as we move from one stage to another, and become terribly, terribly violent towards one another, you know.

KD: In the 1970s, Jamaica went through a strong period of transformation and social and political upheaval. There was an increased sense of Africa, of blackness, and a strong Socialist bent to what was being said and done politically. Do you regard those as shaping periods for you?

AC: Most definitely. I will answer the last part of the question first. I mean the '70s have shaped my life, period. Because I was fortunate to come of age at the time. It's funny because I went to Camperdown High School, and when Nikky Finney came to Toronto to do a launch, I was talking to her about how creative my school years were in my high school because all these things were happening. And then a woman was there (at the launch) and she said, "Well, I went to that school and it was the most racist experience of my life." So I said, "When did you go there?" She said 1959, she was the first scholarship child, in that first batch of scholarship children to go to Camperdown High School. So I said, of course, it was a different period, and my mother told me about those first scholarship children. White people and brown people were so upset because they said all these black people were going to go to school with their children. But the '70s were tremendous, at least in my school. We were downtown and in a working-class neighborhood, and maybe that made a difference. Not just the '70s, because things had started to change in the late '60s. I remember when Walter Rodney was about to be expelled from Jamaica and you had these huge demonstrations in Kingston and riots—rob de store an' bomb up de bus dem an' all kinda nice tings that was just so exciting. And that went right into the '70s, that whole impatience with the status quo. And then Michael Manley won the elections in '72. But also, the influence that Rasta had, coming from the '60s into the '70s. I was in the middle of all of that. I was downtown, my school was downtown and I lived downtown, so you were right in it, you know, in Rasta culture, working-class culture and the music. It shaped how I thought and still think. It was during that time that I figured that I was interested in history. We were all so impressed with and influenced by Walter Rodney that you figure, "Bwoy, if he can do this, that's what I'm gonna do too." And just the whole consciousness of Africa, that you are an African and you come from Africa and learning African history and doing African studies. All that happened at that time. And then you had a prime minister who loved African people. And we loved him, we thought he was God. And he went and visited Africa, and he went to Cuba and all those places. It was tremendous and it shaped my politics and the politics of people like me. Some people just hate that period because it was a period when black people kinda rise up and say black is beautiful, and if yuh dark skin, you feel affirmed and more people start wear Afro and things like that. It was just a tremendous era, I think, in Jamaica.

KD: The '70s did not necessarily produce the kind of big outflow of writing, like the big push of the '40s and '50s. But to me the kind of creative center of Jamaican "literature," as far as I was concerned, was in music. Most writers working in the '70s would say that what reggae music did for them was give them a language that they did not quite have before. Suddenly, we had something distinct and liberating. We recognized that this thing could happen—poetic articulation emerging fully from a working-class ethos. I sincerely believe that most of our major writers were seriously influenced and affected by reggae during the '70s. This is why I am asking you how reggae plays into what you do.

AC: It really gave us a language with which to write. And you're right, during the '70s there was the music happening and those of us who came of age during that time started producing in the '80s and '90s, and the things that we were absorbing in the '70s, they were kind of percolating in us until we had the confidence to write it out. But DJs had a tremendous impact on me, an essential influence. Big Youth, for one—and it was not just the music; it was the language, the literature, the lyrics. And you know, Big Youth, he used to recite a lot of Psalms and t'ing, right. So when you hear that to music and somebody chanting that lyrically, it was like wooh! like a whole new world just open up. And you think, not that we can do it too, 'cause mi never wan' be a DJ, but it was that this was good stuff. Of course there was Bob Marley, but the DJs did it for me. Because dem could tek de language an' do all kinda sumptn wid it. That whole chanting from the DJs was tremendous.

KD: I think of Burning Spear and his repetition—finding a phrase that really contains psychological complexities: "Do you remember the days of slavery?" Repeating and repeating the line and changing its texture every time, and so on.

AC: Those two artists were to me most influential: Big Youth and Burning Spear.

KD: When did you start writing or seeing yourself as somebody who could write?

AC:: I started writing when I was ten.

KD: What were you writing?

AC: I was writing poetry. I started writing early. I had books of poetry. When I look at them now I say, "Oh God." But I used to write books, exercise books. But it wasn't really until I came to Canada that I thought, well, I could do this and start publishing. Because I started reading a lot and it seemed like it was something I could do and should do. You know, like you write—some people can draw, some people can sing, some people can run, you have a little talent, a little gift. I shouldn't be so modest. I had a little talent, and you not going to enter into the field without having a little talent, right? Of course, you start writing the usual thing, nature and all that.

KD: You started to write with publishing in mind when you came to Canada?

AC: That's right.

KD: How do you relate issues of autobiography and "fiction" to what you do as a writer?

AC: I see the world through my eyes and through my body. I write like that, so even if I am writing a novel with different characters and so—one is a man from St. Thomas and the other is from New Brunswick—I am the one who is going to be shaping that character and looking at the world from his point of view. You can't help being what you are. This man from B.C. wrote to tell me how awful it must have been for me, all the things that I went through, after he had read my work. I said "What 'im a talk 'bout?" He took it quite literally. I mean you do write things which are about you and your life, but not everything. When I sit down to write I am not writing about Afua and her life, but, of course, some of that comes in your writing. In that sense it is autobiographical. One psychoanalyst says that everything you write is autobiographical, so I don't know. I don't worry about that too much in terms of critics. The thing is about living in my voice, and I don't see how I can be detached from that. Because for me, so much is about writing from my body, what my body feels, and the voice that is trying to come out of my body, so I don't think you can be detached.

KD: So, how do you define your audience?

AC: I am happy when anybody and everybody reads me wherever that person is coming from, racial-wise, politics-wise, gender-wise and so on. I want to be accessible to a wider community. At the same time I am aware that some people will read your work and not quite understand it because of cultural barriers, where a black person might immediately connect with it. So, while I wouldn't say I write specifically for black people, these are the people from whom I come. Black people's lives and experiences have shaped me and my life and my work. Me nuh care if it sound "parochial," I want my words to be accessible to black people, especially the Diaspora community. I am not saying I am writing for them, because I think when you get down to it in the final analysis, you are probably writing for yourself. But that's how I would define my community, really. Not even so much the Caribbean, but more like a Diasporic African community.

KD: Do you think coming to Canada has led to that wider sense of audience? In other words, do you think that if you had stayed in Jamaica and written there your work would have been different?

AC: Well, in Jamaica we so international anyway that I would probably say the same things. Maybe I would have a larger Caribbean sensibility. But we are so close to North America and many of us migrate and people come from England and some move to live in continental Europe and so on, you start to have that same sort of Diaspora connection. So maybe I would say the same things. I feel my community and the people dem weh me a write fa, I feel are those people — black people, which includes women, of course. I mean, I do have a particular feminist sensibility which is important.

KD: You are read as a feminist voice...

AC: Yeah, but I want people to read the work. The more the merrier. After all, they say they want poetry to change the world, so that's fabulous. I always wonder why some poets become "international"? I guess they were tremendously good. I think of people like Pablo Neruda. He crossed all sorts of geographical lines. But he was also from that place, located in that place.

KD: I am curious about this issue because I am aware that every time I move to another place, I have to define or redefine my politics in that place. I have to decide what the battles are and which ones should I get involved in. And there's always a point at which one asks oneself, "What is my community?" When I say "my people," who am I talking about? How does it work for you?

AC: When I look at the poets that come out of Jamaica, they speak about local concerns because they live there and they write out of that experience. But they are also vastly Diasporic. I think that this concept of displacement makes sense. I am a displaced person and I feel displaced—I come from Jamaica or the Caribbean and the experience shaped me. Those people from whom I come, that sensibility which I have, that is like the source, the feeding ground—and then you are sort of hurled, you are shot as from a rocket into different areas and spaces. What do you do with that? I don't know what I would do if I was living in Toronto and there were no black people here. Maybe I wouldn't write. It would be a problem. I don't know if you remember when a woman on a panel at the Griot Speaks conference was giving us a history of this woman from New Brunswick, a black woman poet. Nobody at the time knew this woman was black, so she could publish poems in the newspapers and so on. At that point she was colorless, raceless. In her work, only one or two poems hinted at her blackness—and even then, the poems could still have been written by a white person. And then she started writing letters to certain people in which she started talking about what it's like to be black in Ottawa and in Canada. But she never had a community of black people in Ottawa or a community of black writers from which to draw succor, so that was her way of dealing with it. People say you are a human being and ultimately, you have to write what you know. Black people, we are human beings, too, and we have the universal experiences as well. So I come from that place and I write from that place. Issues that concern me, really, as a human being and as a writer, issues that affect oppressed people and black people being of that group, and I am black, and my experience as a black person is so immediate, everyday, that you can't escape from it.

Eventually, it will catch up with you—look at O. J. [Simpson], who was trying to run from blackness...

KD: Could you talk about the question of being a historian and being a poet?

AC: I never thought about it, it was just something I did. My two best subjects in high school were English and history. When I graduated I won the English prize and the history prize. So I love these two subjects. Then I was so influenced by Walter Rodney that I decided that I would be a historian. I was going to study Africa and all of that. I wanted to do history and I wanted to write. Interestingly, I never went to school and did a degree in English because I figured I didn't have to. I had no intention of teaching English. I just wanted to write creatively, poetry, fiction, all those things. I never saw it as problematic or that there was any tension until people started asking me questions. And it's two different things. To study academic history, you have to go into another headspace. So when I am doing that, I can't write poetry until I am tremendously inspired. So it depends on the headspace I am in. It takes me a while to come out of one headspace. I am not complaining. I like to be in that mode because it develops your mind in a different way. You become very analytical and question things a lot and try to get different interpretations. That doesn't mean you are not creating.

KD: What are you looking at?

AC: My thesis entails a biographical study of Henry Bibb, a Kentucky-born African American abolitionist. Bibb escaped from slavery in 1842 and rose in the abolitionist ranks to become one of the most prominent abolitionist activist/orators. In 1850 Bibb came to Ontario (with his wife Mary, and his mother Mildred). He continued his black freedom struggles here and died in 1854.

Therefore my thesis looks at the transnational consciousness and identity of Canadian (antebellum/pre-Confederation) blacks. I like doing that and I like to write creatively. This year I have not renewed my membership with the League of Canadian Poets because I have decided I am not doing as many readings. I have done some readings, but I will not be out there like I have been in the past because I have decided that I just want to focus on this thing and commit to it and finish it. I am doing it at U of T. I want this stage of my life to end. Yet the thing that is looming in front of me is the question, am I going to use this degree in the sense of am I going to be teaching?

And the older I get the more I am not sure about it because I am not sure that is what I want to do after spending half my life studying. I am more into things like social studies—the interdisciplinary area—the whole business of historical methodology and so on does not appeal to me. I have been interested in so-called "Atlantic Issues" All these new terms.

KD: What is that?

AC: It's the study of the people on this side of the world—this side of the Atlantic. Studies of, for instance, the movement of vegetables across the Atlantic—maize leaving South America and going to West Africa and so on. I am not even sure if a so it did go, but a soh dem say. But the transferal of goods and the movement of people, for example, the European trade in captured Africans, and foods and so on—that whole business interests me. And then, because I have this strong historical sense, even before I studied history academically, I always had an interest in history. I can't imagine somebody coming from Jamaica and not being interested in history because everybody in Jamaica claims to be a historian. There was always this sense of history, of people talking history and it did not matter if it was true, if it was fact, there was always this historical sense about the place and the people living there. Even people's private histories, family histories, and personal histories—who come from Panama, who come from Englan', who gone a St. Thomas and so on. I grew up with that and liked it. And it has shaped my work. A lot of the poems in my book are about history. At least it gives me material. On the other hand, I don't say I have discovered this interesting historical fact and I am now going to write a poem about it. You don't just sit down and do that unless it's something that really dread—like, let me see, like someone told me something the other day. "FUCK." You know what "F-U-C-K" means? Fornication and Unlawful Carnal Knowledge. And it was usually women it was attributed to even though men engaged in carnal knowledge, sexual knowledge. And they would write it on their foreheads: "F-U-C-K." And when you saw a woman had that, you knew that she was either an adulteress or a fornicator.

KD: Like *The Scarlet Letter*.

AC: Yeah. Shit, now that's a poem. You know what I mean. That is a jerking piece of information that can stir a poem. You do have a large body of work from which to draw. Like your poem "Flight," which draws from a long Diasporic history, you know.

KD: What creative stuff are you working on?

AC: A manuscript of poetry. And it has a lot of historical things in it. I try to talk about reincarnation and the environment—the woman as the earth and the destruction of the earth. It is not quite done.

KD: So you write a volume as a book?

AC: I may place poems in certain places, but, yes, I write a book. I will write maybe forty poems that can be published together.

KD: And you are in a kind of mental space that gives the body a focus.

AC: Yes. And I want to write a poem about this "FUCK." Because a lot of these things just grab me, you know.

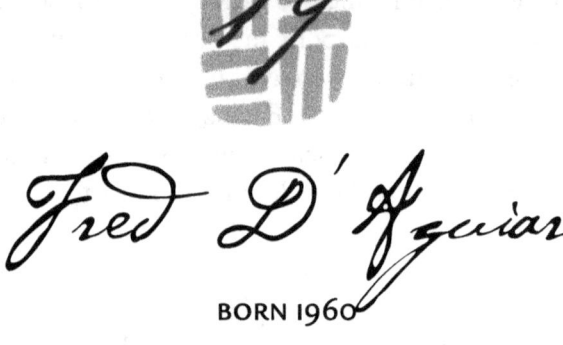

Fred D'Aguiar
BORN 1960

BORN IN ENGLAND to Guyanese parents, Fred D'Aguiar was flown to Guyana at an early age to live and grow under the guiding eye of his grandmother, the prototype for Mama Dot and other strong matriarchal figures that recur in his poetry and some of his prose fiction. At the age of thirteen, however, circumstances made it possible for him to return to England. He completed high school in England and then went on to train as a psychiatric nurse and to work in that capacity for a few years.

In 1985, at the age of twenty-four, D'Aguiar entered the world of poetry in Britain with the publication of his first collection of poetry, *Mama Dot,* which won the Guyana Prize for Poetry. The poems' control, formal dexterity, and carefully rendered sentiment, along with their fresh articulation of the Guyanese experience in a language that was clearly shaped by British life, combined to assure D'Aguiar a strongly positive critical response to his work.

While his reputation as a poet grew, D'Aguiar also became interested in other literary genres, including screenplays and theatrical plays. His successful play *A Jamaican Airman Predicts His Death* explored some of the complexities of race and identity that surround the life of a black person in Britain. D'Aguiar has published three novels. His first, *The Longest Memory* (Chatto & Windus, 1995), won the Whitbread Prize for Best First Novel and was produced as a television drama for the BBC. *Dear Future* (David McKay, 1996) takes him back to Guyana and from there to Britain, tracing in prose much of the ground covered in his first poetry collection. His most recent novel, *Feeding the Ghost* (Chatto & Windus, 1997), examines the capacity of

Africans to survive the Middle Passage. His other collections of poetry are *Airy Hall* (Chatto & Windus, 1989), *British Subjects* (Bloodaxe, 1993), *Bill of Rights* (Chatto & Windus, 1998) and *English Sampler: Selected Poems* (Chatto & Windus, 1998).

Fred D'Aguiar lives in Miami, Florida, and teaches English and writing at the University of Miami.

KWAME DAWES: It has been suggested that you spent much of your apprenticeship as a poet "mimicking" the Western masters, a practice that is rife with all kinds of problematic questions of tradition and identity for many. You describe an awakening to your "voice" as one that revolved around the business of language—Nation Language. Yet you are not what one would readily call a "Nation Language" poet in the strict sense, and your fascination with form suggests that your apprenticeship has not left you untouched by Western (I suspect largely British) models. How do you encounter this business of "voice" first, and "tradition" second, as an Englishman of Guyanese heritage?

FRED D'AGUIAR: My education at the secondary (age twelve to eighteen) and university levels was in England. Poetry writing during my teens evolved out of my encounter at school with the Romantic poets—Keats, Shelley, Wordsworth, Coleridge—the Keats of the Odes, Shelley's "Ode to the West Wind," Wordsworth's "Tintern Abbey," and Coleridge's "Frost at Midnight" and "Kubla Khan" were the kinds of things I returned to again and again during that time (guided by an excellent English teacher, Mr. Hardy, at my secondary school in South London). These poems moved me. The authors used words with passion and love—not just for nature and humanity, but for language itself. To me this was clear though I wouldn't have put it that way at the time. This is the kind of wisdom accrued miles after the event. I shouldn't forget Blake. His *Songs of Innocence* and *Songs of Experience* reminded me of the poem's affinity with song. There were others from an earlier era—Milton, for example, whose study of the devil was enormously attractive to me; rather than scary and instructive about the failure of evil, I saw the devil as a worthy foe of God, as someone or thing imbued with godhead. He was in heaven for a time before he fell, and what struck me was how his powers of creation were deployed towards evil ends with remarkable effect—just like God's hard work over a week. I think Milton refuted for me the idea of God and a paradise creating its opposite using the same material—words—as a foundation. My view then (not now) was that if words can make God, they can unmake God, too. It's really the earliest example I have in my head of recognizing that language possesses as much power as actions. I read Shakespeare, too. Particularly the tragedies and a handful of his 154 sonnets.

The other strand to this "roots" question is my years in Guyana—from age two to twelve. My parents are Guyanese. They emigrated to London in 1958, chasing what every West Indian who made that journey chased, namely prosperity. Perhaps it didn't work for them, since they returned to Guyana for a while. Then they went back to London, leaving my brothers and I with my paternal grandparents in the country and later with my brothers after ten years, by which time my parents had separated, leaving us with my mother.

Guyana gave me a country setting and experience and Creole or Nation Language or Patois (depending on your politics). All three rolled into one in my view. Creole and Standard English forked my tongue in ways that would encourage ambiguity in my utterances and twin loyalties in my beliefs. I began with those two. The canonized texts of the West gave me something else. I arrived in England with a lot of Sparrow songs (and songs from Hindi films, since the village we lived in had a majority of Indians, mainly Hindu) committed to memory.

During the 1970s, I got caught up in the reggae explosion in London; prereleases from Tapazukie, U-Roy, I-Roy, Burning Spear, the Upsetters, Lee Perry, Marley and the Wailers, and many more were the stock and trade alongside U.S. funk and soul and a little jazz-funk. At that time, England was spawning its own reggae groups—Steel Pulse, Misty in Roots, Aswad—and we also had Linton Kwesi Johnson, the dub poet. So although my writer's sensibility is made in England, there are Caribbean undercurrents informing the form and content of my writing.

KD: I also noted an observation you made in the company of Derek Walcott about your sense of indebtedness to him and his generation of West Indian poets for making it possible for you to regard a breadfruit with the same passion and poetic validation as you would an apple. I want to ask you about the influence of certain specific poets, so I am beginning with Derek Walcott. Can you talk about your own encounter with his work, with his "twilight" trope and his use of language? You have written about both issues.

FD: I first met Derek Walcott when I was twenty-six. By that time, I'd read everything he'd written up to then and studied his work at university (but not in school). His poems filled in an absence for me, an absence of place. He seemed to retain in his standard English usage rhythms more akin to Creole. A strong visual and sensual impulse permeates his work. I found these qualities wonderful and true. I didn't want to argue with his poems at all, just embrace them, which is unusual for a "lit crit" mind always on the lookout for fault lines in a writer's work. The other poet who wowed me in a similar way was Kamau Brathwaite. His *Arrivants* trilogy remains the single most powerful imaginative statement from a Caribbean writer about our debt and connection to Africa. In prose I found Wilson Harris's *Palace of the Peacock* startling. I'd never seen anything like it before in prose. I couldn't believe he was from this planet, never mind Guyana! I found his ideas, his philosophy about the region, generous and inclusive and not constrained by history alone or race alone, but indebted to myth and landscape in a way untypical of his contemporaries, say the great stylist Naipaul. This might have to do with the fact that Wilson Harris originates from a country on the continent and not an island. Who knows?

How I understand Derek Walcott's notion of twilight in terms of his art is like this: since twilight is that in-between time, both day and night occupy it, somehow it affords the poet a contemplative space and scrutinizing privilege otherwise denied to him by society. Twilight becomes instructive to the poet even as it allows the poet to instruct his readership about his outlook. Twilight is instructive about the past and it enables the poet to take stock of society and by extension his craft and its ability to match up to the task at hand. This might read like a strange riff on a straightforward notion, but I am coming at the idea as a writer under the influence, as it were, of the same intoxicating trope.

KD: Wilson Harris, also a poet, but better known for his fiction, is quite clearly an influence. Having said that, one is at once struck by the points of separation that seem to exist between yourself and Harris. I am thinking of the absence of his fascination with the interior of the Guyanese landscape and his profoundly constructed mythic recuperation in his fiction. In *Mama Dot* and *Airy Hall* you use memory to shape your own, deeply personal, myths. Am I creating a distinction that is not really there? What do you take from Harris? What impact has he had on your own writing?

FD: I can't write like Wilson Harris. If I could, I would! My love for Guyana is restricted to a childhood there. Harris was in his late thirties when he left. Harris had a working relationship with Guyana in his years spent as a surveyor in the interior. I just grew up in the place, pissed against a few of its trees, that sort of thing. All I have are memories of Guyana based on those early years. I lack a model like Harris's, which is clearly derived from his encounter with landscape and the artifacts associated with it. In this sense, it is inevitable that I'd depart from Wilson Harris when it came to writing, however much I adore his originality and integrity as a writer.

KD: The third writer is the politically engaged poet Martin Carter. Many of the poems in *British Subject* are overtly politicized, and seek to offer ways to understand race in British society, sometimes in language and tone that remind me of Carter. To what extent do you regard your reading of Carter as a way to discover your own voice? Are there other writers who have had a similar impact?

FD: Martin Carter made the supreme sacrifice a writer could make when he dedicated his art to the politics of Guyana. Instead of veering away from politics when it dictated his art, he remained engaged. His *Poems of Resistance* (1954), particularly the poem, "University of Hunger," testify to an original talent grappling with notions of what makes a nation, siding with the oppressed, and extirpating a tenacious colonial power from the imagination of a people. I can't really estimate his worth other than in hyperbole. We went on a five-city tour in England in the spring of '92. I had a chance to listen to him closely. I was aware I was moving with the best aspect of a country, Guyana, I'd hardly grown to know. Martin Carter stayed in Guyana and so he is one of the few writers to remain in the region when being a Caribbean writer meant living in digs in London and broadcasting your poems on Caribbean Voices on the BBC. He stayed because of the ferment around him at that time, and he played a leading role in it. He exemplifies what it means to be a political poet, not just by his writing but by his life.

My overt political poems belong to this tradition of engagement with politics that can be traced in the work of all the poets mentioned. Poetry as an art form is ideally suited to political ends. It can be parody, satire, dramatic monologue, elegy, irony, all of which work wonderfully when directed at politicians!

KD: In your novel *The Longest Memory* the most obvious risk you take is to write a narrative about an African American slave of over a century ago. There is something about the novel form that is not sympathetic to nonrealism—a certain naturalistic authenticity; an expectation that is far less common in our expectations of poetry. Why did you chose to offer this story in this form?

FD: *The Longest Memory* began as a long poem. The first chapter was a long poem which I converted into prose when the meter (alexandrines) collapsed and other insistent voices began to intrude on the main speaker's story as if to argue and disagree with his take on events. Realize I'd always written about slavery from the very first poem in my 1985 book *Mama Dot* ("Born on a Sunday / In the kingdom of Asante. / Sold on Monday into slavery," etc.). The poem is about the death of my grandmother, but because she was old and of African descent, I traced her beginnings back to West Africa. She was my oldest living relation and she'd died so my impulse must have been to connect her to an older tradition that would never die, that would always be there for me to draw sustenance from.

The Longest Memory is really a debate between two types of slave—one rebellious, the other conformist—and an exploration of the difficulty of being a father when you are a slave. A lot of other voices butt in with their twopence worth to give the debate some depth and resonance, but basically, it's a father and a son having a rumble. The novel is good for this variety of extended talk by a character. Expository bits of writing would kill off a poem in no time but in prose it works if uttered by a strong voice. Tone is important, too. Modulations of tone between different characters are easier to register in prose than poetry. Understand, too, that I have always written narrative poems, so *The Longest Memory* is just an extension of that activity.

KD: The power of that piece epitomizes your own creative powers—the capacity to grasp and express the contradictory sentiments of people in words. You seem somewhat uncomfortable with absolutes and the absence of irony. Is the process of questioning what drives your own instinct to write?

FD: Yes, Kwame, you are right. If there is an affinity between our poems (and I believe there is), it resides in a certain inquisitiveness, a definite curiosity about the world and a refusal to settle for things as they seem.

KD: Can you talk a bit about music and your poetry?

FD: When I come round again, I want to be a musician! I love music even though I can't read it and don't play an instrument. Can you believe that?! My first understanding of poetry was its expression in song. My first piece of literature committed to memory were songs from my Guyanese days. During the '70s in London, I frequented discos and blues dances [reggae parties organized in systems]. I used to dance to funk and the DJs of reggae. I went to a lot of concerts. My older brother (like yours) had a great record collection. My mother, too. She introduced my brother and I to her music collection: Marvin Gaye, Millie Jackson, Aretha Franklin, Percy Sledge, Billie Holiday, to name some. She had a good record player in the house and when she went to work, we used to turn it right up and dance to our own records.

All this is leading to my notion that poetry holds for me a solid musicality. It has a lot of the features of music and so I must have been drawn to it for the same reasons that I found music irresistible. These days I find it useful to write against those very qualities.

KD: Mervyn Morris sometimes suggests that the business of detachment is not necessarily a negative in poetry, arguing, in fact, that the wearing of masks represents the ultimate posture of poetic detachment and that poets are constantly wearing masks. In his paradigm, it seems, the mask protects the "poet," reducing his/her vulnerability. His mask is most often irony. Are you tempted by this mask, this almost Eliotesque detachment, or is there another model that you are drawn to as a poet?

FD: I like Mervyn's idea of the mask. Detachment is necessary if the poet is to function as an artist. But so is its opposite—engagement. A balance has to be found between them. Insofar as I take on certain personas to write or adopt certain postures depending on the poem I'm writing, I wear a mask. Behind all those disguises, there is a tone which I hear as mine however much I might turn up or down the volume. (Am I mixing my metaphors here? What the hell!) In Derek Walcott's long autobiographical poem, *Another Life,* the teenager Walcott is falling in love. Suddenly he catches himself watching the experience of falling in love and he recognizes that he is already writing that moment even as it happens. That is the kind of detachment that the writer needs, and the young Walcott actively indulged in recognition of his vocation.

KD: In "Pyramus to Thisbe," you offer an idealized world: "we'll go where love's color- / Blind and therefore colored," which reminds me of Lucky Dube's (South African reggae singer) song "Lovers in a Dangerous Time," which tells the story of a biracial couple who flee to Chicago "where they thought things would be better for them." Like in Dube's song, tragedy faces Pyramus and Thisbe in your poem, but the ideal is still there. More often than not, you discuss race in the context of sexuality, entering, I suspect, the most complex, yet germane, area of the politics of race. Can you talk a bit about the idealism suggested in some of your poems and about the apparent ambivalence that you yourself seem to express particularly because of the seemingly "colored" world from which you emerged in Guyana?

FD: I wish I knew Lucky Dube's music, but I don't. My view is simple: love must transcend race. Loyalties to race must be overruled by the impulses of the heart. Poetry is an intuitive art so it overindulges these kind of insights. Love in a life is hard to find and when found to keep, so why confine it? Guyana is replete with race problems. A civil war was fought along racial lines back in the early '60s. Successive governments have used race to gain votes and foster fear so that the country has become infected with this long-standing virus of essentialism. This is not a Guyanese problem by any stretch of the imagination, but a problem of a recent civilization built on slavery on the right to exploit a people based on the color of their skin. Britain and the U.S. are suffering the ramifications of this racist outlook today and it prevents progress precisely because it impedes love, the capacity to love across boundaries.

KD: Your poem "Dread" is an anthem to Bob Marley and more. Please talk a bit about Marley and his place in shaping the directions of Caribbean poetry, and Caribbean arts in general. I suspect that he represents an important influence. The "anthem" locates Marley in the middle of the quintessential London landscape . . .

FD: I saw Marley a few months before he died in a concert at the Crystal Palace Bowl in South London. He was magisterial on that stage. His dreadlocks were shaken at the London Stock Exchange and at the Houses of Parliament. He stomped on the spot as if to put out the fire of despotism. He crooned some unforgettable lovers' lyrics as if to confirm that even the warrior has to love. His songs are anthems for me. They celebrate Africa, berate politicians, lament slavery, invigorate the spirit. Looking over the century as it closes, I see Marley up there with the best six popular songwriters—Gershwin, Bob Dylan, Michael Jackson, Billie Holiday, the Beatles . . . I know we all have our own lists.

KD: How then do you speak of issues of home? You confess a love of the London space, yet your engagement with Guyana is unquestionably that of a child to a mother. Are these conflicting realities? Is there ever a danger of romanticism spawned by static nostalgia?

FD: Home, as Rushdie says, is always "imaginary," or, as Brodsky would have it, always "elsewhere." For it I have two landscapes in mind and heart when I think of home. The more adult perspective is London; the more idealistic one is Guyana. Nostalgia is an awful sentiment to indulge, so I try not to get nostalgic about Guyana or England; I always maintain a sternly critical eye even as I promote certain sweet judgments about them. A lot of my poems are generated by how the landscape and cityscape and the light of a place can carry ideas, so inevitably I write a lot about Guyana and England.

KD: You have been in the United States for several years now, and predominantly in the South. *The Longest Memory* begins to reveal something of your encounter with this landscape, but can you talk a bit about how you have experienced this country and how it has influenced your writing?

FD: America has given me a job teaching creative writing. This is hard to find in England. I'd exhausted all those avenues before I made the move to the States. Here the idea of creative writing as part of the curriculum is firmly established right through the school and university system. This is good for writers and writing. So I like America right now. I've seen how creative writing has got students reading living writers and many younger writers who would not otherwise have found their ways into the curriculum.

Coming to America has got me reading a lot more fiction and poetry written by Americans than I ever read in England. I am back on a continent (just like Guyana). I am very near the Caribbean here in Florida. Right now the relationship with the place is fertile. Of course I look with trepidation at the politics, but I felt the same way about British politics. The black intellectual community here is bigger and more diverse, which is a plus. There are more black writers and there is a longer tradition of black writing. All this is good for the soul. I don't think I could have written a slave novel had I not left London. Somehow slavery—a British invention—is seen as American. Maybe it's because slavery was established here whereas it never took root in England beyond a few hundred black servants. Slavery came to the English ports but it never really docked except to wash and examine slave stock for re-export to the U.S. and the Caribbean. The British made slave triangles; dropped off slaves elsewhere.

Race in America is more advanced (and curiously backward at the same time) than it is in the U.K. Paternalism from above towards black people still reigns alongside the terror of neo-Nazi groups from below in the U.K.

KD: You have written about many writers of your generation writing from a Caribbean milieu today. Can you talk about some of your own "takes" on how Caribbean literature is taking shape and about the directions in which it is going?

FD: I read the literature published by Peepal Tree and other houses which feature Caribbean writers in a prominent way. The Black Diaspora interests me right now, since writers wholly removed from the Caribbean are springing and writing with this dual loyalty as twin motors of their art. Creole is much more international as a result, and these writers are far more integrated in the arts movement of the countries they were formed in than in the '50s when Lamming, Naipaul, Selvon, and others were struggling and not taken seriously or else were seen as foreign.

Index

Inclusive page numbers of interviews are given in italics.

Adisa, Opal Palmer, xv, *183–95*; *Bake-Face and Other Guava Stories*, 183; *Caribbean Women Writers*, 183; *Daughters of Africa*, 183; "Ethiopia and the Mango Trees," 192; "Feeding," 189, 226; "First Sound," 194; "Let Them Laugh," 194; "Market Woman," 188; *Pina, The Many-Eyed Fruit*, 183; *Tamarind and Mango Women*, 183; "Will the Real Island Please Stand Up," 183, 184
aesthetics, Caribbean, 22
Africa, 2, 3, 5, 7, 22, 34, 35, 56, 61, 65, 66, 68, 69, 70, 78, 81, 82, 83, 85, 96, 98, 108, 122, 123, 127, 128, 137, 138, 140, 142, 145, 151, 154, 158, 165, 187, 190, 191, 192, 194, 195, 197, 198, 199, 200, 202, 203, 210, 218, 219, 221, 223, 224, 227, 229, 231, 233, 234
African American people and culture, 69, 165, 187, 194, 195, 223, 231
African-Caribbean people and culture, 5, 93
Afrocentrism, 81, 83, 115, 137
Agard, John, xvi, 8, 28, 135, 144
Ai, *Cruelty* and *Killing Floor*, 122
Akhmatova, Anna, 94
Allen, Lillian, 144, *148–60*; *Nothing But a Hero Dub*, 148; "Riddim on Hard Times," 160; *Some Imagining Women*, 148; *Why Me*, 148; *Women Do This Every Day: Selected Poems*, 148
Amerindian people and culture, x, 123, 138, 200
Anancy, 2, 144, 197, 206
Arawak, x, 77
Asian people and culture, 7, 96, 138
Atwood, Margaret, 159
Auden, W. H., 93

Baldwin, James, 101, 102
Barbados, 22, 23, 25, 34, 35, 124, 128, 173
Barston, Stan, 102
Basement Theatre Workshop (Trinidad), 120
Baugh, Edward, xii, *38–46*, 50, 51; "Capricorn," 44, 45; "The Carpenter's Complaint," 40; "The House of Poems," 40; "Lignum Vitae," 45; "Mistaken Identity," 44; "Nigger Sweat," 41, 43, 44; "The Poet Bemused," 44, 51; "A Rain-Washed Town by the Sea," 44; "Responsibility," 43; "Small-Town Story," 43; *Tale from the Rainforest*, 38, 39, 41, 42, 43, 51; "Tale from the Rainforest," 40; "There's a Brown Girl in the Ring," 29, 40, 41, 100; "Truth and Consequence," 44
BBC's Caribbean Voices (radio program), 22, 25, 94, 230

Bennett, Louise, 56, 101, 144, 149, 150, 157, 158, 205
Berry, James, *1–10*; *Bluefoot Traveller*, 1; *Chain of Days*, 2; *Classic Poems to Read Aloud*, 1, 7; "Fantasy of an African Boy," 1; *Fractured Circles*, 1, 4; *Hot Earth Cold Earth*, 2, 3; "I Am Racism," 6; "Letter to Mother Africa," 3; "My Name Is I Don't Know," 8; *News for Babylon*, 1; *When I Dance*, 1; "White Child," 7
Berry, Wendell, 165
Best, Lloyd, 109, 226
Bhagavada Gita, 98
Bhatt, Sujata, 122
Bibb, Henry, 223
Bible, the, 2, 7, 32, 125, 131
Big Youth (Manley Buchanan), xv, 219, 220
Bim (journal), 25, 43, 50
Birbalsingh, Frank, 91
Birney, Earle, 94
black writers: American, 142, 158; British, 7, 8
Black Power, xiv, 50, 150, 153, 160
Blake, William, 7, 10, 203, 227; "The Sick Rose," 10; *Songs of Experience*, 227; *Songs of Innocence*, 227; "Tyger," 7
blues, the, 105, 132
Bosle, Asha, 98
Braine, John, 102
Brathwaite, Kamau, xi, xii, xv, *22–37*, 52, 81, 91, 93, 96, 105, 128, 188, 196, 229; *The Arrivants*, 22, 35, 36, 37, 142, 202; *Barbajan Poems*, 26; "The Cabin," 36; *Conversations with Nathaniel Mackey*, 35; *DreamStories*, 22, 23, 37; *Islands*, 34, 36, 86, 193; *Jah Music*, 23; *Masks*, 34; *Middle Passages*, 23; *Mother Poem*, 23, 35; "Negus," 164; *Other Exiles*, 23; *Rights of Passage*, 34, 36, 128; "Rites," 209; *Shar*, 23; *Soweto*, 23; *Sun Poem*, 23, 35; *Trench Town Rock*, 23, 30, 45; *The Zea Mexican Diary*, 23
Breeze, Jean Binta, 206

British-Asian poets, 7
British English, 16
British Guyana, 15
Brodber, Erna, x, xi, 32
Brodsky, Joseph, 234
Brooks, Cleanth, 48
Brown, Wayne, 41, 56

cadence, 36
Calling the Caribbean (radio program), 94
calypso, xv, 66, 97, 122, 145, 146, 164, 194
Campbell, George, 101
Carew, Jan, xii, 95, 144
Caribbean aesthetic, 22
Caribbean-British people and culture, xii, 5, 7
Caribbean-British anthology, 7
Caribbean cosmology, restoration of, 31
Caribbean literature, 26, 31, 33, 102, 129, 141, 142, 161, 235
Caribbean Nation Language, 6
Caribbean poetry, 108, 126, 133, 142, 167, 206, 233
CARIFESTA, 35, 148
Carnegie, James, 25
Carter, Martin, *11–21*, 25, 92, 94, 109, 142, 165, 230; "Bent," 19; *The Hidden Man (Other Poems of Prison)*, 12; *The Hill of Fire Glows Red*, 12; *Jail Me Quickly: Five Poems*, 12; *The Kind Eagle (Poems of Prison)*, 12; *Poems of Affinity*, 12; *Poems of Resistance from British Guiana*, 11, 94, 230; *Poems of Succession*, 12; *Selected Poems*, 11, 12; "University of Hunger," 17, 230
Charles, Faustin, 209
Chaucer, Geoffrey, 129, 137
Christian, Barbara, 193
Christianity, 57, 81, 98, 123, 124, 125, 129, 133, 193
classical literature, 7
Cleaver, Eldridge, 93
Cliff, Jimmy, xv
Clifton, Lucille, 188, 189

Coleridge: "Frost at Midnight," 227; *The Keats of the Odes*, 227; "Kubla Khan," 39, 227
Collins, Merle, xvi
Commonwealth Poetry Prize, 61, 135, 136
Constable, John, 211
Cook, Eliza, 2
Cooper, Afua, x, xv, 144, *215–25*; *Breaking Chains*, 215; *Memories Have Tongue*, 215; *The Red Caterpillar on College Street*, 215
Cooper, Ibo, 104
cosmology, 34, 164
Craig, Christine, 142
creole, 110, 120, 121, 137, 139, 144, 185, 228, 229, 235; and creolization, 199, 202, 209, 210. *See also* dialect; Jamaican language; Nation Language; patois
cricket, 28, 33, 86, 98, 209–11

Dabydeen, Cyril, *86–98*; "Absences," 96; *Born in Amazonia*, 87; *Coastland: New and Selected Poems*, 86, 91, 94; *Dark Swirl*, 90, 91, 97; *Discussing Columbus*, 87, 97; *Distances*, 86; *Goatsong*, 86; *Islands Lovelier than a Vision*, 86; "Jogging in Havana," 95; "Methuselah," 95; *Poems in Recession*, 88, 94; "Racism," 90, 115; *A Shapely Fire*, 95; *Sometimes Hard*, 92; *Stoning the Wind*, 87; "A Tide at Beachhead," 87; *The Wizard Swami*, 94
Dabydeen, David, 8, 9, 168, *196–214*; *The Black Presence in English Literature*, 196; *Black Writers in Britain, 1760–1890*, 196; "Caliban," 37, 205; *Coolie Odyssey*, 197, 199, 201, 210, 211, 213; *The Counting House*, 196; *Disappearance*, 196; *A Harlot's Progress*, 196; *Hogarth, Walpole, and Commercial Britain*, 196; *The Intended*, 196; "Love Song," 205; "Miranda," 205; "New World Words," 205; "Rebel Love," 205; "For Rohan Babulal Kanhai," 209–11; "Sir James Douglas," 91; *Slave Song*, 197, 198, 199, 200, 201, 207, 211; *Turner: New and Selected Poems*, 197; "Turner," 197, 198, 199, 200, 201, 202, 203, 204, 205, 213; "Water with Berries," 205
D'Aguiar, Fred, xv, 8, 12, *226–35*; *Airy Hall*, 227, 230; *Bill of Rights*, 227; *British Subjects*, 227; *Dear Future*, 226; "Dread," 124, 130, 233; *English Sampler: Selected Poems*, 227; *Feeding the Ghost*, 226; *A Jamaican Airman Predicts his Death*, 226; *The Longest Memory*, 226, 231, 234; *Mama Dot*, 226, 230, 231; "Pyramus to Thisbe," 233
dance hall, 194, 195
Dandelion (journal), 61
Danticat, Edwidge, 25
Das, Mahadai, xvi, 119, 122
Davie, Donald, 55
Davis, Miles, 104
Dawes, Kwame, 2, 24, 38, 48, 62, 74, 87, 99, 109, 125, 135, 148, 162, 173, 183, 197, 215, 227; "Flight," 225; *Jacko Jacobus*, 32
Dawes, Neville, xii, 101
decolonization, 200
Devakaruni, Chitra, 122
Dia-African. *See* diaspora
Dia-African writers, 69
dialect, 4, 5, 16, 17, 43, 83, 84, 91, 93, 96, 105, 164, 211. *See also* creole; Jamaican language; Nation Language; patois
dialectic triad, 199
diaspora, 68, 69, 71, 108, 118, 137, 191, 192, 221, 222, 225, 235
Dickens, Charles, 208
Dickinson, Emily, 121
dislocation and displacement, 13, 109, 111, 222. *See also* exile
Donne, John, 101
Douglas, Marcia, xvi
Drummond, Don, 104
Dryden, John, 97
dub poets and poetry, 27, 35, 93, 104, 148, 150, 151, 157–60, 195, 228

Dube, Lucky, 233; "Lovers in a Dangerous Time," 233
Dubois, W. E. B., 68
Dylan, Bob, 234

Egypt, 37, 190
Eliot, T. S., 4, 42, 48, 55, 92, 93, 96, 197, 198, 199, 201, 205, 206, 208
England, 2, 3, 6, 16, 22, 28, 34, 36, 54, 55, 71, 92, 93, 113, 136, 137, 143, 144, 191, 197, 202, 203, 209, 210, 211, 212, 221, 226, 227, 228, 230, 234, 235
Espinet, Ramabai, *108–23;* "City Blues," 117; *Creation Fire: A CAFRA Anthology of Caribbean Women's Poetry*, 108; "Hosay Night," 111; "In the Jungle," 111; "Lost Cargoes," 111, 112; *Nuclear Seasons*, 108, 117
Eurocentrism, 81, 84, 90, 92, 93
Europe, 6, 64, 65, 68, 69, 72, 82, 122, 138, 141, 154, 197, 205, 221
European literature, 70, 71
exile, 22, 24, 28, 29, 30, 32, 33, 59, 109, 136, 196, 203. *See also* dislocation and displacement

Fanon, Frantz, 68, 69, 191
feminism, 121, 123, 143, 144, 146, 152, 153, 187, 188, 193, 194, 215, 221
Fiddlehead (press), 86, 92
Fifty Caribbean Writers (ed. Dance), 49
Finney, Nikky, 218
Franklin, Aretha, 98, 232

Gajadin, Chitra, 119
ganja, 203
Gaye, Marvin, 232
Ghana, 22, 34, 36
Ginsberg, Allen, 129
Globe and Mail, 70, 92
Goodison, Bunny, 104
Goodison, Lorna, xv, *99–107*, 120, 138, 142, 163; *Heartease*, 99; "Heartease," 40; *I Am Becoming My Mother*, 99; *Selected Poems*, 91, 99; *Tamarind Season*, 99; *To Us, All Flowers Are Roses*, 99

Grand Prix Smarties Prize, 1
Graves, Robert, 55, 60
griot, 75, 76, 126, 140, 154, 167
Gunn, Tom, 174
Guyana, xiv, xv, 11, 14, 17, 24, 25, 83, 86, 87, 88, 91, 93, 94, 95, 96, 98, 110, 135, 136, 137, 142, 145, 196, 200, 207, 208, 209, 210, 211, 214, 226, 228, 229, 230, 233, 234

Halifax, Nova Scotia, 159
Harlem Renaissance, 191
Harris, Claire, xv, 28, 29, *61–72;* The *Conception of Winter*, 62; *Dipped in Shadow*, 61, 62, 71; *Drawing Down a Daughter*, 61, 62, 65, 67; *Translation into Fiction*, 62
Harris, Wilson, x, 32, 95, 196, 198, 201, 205, 206, 213, 229, 230; *Palace of the Peacock*, 95, 229; *The Secret Ladder*, 205
Hayden, Robert, 165
Hearne, John, xii, 156
Heinemann Book of Caribbean Poetry, The, 161
Hindus and Hinduism, 123, 199, 203, 210, 228
Hippolyte, Kendel, xiii, 24, 41, 127, 128, *161–72*, 173, 181; *Bearings*, 161; *Birthright*, 161; *Island in the Sun*, 161, 163, 167; *Island in the Sun-Side Two*, 161, 167; *The Labyrinth*, 161, 168; "Villanelle for Blake," 170; "Worker Chant," 163
Holiday, Billie, 232, 234
Homer, 205, 208; *Iliad*, 208
Hopkins, Gerard Manley, 174; "The Wreck of the *Deutschland*," 174
Hopkinson, Nalo, *Brown Girl in the Ring*, 29, 40
Hughes, Langston, 81, 189
Huxley, Aldous, 67

iambic meter, 13, 40, 41
In Focal (magazine), 136
India, 109, 111, 200, 202, 203
Indian writers, 42, 113, 196
Indo-Caribbean people and culture, 113, 115, 118, 119, 200, 210

Indo-Presbyterian-Naparima community, 110
Indo-Trinidadian people and culture, 115, 116
Irish folklore, 120
I-Roy (musical group), 228

Jackson, Mahalia, 98
Jackson, Michael, 234
Jackson, Millie, 232
Jamaica Journal, 73
Jamaican Daily Gleaner, 101
Jamaican language, 46, 185. *See also* dialect; creole; Nation Language; patois
Jamaican music, xiv, 104, 105
Jamal, Mahmoud, 7
James, C. L. R., 113, 141, 191, 209
Jarret, Keith, 104
jazz, 32, 35, 36, 62, 104, 163, 174, 194; jazz-funk, 228
Jennings, Elizabeth, 174
Jerry, Bongo, 25
Johnson, Linton Kwesi, 150, 228
Jones, Barbara, 121; "Among the Potatoes," 121
Joseph, Clifton, xvi, 148, 151, 159; "Looking for a Job," 159
Joyce, James, 200

kaiso, 28, 36. *See also* calypso
Kanhai, Rohan, 98, 209, 210
Karnac House, 142
Kay, Jackie, 8
Keats, John, 85, 101, 227
Kellman, Anthony, xvi
Kincaid, Jamaica, 25
King, Jane, xiii, xv, *173–82;* "Dream Poem," 177; *Fellow Traveller*, 173, 178; "Fellow Traveller," 173, 178; "How Not to Write a Poem," 180, 181; *Into the Centre*, 173, 178; "Kingston Ramble," 180; "Mandala Dream Song #3," 177; "Moments," 180, 198; "Negative Space," 174, 179; "Neighbors," 174; "Of Men and Mermaids," 174; "Postulant," 174
koumbla tradition, 32
Kumar, Hemant, 98

Kyk-Over-Al (journal), 25
Kyk-Over-Al Anthology of West Indian Poetry, 27

La Rose, 36
Lai, Wally Lok, 199
Lamming, George, xi, xii, 27, 30, 205, 206, 210, 235; *Pleasures of Exile*, 205
Larkin, Philip, 52
League of Canadian Poets, The, 94, 223
Lee, John Robert, xiii, 24, *124–34,* 163; *Clearing Ground: Poems*, 124, 129, 130; *Dread Season*, 124; "Dread Season," 130; "Hologram," 132, 133; *Possessions*, 124, 129; *The Prodigal*, 124, 129; "The Prodigal," 130; *Saint Lucian*, 124; "Sighting," 129; *Translations*, 124, 129, 130, 131, 132; "Translations," 124, 129, 130, 131, 132; *Vocation and Other Poems*, 124
Listener, The, 54
literary allusions, 187
Lorde, Audre, 122
love poems, 59, 186
Lovelace, Earl, 206
Lowell, Robert, 93, 129
Lyman, Frankie, 105
lyrics, 122, 151, 219, 234

MacKay, Claude, 93
MacNeice, Louis, 93
MacNeill, Anthony, 163, 165
Macullum, Shara, xvi
Mahabarata, The, 199
Maharaj, Niala, 119
Mais, Roger, 27, 31, 188; *Black Lightning*, 31; *The Hills Were Joyful Together*, 27
Manley, Michael, 216, 218
Manu, 199, 200, 201, 202, 210
Markham, Archie, xvi, 7; *Hinterland*, 7, 8, 49
Marley, Bob, xiv, 34, 37, 104, 121, 129, 157, 158, 186, 194, 220, 228, 233, 234; "Is This Love," 186; "Natty Dread," 154; "No Woman No Cry," 186, 194

Maroons, 217
Marshall, Paule, 100, 102; *Brown Girl Brownstone*, 100
matikor, institution of, 112, 123
McNeill, Anthony, xvi, 163
mento, 36, 37
metaphor, 37, 64, 65, 66, 73, 81, 87, 88, 89, 117, 128, 165, 166, 171, 175, 177, 179, 197, 204, 205, 209, 210, 211, 212
metaphysical poetry, 55, 56
Millay, Edna St. Vincent, 101, 121
Milton, John, 12, 13, 227; "Lycidas," 12
Miss Lou. *See* Bennett, Louise
Mistral, Gabriela, 121
Misty in Roots (musical group), 228
Mittelholzer, Edgar, 141
Monar, M. R., 91
Mordecai, Pamela, xvi, 49
Morris, Mervyn, 41, *47–60*, 97, 179, 183, 188, 232; "Behind the Poems," 49; "The Day My Father Died," 55; "A Drowning," 50; *Examination Centre*, 48, 58, 59, 97; *The Faber Book of Contemporary Caribbean Short Stories*, 48; "For Consciousness," 51; "The Forest," 57; *Jamaica Woman*, 48; "Love Is," 53, 59; "My Rodney Poem," 50, 51; *On Holy Week*, 48, 52, 57, 59, 60; "Outing," 50; *The Pond*, 47, 48, 50, 57, 59; "The Pond," 59; "Recreation," 58; *Shadowboxing*, 48, 50, 59, 60; "The Stripper," 59; "Thomas," 55, 57, 58, 220, 224; "Version," 58; *Voiceprint*, 48, 162; "West Indian Love Song," 55; "Womansong," 60
Morrison, Toni, 187, 198, 199; *Beloved*, 198, 199
Mosaic Press, 92
muse, 27, 40, 42, 59, 60, 131, 138
music and musicality, 4, 9, 10, 12, 22, 28, 31, 36, 37, 40, 67, 69, 82, 84, 98, 103, 104, 122, 130, 133, 145, 146, 150, 151, 152, 156, 157, 158, 159, 160, 162, 163, 164, 165, 181, 187, 194, 195, 208, 209, 219, 232, 233.
See also blues, the; *cadence*; calypso; jazz; *kaiso*; La Rose; *mento*; reggae; ska

Naipaul, V. S., xii, xv, 25, 27, 94, 97, 101, 109, 111, 113, 114, 141, 196, 200, 205, 208, 210, 211, 212, 229, 235; *A Bend in the River*, 113; *The Enigma of Arrival*, 114; *The House of Mr Biswas*, 113; *Miguel Street*, 101; *The Mimic Men*, 109
Nation Language, 5, 91, 185, 227, 228. *See also* creole; dialect; Jamaican language; patois
Native Americans, 217
nativism, 36
Negritude, 191
Neruda, Pablo, 11, 222
New Directions, 23, 37
New Statesman, The, 54, 200
Nichols, Grace, xv, 8, 9, 28, 81, *135–47*; "Dove and Pigeon," 145; *The Fat Black Woman's Poems*, 9, 135, 139; *Lazy Thoughts of a Lazy Woman*, 135; "Manna Come Home," 136; *Sunris*, 135, 137, 146; *Whole of a Morning Sky*, 135, 136
Nigeria, x, 61, 191
Nkrumah, Kwame, 191
Nobel Prize for Literature, 121
North America, 30, 108, 122, 186, 187, 217, 221
Nourbese Philip, Marlene, xvi, 29, 194

obeah, 79
Oku, Onuora, 148, 150, 151, 158, 160
Orishas (African deities), 82

pan-African Caribbean, 113
pan-Africanism, 155
pan-Caribbeanism, xv, 114
patois, 83, 185, 228. *See also* creole; dialect; Jamaican language; Nation Language
Patterson, Orlando, xii
Peepal Tree Books, 34, 86, 87, 90, 161, 168, 235
Penguin Book of Caribbean Verse in English (ed. Burnett), 162, 200

People's National Party, 102
Perry, Lee ("Scratch"), xv, 156, 228
Philps, Geoffrey, xvi
Pintard, Michael, 194
Plath, Sylvia, 93
Pollard, Velma, xvi
popular culture, 22, 157, 162
postcolonialism, 70, 76, 102, 140, 141, 146, 150
Pound, Ezra, 121
Pratt, E. J., 94
Preston, Rohan, xvi, 28
prose rhythm, 12, 13, 20
prosodic craft, 12, 13
Psalms, 2, 4, 130, 131, 219
pukkumina, 36
Punch, 54

Queh-Queh ceremony, 145

Radjkoemar, Asha, 119
Ramayana, The, 199
Rankine, Claudia, xvi, 28, 29, 179; "elsewhere, things ten," 29
Rastafarians and Rastafarianism, xiv, 102, 103, 190, 192, 193, 203
reggae, xiv, 28, 32, 33, 35, 36, 104, 145, 150, 156, 157, 158, 162, 163, 194, 195, 219, 228, 232, 233
Reid, V. S, xii, 101, 141, 188
Rhys, Jean, 76
rhythm, 10, 12, 13, 26, 36, 57, 62, 63, 64, 65, 66, 71, 84, 85, 90, 91, 93, 105, 130, 131, 145, 146, 151, 152, 157, 158, 160, 163, 164, 195, 202, 205, 208, 229
Rich, Adrienne, 122
Rilke, Rainer Maria, 171
Roach, Eric, 25
Rodney, Walter, 129, 199, 218, 219, 223; *How Europe Underdeveloped Africa*, 199
Roethke, Theodore, 93
Rohlehr, Gordon, 34, 37
rootlessness, 168, 169
Rushdie, Salman, 234
Rwanda, 22, 34

Salkey, Andrew, xii, 26, 29, 144; *Breaklight*, 26
Sanchez, Sonia, 189
Sandberry Press, 38, 173
Sankofa (film), 191
Scott, Dennis, 56, 163
Seecharan, Clem, 209
Selvon, Samuel, xii, xv, 29, 30, 97, 101, 114, 115, 141, 188, 196, 205, 207, 235; *An Island Is a World*, 114; *Lonely Londoners*, 97, 114; "Three into Two Won't Go," 115; "Turning Christian," 114
Senghor, Léopold, 113
Senior, Olive, x, 73–85, 120, 138, 142, 157; "Ancestral Poems," 75; *The Arrival of the Snake-Woman*, 73; "Cockpit Country Dreams," 75; "Colonial Girls School," 75; *The Discerner of Hearts*, 73; "Eighth Birthday," 75; *Gardening in the Tropics*, 73, 74, 75, 77, 78, 81, 83; "Gardening in the Tropics," 85; "The Immovable Tenant," 84; "My Father's Blue Plantation," 79; "Mystery," 82, 85; "Nature Studies I," 75; "Nature Studies II," 75; "Seeing the Light," 80; "Stowaway," 84; *Summer Lightning*, 73; *Talking of Trees*, 73, 74, 75, 77, 81, 83; "Tree of Life," 79, 80
sensuality, 151, 186, 187, 188, 189, 199, 208
Sexton, Anne, 93
sexuality, 59, 118, 121, 186, 187, 188, 189, 212, 233
Shakespeare, William, 37, 39, 66, 67, 70, 71, 129, 137, 205, 213, 228; *Hamlet*, 39, 71; *King Lear*, 209, 213; *The Merchant of Venice*, 71; *The Tempest*, 71 (see also Sycorax writing style)
Shange, Ntosake, 187
Shelley, Percy, 13, 85, 227; "Ode to the West Wind," 12, 13, 227
Sherlock, Philip, 27, 101
Shinebourne, Janice, 91

Sillitoe, Allan, 102
Silvera, Makeda, 215, 216
Singh, Rajkumari, 205
ska, 36, 194
Sledge, Percy, 232
Smith, Mikey, 34
Soyinka, Wole, x, 81; *Death and the King's Horseman*, ix
Sparrow (Slinger Francisco): "Cricket in the Jungle," 28; "Lion and Donkey," 28
Spear, Burning, xv, 104, 156, 220, 228
Spender, Stephen, 93
St. Lucia, xiii, 22, 24, 25, 36, 124, 128, 134, 161, 166, 167, 168, 173, 180
standard English, 6, 16, 71, 83, 105, 121, 137, 139, 204, 228, 229
Stevens, Wallace, 121
Sunday Chronicle, 87
Sycorax writing style, 22, 37
Sylvester, Everton, xvi

Tagore, Rabindranath, 93, 98
Taino, x, 78, 217
Tapazukie, 228
Tennyson, Alfred Lord, 93
terza rima, 13
Third World, 76, 90, 104, 140, 150
Thomas, Dylan, 42, 54, 56, 105
Thomas, R. S., *Poetry for Supper*, 55
Tosh, Peter, xiv, 104
Trinidad, xiv, xv, 61, 69, 108, 110, 114, 115, 116, 118, 121, 122, 173, 194, 209
Turner, Joseph Mallord William, 201, 205

Upsetters, The (musical group), 228
U-Roy (musical group), 228

Vedic scripture, 200
violence, 33, 45, 186, 217, 218
voice, 89, 94
Voznesensky, Andrei, 94

Walcott, Derek, x, xii, xv, xvi, 25, 27, 41, 42, 43, 44, 52, 53, 56, 67, 73, 86, 89, 93, 94, 101, 102, 114, 120, 121, 127, 128, 129, 131, 138, 141, 142, 143, 161, 163, 164, 165, 166, 167, 169, 174, 176, 180, 190, 196, 199, 201, 205, 208, 228, 229, 232, 233; *Another Life*, 44, 142, 232; "Choc Bay," 56; "A Letter from Brooklyn," 56; *Omeros*, 27, 52, 205; *The Sea at Dauphin*, 120; *Sea Grapes*, 53; "Tales of the Islands," 43, 56; *Twenty Poems*, 120
Walker, Alice, 187
Walker, Margaret, 188, 189
West Indian literature, 49
Whitman, Walt, 129
Williams, Aubrey, 201, 206
Williams, N. D., 25
Wilson, Jackie, 105
womanism, 152, 187, 188
Woolf, Virginia, *The Waves*, 175
Wordsworth, William, 85, 101, 171, 211, 227; "Tintern Abbey," 227
Workers Movement, 157

Yardan, Shana, 119
Yeats, William Butler, 101, 120, 174, 181; *The Oxford Book of Modern Verse*, 101
Yevtushenko, Yevgeny Alexandrovich, 94
Yoruba, ix, 82

Zephaniah, Ben, 8

www.ingramcontent.com/pod-product-compliance
Lightning Source LLC
Chambersburg PA
CBHW071834230426
43671CB00012B/1957